ASTROLOGY: OLD THEME, NEW THOUGHTS

D1512141

ASTROLOGY: OLD THEME, NEW THOUGHTS

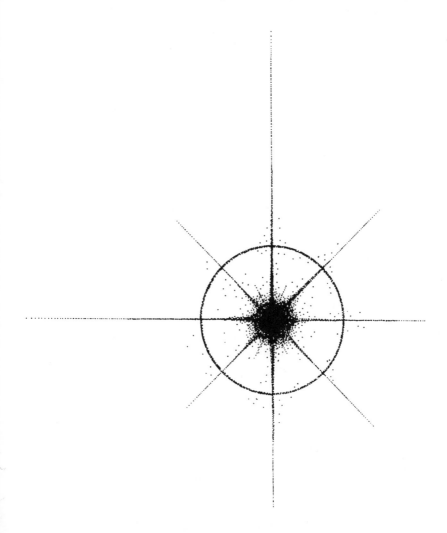

by MARION D. MARCH & JOAN McEVERS

Chapters previously published:
"Family Patterns: How to Find Heredity in the Chart,"
©by Clancy Publications.
"The Many Faces of Pluto,"
©by Clancy Publications.
"A Different Approach to Vocational Indicators,"
© by Clancy Publications.
Articles are being used by permission.
Chapters in BULLETIN of American Federation of Astrologers, Inc.:
"SATURN: Teacher, Taskmaster and Friend"
appeared in the
August 18, 1982 BULLETIN.
"A TRIBUTE: H.S.H. Princess Grace of Monaco"
appeared in the June 10, 1983 BULLETIN.
"A Positive Approach to the Teaching of Astrology"
appeared in the October 1977 BULLETIN.
This material has been released for publication in this book.

International Standard Book Number 0-917086-62-7

Printed in the United States of America

Published by ACS Publications, Inc.
P.O. Box 16430
San Diego, CA 92116-0430

DEDICATION

In memory of my enlightened parents Kathryn & Edward Wessels who gave me the foundation for understanding my fellowman.

Joan

In memory of my uniquely wonderful parents Franz & Grete Dispeker and to Leo, the man who taught me to "see" and "hear".

Marion

Also by ACS Publications, Inc.

The American Atlas
The American Book of Charts (Rodden)
The American Book of Nutrition and Medical Astrology (Nauman)
The American Book of Tables
The American Ephemeris for the 20th Century [Midnight]
The American Ephemeris for the 20th Century [Noon]
The American Ephemeris for the 21st Century
The American Ephemeris 1901 to 1930
The American Ephemeris 1931 to 1940
The American Ephemeris 1931 to 1980 & Book of Tables
The American Ephemeris 1941 to 1950
The American Ephemeris 1951 to 1960
The American Ephemeris 1961 to 1970
The American Ephemeris 1971 to 1980
The American Ephemeris 1981 to 1990
The American Ephemeris 1991 to 2000
The American Heliocentric Ephemeris 1901 to 2000
The American Sidereal Ephemeris 1976 to 2000
The Asteroid Ephemeris: Dudu, Dembowska, Pittsburgh & Frigga
    (Stark & Pottenger)
Astrological Insights Into Personality (Lundsted)
Astrological Predictions (Whitney)
Basic Astrology: A Guide for Teachers and Students (Negus)
Basic Astrology: A Workbook for Students (Negus)
The Body Says Yes (Kapel)
The Cosmic Clocks (Gauquelin)
Cosmic Combinations (Negus)
Expanding Astrology's Universe (Dobyns)
The Fortunes of Astrology (Granite)
The Gauquelin Book of American Charts (Gauquelin)
Healing With the Horoscope (Pottenger)
The Horary Reference Book (Ungar & Huber)
Interpreting the Eclipses (Jansky)
The Lively Circle (Koval)
The Only Way to. . .Learn Astrology, Vol. I
    Basic Principles (March & McEvers)
The Only Way to. . .Learn Astrology, Vol. II
    Math & Interpretation Techniques (March & McEvers)
The Only Way to. . .Learn Astrology, Vol. III
    Horoscope Analysis (March & McEvers)
Planetary Planting (Riotte)
Planting by the Moon 83/84 (Best & Kollerstrom)
The Psychic and the Detective (Druffel)
The Psychology of the Planets (F. Gauquelin)
Small Ecstasies (Owens)
Stalking the Wild Orgasm (Kilham)
Tomorrow Knocks (Brunton)
12 Times 12 (McEvers)

TABLE OF CONTENTS

POTENTIALS AND LEVELS OF SEXUALITY
IN THE HOROSCOPE
by Marion D. March 143

IN-DEPTH DELINEATION: The Profile of a Rapist
by Joan McEvers 165

OUR HIGHEST PHILOSOPHICAL
AND SPIRITUAL POTENTIAL
by Marion D. March 193

DATA FOR HOROSCOPES

Cher Bono Allman
El Centro, CA   May 20, 1946
7:25 Zone +8, 32N48 115W34
Source: Quinn quotes "her mother" birth
    certificate (A)

David Bowie
Brixton, England   January 8, 1947
23:50 Zone 0.0, 51N28 0W6
Source: *The American Book of Charts*
    (B)

Frederick Harlan Coe
Spokane, WA   February 2, 1947
23:52 Zone +8, 47N40 117W24
Source: Spokane Health Dept. birth
    certificate (A)

Ruth Enfield Coe
Spokane, WA   June 30, 1920
11:00 Zone +8, 47N40 117W24
Source: Spokane Health Dept. birth
    certificate (A)

Charles Dickens
Portsmouth, England   February 8, 1812
0:05 LMT, 50N47 1W5
Source: Church of Light (DD)

Marlene Dietrich
Berlin, Germany   December 27, 1901
22:08 Zone -1, 52N30 13E23
Source: Copy of birth certificate (A)

Christian Dior
Sceaux, France   January 21, 1905
1:30 Zone 0.0, 48N57 2E20
Source: Penfield quotes Tager
    Germany Archives (C)

Walt Disney
Chicago, IL   December 5, 1901
0:35 Zone +6, 41N52 87W39
Source: Lyndoe, *American Astrology
    Magazine* (C)

Ralph Waldo Emerson
Boston, MA   May 25, 1803
13:16 Zone +5, 42N22 71W04
Source: Father's diary "while at Sunday
    dinner" (B)

George Gershwin   New York, NY   September 26, 1898
                        11:19 Zone +5, 40N45 73W57
                        Source: *Sabian Symbols* #384 (C)

Ira Gershwin   New York, NY   December 6, 1896
                        4:50 Zone +5, 40N45 73W57
                        Source: Rectified by Joan McEvers (DD)

Ferde Grofe   New York, NY   March 27, 1892
                        4:05 Zone +5, 40N45 73W57
                        Source: *Sabian Symbols* #412 (C)

Xaviera Hollander   Soerbaja, Java   June 15, 1943
                        6:14 Zone -7.5, 7S15 112E45
                        Source: *Profiles of Women* (C)

James Joyce   Dublin, Eire   February 2, 1882
                        6:00 AM Zone 0.0, 53N20 6W15,
                        Source: Lockhart quotes Storme (C)

Grace Kelly   Philadelphia, PA   November 12, 1929
                        5:31 Zone +5, 39N57 75W10
                        Source: Secretary quotes birth
                           records (A)

Robert Kennedy   Brookline, MA   November 20, 1925
                        15:11 Zone +5, 42N20 71W07
                        Source: CL/*Horoscope Magazine*
                           Sept. 1970 quotes Harmon (C)

Elisabeth Kubler-Ross (#1)   Zurich, Switzerland   July 8, 1926
                        17:30 Zone -1, 47N23 8E32
                        Source: Bio by Derek Gill (B)

Elisabeth Kubler-Ross (#2)   Zurich, Switzerland   July 8, 1926
                        22:15 Zone -1, 47N23 8E32
                        Source: Elisabeth Kubler-Ross (A)

Elisabeth Kubler-Ross (#3)   Zurich, Switzerland   July 8, 1926
                        22:45 Zone -1, 47N23 8E32
                        Source: Elisabeth Kubler-Ross (A)

Chris Evert Lloyd   Ft. Lauderdale, FL   December 21, 1954
4:30 Zone +5, 26N7 80W8
Source: *Profiles of Women* (C)

Charles Manson   Cincinnati, OH   November 12, 1934
16:40 Zone +5, 39N06 84W31
Source: *Contemporary Sidereal
Horoscopes* (A)

William Masters   Cleveland, OH   December 27, 1915
19:20 Zone +5, 41N30 81W42
Source: *Gauquelin Book of American
Charts* (A)

Marliyn Monroe   Los Angeles, CA   June 1, 1926
9:30 Zone +8, 34N4 118W15
Source: Photo of birth certificate in
biography (A)

Leontyne Price   Laurel, MS   February 10, 1927
6:15 Zone +6, 31N41 89W8
Source: *Profiles of Women* (A)

Prince Albert   Monte Carlo, Monaco   March 14, 1958
10:50 Zone -1, 43N45 7E25
Source: Secretary quotes birth
records (A)

Prince Rainier   Monte Carlo, Monaco   May 31, 1923
6:00 Zone -1, 43N45 7E25
Source: Church of Light old file (C)

Princess Caroline   Monte Carlo, Monaco   January 23, 1957
9:27 Zone -1, 43N45 7E25
Source: Secretary quotes birth
records (A)

Princess Stephanie   Monte Carlo, Monaco   February 1, 1965
18:25 Zone -1, 43N45 7E25
Source: Secretary quotes birth
records (A)

Richard Pryor   Peoria, IL   December 1, 1940
                                 13:02 Zone +6, 40N42 89W36
                                 Source: *Gauquelin Book of American
                                     Charts* (A)

Tom Selleck   Detroit, MI   January 29, 1945
                                 8:22 Zone +4, 42N20 83W3
                                 Source: Barbara Ludwig quotes birth
                                     certificate via Penfield (C)

Frank Sinatra   Hoboken, NJ   December 12, 1915
                                 13:19 Zone +5, 40N44, 74W02
                                 Source: First Temple of Astrology,
                                     Karma Welch (C)

Gertrude Stein   Allegheny, PA   February 3, 1874
                                 8:00 LMT, 40N28 80W01
                                 Source: *Profiles of Women* (B)

Tennessee Williams   Columbus, MS   March 26, 1911
                                 2:30 Zone +6, 33N30 88W25
                                 Source: Lockhart, Emma Cates from
                                     him (C)

Private Individuals
Charles   Confidential   October 5, 1943
                                 4:25 Zone +5, 33N31 86W48

Daughter   Confidential   November 16, 1969
                                 3:43 Zone +8, 37N20 121W53

Ellen   Confidential   November 12, 1921
                                 17:15 Zone +5, 39N37 82W50

Father   Confidential   June 24, 1937
                                 13:20 Zone +8, 34N03 118W15

Female Client   Confidential   June 16, 1927
                                 0:02 Zone +4, 41N57 85W0

Francis   Confidential   January 22, 1947
                                 14:10 Zone -1, 46N10 8E48

Frank   Confidential   February 1, 1888
                         22:50 LMT, 49N19 12E52

Laura   Confidential   March 29, 1946
                         5:05 Zone +6, 36N10 86W47

Millie   Confidential   March 6, 1951
                         02:48 Zone +8, 34N04 118W15

Mother   Confidential   May 28, 1940
                         8:33 Zone +8, 34N03 118W15

Rick   Confidential   October 28, 1953
                         00:14 Zone +8, 34N06 118W20

Son #1   Confidential   March 5, 1959
                         8:21 Zone +8, 34N01 118W29

Son #2   Confidential   Sept. 20, 1961
                         5:15 Zone +8, 34N03 118W15

Son #3   Confidential   January 4, 1964
                         13:30 Zone +8, 34N03 118W15

Werner   Confidential   August 13, 1909
                         21:30 Zone -1, 51N50 12E17

INDEX OF HOROSCOPES
OF FAMOUS PEOPLE

A POSITIVE APPROACH TO THE TEACHING OF ASTROLOGY

by Joan McEvers

In teaching astrology for many years, I have tried to impress my students with the need to use the energies indicated by the planets positively and to make them realize that this usage is a matter of free will. There is nothing that forces them to use the powers Neptune symbolizes for confusion and delusion, but instead, by tuning into the higher vibration of Neptune's meaning, people can find spiritual enlightenment and creative inspiration.

In the beginning when you are trying to grasp the basic rudiments of a very complicated study, there is a distinct tendency for you to see only the negative side of a planet, sign or aspect. Just as reading about crime, murder, kidnapping and perversion in the daily newspaper is much more titillating than the ordinary humdrum things of life — or keeping abreast of the latest jet set or movie star goings-on is much more interesting than knowing who got an "A" on a geometry test — so it is with astrology. The fact that a Mars/Pluto square can indicate violent action at times is much more exciting than the fact that it can show energy (Mars) challenged (square) to uncover a hidden meaning or source of supply (Pluto).

Beginning students who come to my classes with a slight knowledge of transits often say something like, "I'm really scared of Uranus making a station on my Sun or Ascendant because it is going to make me accident-prone or cause sudden changes that I don't think I can handle." I ask them to realize that if they choose to use Uranian energy in a positive way, they can have an awakening...a sudden flash of genius or an idea for a new book or invention. The choice is theirs to use this energy in a productive way.

Saturn

The biggest problem in this area of positive or negative use of planetary characteristics seems to be Saturn. Granted, Saturn represents, among other things, the principles of limitation, contraction, crystallization and delay. But aren't these principles necessary in everyone's life? Certainly, without your skin and skeleton, both Saturn ruled, your flesh wouldn't have anything to hang on to or be confined by, and you would just be a blob. I tell my students that where Saturn is by house, you have something to learn so that you can teach it to others. As they learn the basic principles, they are able to see this and understand that Saturn's delays and limitations are as necessary to the horoscope as brakes are to a car.

Another challenge is when the novice astrologer sees a heavy Saturn transit or a Saturn return approaching. The usual reaction is to panic and feel a fear of coping with limiting, denying Saturn. The positive use of this energy is to learn the lessons of timing, self-perception, and concentration that a Saturn transit symbolizes.

Wherever Saturn transits, hard work, application and dedication are required. Properly channeled, accomplishments and status (indicated by Saturn) are rewarded by this hard work and dedication. If you fear working hard and resent dedicating yourself to the task at hand, Saturn's transit can indeed be difficult and fateful. But Saturn is the taskmaster of the zodiac, and mirrors society's demand for justice and consequences of past actions. Where this beautiful planet is, you reap what you sow.

At age 28 to 30, everyone gets a Saturn return. This takes place when the transiting Saturn returns by degree and sign to the place it occupies in the natal chart. For most people this is a challenging turning point in the life, because you have to face up to Saturn's lessons: bear your responsibilities and not hide from your obligations. If you cannot do this, then the Saturn return year can become one fraught with heartbreak and anguish. However, if you are using Saturn qualities (discipline, thoroughness, practicality) in your life positively, you will find that your Saturn return can mature you and prepare you to face the years ahead with wisdom and patience — also Saturn attributes.

You get a second Saturn return around age 58 to 60, when you get a second chance to deal with the Saturn principles. If you are acting out a negative interpretation of Saturn's qualities, you may experience the feeling that life is passing you by, or that just the daily affairs of living are too much for you to deal with. You may be feeling "old;" Saturn rules old age. All of this can be dealt with through a positive attitude and the realization that since your first Saturn return, you have gained wisdom and experience, and this is something that can be shared with others. Sharing is an extension of the teaching experience and teaching is a Saturn principle.

Mars

In the past, Mars has also been given a negative meaning in the birth chart. It has been said that where Mars is, there is temper, careless action, accidents and haste. This is often true, but could you imagine the chart without Mars to characterize drive and energy? And where would we find our soldiers, athletes, test pilots and race-car drivers without a strong Mars in the chart? By a strong Mars, I mean the one with squares and oppositions to it; they show the dynamism to get things accomplished.

The squares, conjunctions and oppositions in each chart enable you to tell where a person is operating. Trines and sextiles are nice and often denote a pleasing and charming personality, but the strength, ambition and drive of any horoscope is shown by the hard or angular aspects. Often the beginning student views these aspects as insurmountable hardship, tragedy, accident and even untimely death. I do not discount these possibilities, but I point out that it is by the challenges in our lives that we learn and accomplish. A square between Mars and Mercury may be a good indication of a hot temper or impulsive speech. The square suggests a quick mind but potential difficulty in expressing your thoughts tactfully. Your free will says that you can use this square by learning to control your temper and developing an original way of expressing yourself. True, this may not come easily, but lessons learned the hard way are seldom forgotten.

Houses

Another area where we are misled into a negative interpretation is house position. In looking at a natal chart with many 6th and 12th house planets, you might immediately think: illness and/or hospitalization — and this is always a possibility; but don't ever forget that the person has the right to exercise free will.

Several years ago I had a client with a heavy 6th/12th axis: Moon in Taurus in the 12th opposed by several Scorpio planets (including the Sun) in the 6th. I had never met her, and in the course of her consultation I asked if she was using this energy in a service-to-others capacity, perhaps working as a nurse or doctor's assistant. She replied that, though she had always been interested in the medical field, she was just a poor frustrated housewife with a lot of health problems, not the least among them a partial hysterectomy.

I explained to her about the energy symbolized by the planets in these particular houses and suggested that perhaps if she went to work in some area of the medical field, the energy would be positively used and her health might improve. A year later I saw her again; her health was better and she was working as a doctor's receptionist and enjoying it, although her marriage was falling apart. The next time I heard from her, she was ill, separated from her husband and unemployed. After the divorce she again went to work, but in the banking field; had a partial mastectomy, nervous upsets and other health problems. When I next heard from her, she was back in the medical field as a technologist after taking some training. Her health was improving, she had remarried and was looking forward to a good year — a year, I might add, that found transiting Uranus conjunct her Scorpio stellium and Saturn squaring it. But she was using these transits in the most positive way possible to change her work habits (Uranus in the 6th) and to stabilize her thinking patterns (Saturn in the 3rd).

Kennedy vs. Manson

Another example of positive or negative use of houses and planetary energies is to compare the charts of Robert Kennedy and Charles Manson. The horoscopes are quite similar and I have a class project where I give both charts to the students and ask them to tell me which is the upholder of the law and which is the fugitive from the law. Rarely can they tell them apart. To me this indicates the positive and negative use of similar planetary energies. One man chose to deal with crime from the side of the law; the other took the opposite way.

Kennedy and Manson both have Taurus rising. Kennedy's Ascendant ruler, Venus, is in Capricorn in the 9th house suggesting an interest in the law and, since it opposes Pluto, it could be criminal law. Manson has Venus in Scorpio in the 7th house conjunct his Sun, indicating interest in the law since the 7th is also a legal house. Both have 7th house Suns in Scorpio symbolizing the need to deal with people on a face-to-face basis. Both have the Moon in the 10th house which is often the case with those who come into the limelight in some way and attract notice or notoriety. Manson's Moon is in sometimes erratic Aquarius (it could have been humanitarian), while Kennedy has a more conservative (and sometimes hard) Capricorn Moon. However, it is not the sign the Moon is in so much as it is the aspects it makes.

Kennedy's Moon squares Mars indicating a hot temper and the ability to use biting sarcasm to get his point across — boundless energy and the ability to move mountains. There is also an opportunity sextile to the Sun.

Robert Kennedy
November 20, 1925
3:11 PM EST
Brookline, MA
42N20 71W07

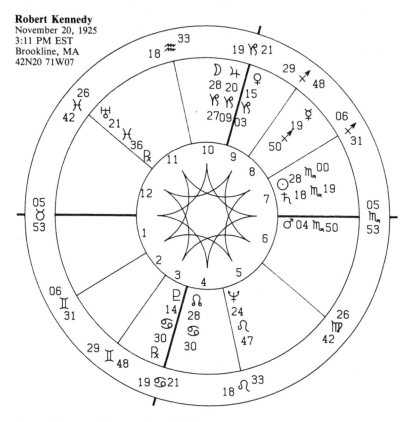

Source: *Horoscope Magazine* Sept. 1970 (C)

Manson's Moon is caught up in a frustration-indicating grand cross; opposing Pluto (widely) across the parental houses symbolizing the parental problems; square both Uranus and the Mercury/Jupiter conjunction, indicating a need to control his powerful ego, his stubbornness, fanaticism and high nervous tension. There are no easing aspects to help him find acceptable outlets for his frustration. (Some people express the powerful potential of similar patterns through highly aggressive, competitive business or sports activities.)

Mercury shows the reasoning and communicative abilities. Manson's Mercury is stationary direct in Scorpio just below the 7th house cusp and indicates his ability to spellbind and influence others in a (negative) Scorpio way. Others have used such a placement for research and depth analysis. Mercury conjuncts Jupiter suggesting an interest in the law in some capacity. Kennedy's Mercury is in Sagittarius in the 8th (Scorpio) house suggesting similar interests and outlook, and it has a trine to Neptune as well as a square to Uranus. The aspect to Neptune symbolizes compassion and concern for others, especially those he loves and cares about (although it could manifest as overidealism). Neptune is in the 5th house.

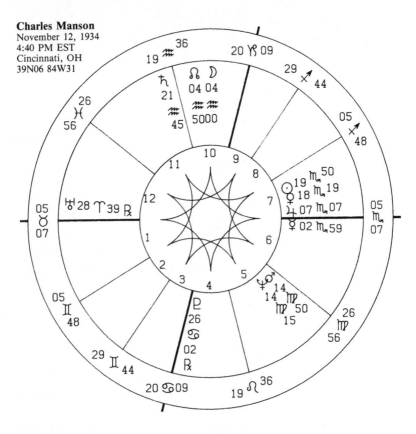

Charles Manson
November 12, 1934
4:40 PM EST
Cincinnati, OH
39N06 84W31

Source: *Contemporary Sidereal Horoscopes* (A)

Manson's Mercury opposes Uranus and Kennedy's squares it. Both of these aspects can indicate genius. Certainly both were highly intelligent and captivating personalities; others were swayed by their arguments. In both cases Mercury rules the 2nd house of values and

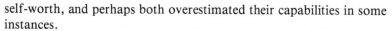

self-worth, and perhaps both overestimated their capabilities in some instances.

Manson's Neptune is also in the 5th house and it was necessary to him to feel that he was "loved;" but since Neptune exactly conjuncts Mars, this need was compulsive and eventually self-destructive (Mars rules the intercepted 12th house). Ruthless, self-centered, he wanted what he wanted, when he wanted it, regardless of the consequences. According to his biographer, Manson had an interest in music as a youngster, but he felt circumstances never allowed him to pursue it. Neptune in the 5th house with sextiles to Venus and the Sun often indicates this ability. These same aspects symbolize his almost hypnotic effect on his followers. Neptune glamorizes.

Even the nodal axis falls across the same houses, though it is reversed. Kennedy has the south node in the 10th house, hence he was comfortable in a public position; Manson's south node is in the 4th house, indicating his need for a "family" type situation.

The only real dissimilarities in the charts are the placement of Saturn, Jupiter and Pluto. In Kennedy's horoscope, Pluto in the 3rd house with its challenging oppositions to Venus and Jupiter indicates his political involvement with his brother (3rd house) and the tragic losses of siblings. These patterns can also show a fine mind with depth as well as breadth. The 4th house Pluto in Manson's chart is verification of the unhappy and unsettled childhood in his case. Other people have families interested in the occult, psychotherapy or it may simply be a deep need to control one's emotions. Jupiter in the 7th house shows Manson's ability to attract others to him and their willingness to do his bidding. The sextile to Neptune enhances his charisma, but his improper use of the challenging aspects and the fact that Jupiter rules the 8th house indicate the sort of macabre hold he had on his "family."

Where Saturn is in the horoscope is often where we overcompensate. Manson's Saturn is in the 11th house and Manson overcompensated in his need to have his friends do his bidding so he could gain notoriety (10th house). Kennedy used his Saturn energy in the 7th house and ruling the 10th to attract support and backing through face-to-face relationships. This support helped him gain a position of power where he wielded authority from a legal position (7th house.).

Pluto

Besides Saturn and Mars there is another planet that is often viewed negatively: Pluto. As a beginning astrologer, I found very little information available on Pluto. It was a mysterious little planet that ruled crime, plumbing and the underworld — all quite negative connotations. Since I try to use the planetary symbolism positively, I have worked hard and long to find some of Pluto's positive attributes. Basically where Pluto is in the natal chart, you can gain a great awareness of yourself in a subtle and gradual way. You can learn to delve into your subconscious to better understand your true conscious self. When Pluto is angular there is strong ability for leadership. Of course care must be taken not to let this take the form of dictatorship. Positively used, natally, by progression or transit, Pluto presents the ultimate opportunity for growth and change through inner transformation. Both Kennedy and Manson had the potential to grow and transform on deep, psychological levels. Each chose to wield the power drive signified in their charts in his own way.

THE MANY FACES OF PLUTO
by Marion D. March

Ever since I started studying astrology some 18 years ago, I've been fascinated by the small, way far out — but oh so significant — planet Pluto. In those 18 years I've observed Pluto's meanings in over 500 private charts, and thousands more of famous people. The deeper I probed, the more convinced I became that Pluto is the most multifaceted of all the planets.

Astronomical Qualities

Pluto is the most distant planet from our Sun (3.64 million miles). Too small to ever be seen with the naked eye, Pluto was the last planet to be discovered in our solar system (1930). Pluto's orbit is more eccentric and its inclination from the plane of the ecliptic is greater than that of any other planet. At perihelion (nearest distance to the Sun) it is closer to the Sun than Neptune is at aphelion (greatest distance from the Sun). It is also the slowest moving of all planets, taking nearly 248 years to traverse the zodiac. Pluto stays longest in Taurus, the probable sign of its detriment (about 32 years), and shortest in Scorpio, the probable sign of its dignity (about 12 years).

Rulership

Rulerships of planets in certain signs have been assigned according to which of the attributes or traits of that sign the planet best represents. After observing Pluto since 1930, astrologers still are debating whether it rules Scorpio or Aries. The majority lean to Scorpio and personally I am convinced that the divergent qualities expressed by Pluto correspond to Scorpionic traits.

I see Aries as impulsive, while Pluto is compulsive (Scorpio). Aries is ardent whereas Pluto/Scorpio are passionate; eager versus intense, independent versus possessive, dynamic versus penetrating, arrogant versus sarcastic, quick tempered versus vengeful, hasty versus deliberate, zesty versus incisive — all key words which fit both Pluto and Scorpio to a tee.

Glyphs

Even Pluto's glyphs are controversial, since there are at least 6 of them still in use. The most used ♇ stood for the first two letters of the word Pluto, as well as the initials of Percival Lowell, the astronomer who had pursued and investigated the mysterious planet for years, but who died before its actual discovery. ♇ is considered by some a more evolved glyph than ♇. Astrologer Isabel Hickey referred to it as the higher side of Pluto and called it Minerva. On the European continent ♇ or ♇ is most often used, which shows their early assignment of Pluto as the ruler of Aries. Some Scandinavian charts employ these gylphs for Pluto: ☉ or ☉ , symbolizing the melding of solar and lunar forces. Some astrologers utilize these two glyphs: ♅ or ♇ .

Mythology

The literal meaning of the word Pluto is riches. Its implied meaning is also surplus, might, treasure, fortune and blessing. The riches supposedly were the fertile earth, the depth of which Pluto, also known as Hades, ruled. In Greek mythology he was the son of one of the Titans, Cronus, and his sister/wife Rhea. After the fall of the Titans, Pluto/Hades and his brothers Zeus/Jupiter and Poseidon/Neptune divided the universe. Zeus and his sister/wife Hera took over the heavens; Poseidon ruled the waters; and Pluto/Hades everything underground.

Just as there are diverse glyphs for Pluto, the mythological tales of this god abound. As Hades he was also called the "Unseen," the god to whom all must go sooner or later; but the living shrank away from giving a face to one who became their lord upon death. He was accorded universal respect and given reverence by those who cared for the condition of the departed. In early tradition his realm was in the west (*Odyssey*, Book X), since the Sun set there. Later it was placed underground and everyone, after being properly buried, arrived at one of Hades' rivers. Pluto is also depicted as the King of the Underworld, seated on a throne of sulfur from which flow the streams Lethe (oblivion), Cocytus (lamentation), Phlegethon (river of fire) and Acheron (river of shadows), all four of which traverse the kingdom of the dead and flow into the sacred river Styx.

The best known Pluto/Hades myth relates to Persephone, daughter of Zeus, and Demeter, goddess of fertility. Zeus gave Hades permission to take Persephone as his wife, whereupon he snatched her while she was picking flowers and bore her off in his black chariot to his kingdom. Demeter's grief while searching for her daughter caused all nature to wither and a famine threatened Earth. Seeing the blackened soil, Zeus relented and sent Hermes to fetch Persephone back, but she had eaten part of a pomegranate and was already beholden to Hades. A compromise was reached and Persephone spent part of the time with her mother where she remained the carefree young girl picking flowers; the rest of the time she reigned with Hades where she was considered a tragic but fearsome queen.

In some myths Pluto was an inexorable god, goading the unwilling into his realm with a pitchfork, hated by gods and men alike. The souls of the dead, accompanied by Hermes, were met by Hades' dog Cerberus who guarded the gates so that no one could ever again emerge. After judgment, the souls were allocated to Tartarus, a place of torment in the lower underworld; if virtuous, they were given a place in the joyous Elysian Fields. For heroes there was also an alternative reward: eternal life in the far-off Isles of the blessed where the Golden Age was recreated.

A pleasant aspect to life after death is also reflected in the identification of Pluto as the giver of wealth, food and corn. This connection leads to one more face of Pluto, namely, as the mysterious son of a goddess, with Demeter's name most often mentioned. That would make Demeter his sister (as daughter of Cronus and Rhea), his mother-in-law (mother of his wife Persephone) and his mother. As the story goes, a young Cretan hunter named Iasion mated 3 times with Demeter in the fertile and plowed fields. The goddess bore the child Pluto — the bearer of riches — and in thanks the earth gave forth a manifold harvest.

The most fascinating discovery is that there is a female Pluto in mythology. According to mythology, "Tantalus, who offended the gods by serving them the cut-up flesh of his son Pelops at a banquet, was himself the son of Zeus and his mother was Pluto, a sea nymph." Some go into even greater detail: "Tantalus' mother was Pluto, the rich one, a daughter of Cronus. Thanks to her, Lydia was famous for its gold — gold in the veins of its mountains and in the sands of its rivers. No name better suited the greatest goddess of this land than the name Pluto.''

Myth and reality, how far apart are they in this world where everything is interconnected? Where does mythology end and folklore or history start? How much of this is inherent in the archetype of Pluto? Pluto the prince of darkness who rules the nether world; Pluto the "unseen" yet respected and revered god; Pluto the tempter who snatched innocent Persephone and offered her a pomegranate; Pluto the relentless one goading his victims with a pitchfork, reminiscent of Christianity's symbolism for Satan; Pluto the great goddess of riches. Pluto, the smallest planet with the most eccentric orbit, was discovered at a time when scientists were studying the possibility of splitting the atom and found that by bombarding uranium with neutrons at a suitable speed, it can be transformed into plutonium, an element not found in nature but needed for a new form of energy — atomic energy.

Meanings

So here we have Pluto's main ingredients — the ruler of the underworld, the androgynous male/female figure and the great Earth mother. (In natal delineation I use the Sun, Mars and Saturn as the three planets describing the father or male principles, with the Moon, Venus and Pluto as the mother or female principles.) Pluto is the bearer of riches to the point of surplus, very visible and "seen" versus hidden, underground and "unseen."

What better way to describe certain covert sexual urges that seem to burst forth from some unknown depth within us than through the allegory of Pluto, god of the dark underworld, seducing his beloved with the forbidden fruit. What better comparison to Pluto's need to exert power or be in control than the god Pluto sitting in judgment over which soul should go to *Elysium* (heaven), or *Tartarus* (hell), or live in eternity (*Nirvana*).

What better explanation for "transformation," astrology's favorite key word for Pluto, than the reality of uranium being transformed into **Pluto**nium shortly after the discovery of the planet.

Collective Unconscious

Astrologer Liz Greene feels that the outer planets Uranus, Neptune and Pluto tune in to the collective unconscious (a Jungian term). I agree with her, particularly where Neptune and Pluto are concerned, and I feel that the Einsteins, Bohrs, Fermis and Oppenheimers of the world "tuned in" when the time was right to discover a new energy, while astronomers simultaneously found a new planet to rule, or astrologically explain that energy. Physicists became the vehicles to bring the subterranean forces to the surface or into the conscious world.

By tuning in to the collective unconscious we can also see why the mythology of the Greeks is closely related to folklore, fairy tales, The *Bible*, the *Talmud*, the *Vedas*, the *Koran*, and so on. The pomegranate, a beautiful flowering tree that produced fruit only when protected, a fruit whose seeds were said to have medical (aphrodisiacal?) properties, is as much a symbol of temptation as the apple that Eve ate.

To relate it to Pluto, it is the forbidden fruit of any age, especially that which is inherent in darkness, night or secret places, all truly Plutonic attributes. It could represent the stolen kiss of the Victorian age, necking or petting in the backseat of a car during the 1930s and 1940s or some sexual orgies of today. The incestuous relations of the gods may raise our eyebrows but were totally accepted then, just as homosexuality was taken for granted during much of the Roman Empire.

In the *Upanishads* (Indian), the creation of the world is the work of a supreme creator. As such, s/he breaks in two parts, male and female, and thus becomes two people. The female thinks: "How can he who just begat me mate with me? Maybe I better hide from him." So she transforms herself into a cow — but he changes into a steer and mates with the cow, and thus it continues in the name of creation, procreation and transformation.

The collectively attuned person can understand why Scorpio's symbolism of the snake was changed into a phoenix. In Indian myths and religions, the powers of *kundalini* are like a snake, coiled at the bottom of the spine, waiting to uncoil its force and reach upward to illumination and insight, or downward to violence and self-destruction. The snake was therefore revered and feared. But Christian ethics, and especially Freud's later equation of snakes with sex in a sinful or guilt-ridden fashion, ruined that symbolism for us in the Western world.

We felt much happier with the phoenix, that sacred Egyptian bird with reddish plumage the color of the Sun and the face as white as the Moon. The phoenix self-immolates by placing itself on the burning altar (martyrdom of Christ) and then, rising from its own ashes as a young and healthy bird, flies away into a new life (resurrection). That symbolism still means death and rebirth, or Pluto's ability to transform, but in a language we can understand today. The collectively attuned person knows that death is a form of transmutation or a changing of form. As Pluto's energies seep into our conscious level, people like Elisabeth Kubler-Ross (author of *On Death and Dying*) can advocate ideas like death with dignity and find willing ears. Doctors can find ways to transplant organs and overcome the body's natural rejection and extend one person's physical life through another's physical death. They can also use Pluto's obsessive traits and prolong life beyond its point of sense or reason through machines and other mechanical means.

The collective unconscious is no guarantee of good or bad. It is a collection of everything: past, present and future. Atomic energy can become atomic destruction through a bomb; sexual equality can come into our awareness as well as sexual misuse through exploitation, child pornography, sado-masochism, etc.

Since Pluto is so far away from Earth, its symbolism is slow, deep, probing and far reaching, both for the individual and the masses. Its meaning cannot be timed because it advances and retrogrades in a restricted area of the horoscope for nearly two years. It is more like a seed sown which sprouts and pierces the Earth's surface in its own good time (free will!).

The Outer Planets

When talking of the transcendentals, we might say that Uranus indicates awakenings, Neptune illuminations, and Pluto transformations by making a transition into a new state of being. For this reason I feel that the higher vibrations of the transcendentals are only achieved after the personality is formed. The child may use the energy Uranus symbolizes to rebel, to be (as adults would interpret it) different, to shock, but not to fulfill some unique function. Few children will think of illumination or enlightenment in their growing years; they might use Neptunian themes to dream their dreams, to imagine their imaginary playmates or to put a veil over realities they cannot face. How can children think of Pluto as transforming when they have not even formed?

It is only at an appropriate point in time that what Pluto portends can project outward or inward. Pluto, planet of mystery, can represent our eventual bridge between the spiritual and material world (the riches versus the unseen), and therewith embody the principle of transition or transformation. Pluto, planet of sex, can be the force to insure the perpetuation of life. In Pluto the processes of creation and death seem to merge. The Plutonian energies often demolish or destroy in order to reconstruct the new from the rubble of the old — by tearing down the old and accepted concepts, it forces us to make way for the new.

Mass Consciousness

Where is the difference between Adolf Hitler — Libra rising, Pluto in Gemini in the 8th house, quincunx the Moon and Jupiter, conjunct Neptune — and my uncle, born the same day, in Fuerth (Bavaria) one hour earlier, same Ascendant, same Pluto aspects, who was blown to pieces by a grenade during World War I at age 17; yet according to his brothers he was a gentle soul who would not hurt a fly. Or humanitarian, doctor and musician Albert Schweitzer, Libra ascending, Pluto in the 8th house involved in a grand cross with Saturn, Mars and Uranus.

Can Pluto tell us why Sissy Spacek, with Virgo rising and Pluto in Leo in the 11th house, inconjunct Mercury and opposition Venus, became an actress while Richard Speck, Virgo rising, Pluto in Leo in the 11th house, trine Mercury, opposition Venus, became a mass murderer?

Obviously Pluto by itself is not the key to a person's total personality or behavior; it is but one of the cogs in the wheel. It can help us identify issues and themes, but does not tell us what the person will do with those issues (free will). Yet those who tune in to that extra vibration (which is neither higher, lower, better or worse) can be propelled into mass consciousness.

Generational Themes

Pluto's transit through the signs of the zodiac is too long to have personal meaning and should be viewed in a historical sense, as its meaning applies to a generation. It can represent that generation's common ideas and ideals, leading into a collective destiny.

A cursory glance at history in capsule form reveals that less happened when Pluto was last in Scorpio, 1737 to 1749, than many another time: no wars, no famines, no great scientific discoveries. But Bering sighted and explored Alaska in 1740. During the previous pass of Pluto in Scorpio, 1491 to 1503, Michelangelo sculpted the *Pieta* and Leonardo da Vinci painted the *Mona Lisa*; Columbus discovered the New World; Vasco da Gama sailed around Africa and found a sea route to India, while John Cabot explored Canada. Again, no report of pestilence, volcanic eruptions or other great disasters.

Could it be that instead of upheavals, major earthquakes, Armageddon and other catastrophic events predicted for the 1983 to 1995 stay of Pluto in Scorpio, we will discover new worlds in outer space? Is it our instinctive fear of the mysterious and unknown that makes us wonder which face Pluto will show next? Could Pluto, ruler of the 8th house of the public's resources, bring the long overdue total change in the world's monetary systems? Or could it be a new approach to medicine? The holistic trend started with Pluto in Virgo could come to fruition through new medical discoveries, leading to less surgery and more natural healing. A new physical method of birth control for men rather than women might also be in the offing, as well as new understanding and acceptance in Third World countries to limit their child-bearing.

It is Pluto's house position, its aspects and the house which it rules that will show us where and how we can personally best meet the challenge of our destiny; and when we find it, we have to solve the problems unaided and alone.

Pluto can be the redeemer, a word which according to the dictionary means "to change for the better, to release and to reform," and can represent another way of transforming. Pluto is like a volcano (volcanic is a synonym for the word plutonic), seething below and waiting to erupt. Which way will you let it erupt?

The choice is yours!

Bibliography

Gehre, Fritz. "Mythologisches." *Astrolog*, No. 13 (April 20, 1983): 10-12.

Greene, Liz. *The Outer Planets and Their Cycles*. Reno, Nevada: CRCS Pub., 1983.

Hickey, Isabel and Bruce Altieri. *Pluto or Minerva*. Bridgeport, Connecticut: Altieri Press, 1973.

Ions, Veronica. *The World's Mythology*. London: Hamlyn Pub., 1974.

The MacMillan Everyman's Encyclopedia. 4th Ed. in 12 Volumes. New York: MacMillan Co., 1959.

New Columbia Encyclopedia. New York: Columbia University Press, 1975.

New La Rousse Encyclopedia of Mythology. London: Prometheus Press, 1968.

Stapleton, Michael. *Dictionary of Greek and Roman Mythology*. New York: Bell Pub. Co., 1978.

World Book Encyclopedia — Greek Mythology. Chicago: World Books, Inc., 1983.

HOUSES AND THEIR RULERS
by Joan McEvers

Basically I am a house-oriented astrologer. I have studied the Ebertin system and have great regard for the research the Ebertins have done, but I cannot give up the use of a house system, because I find that house placement is often as important as and many times more important than the sign the planet is in. I find this to be particularly true in comparison charts as well as in natal interpretation. If you have the Sun in the 1st house, regardless of sign, you will come across with many Arian qualities. Perhaps the foremost research in astrology has been conducted by Michel and Francoise Gauquelin. They found **high** significance in planets in houses — as keys to vocation and basic character traits.*

Placement of the House Ruler

House position is truly significant, and one of the most pertinent parts is the placement of the house ruler. There are 144 possibilities for the ruler of each house in every house in the wheel — the ruler of the 1st house in the 1st, 7th, 10th, and so on. Where the ruler of the house is, is where you function through that house. The way that I view the chart is that the ruler of each house "owns" that particular house.

For instance, if you have Gemini on the cusp of the 2nd house, the planet Mercury rules that house. And even though the Moon or Jupiter may be placed there, Mercury, as the "owner," runs the house and sets the rules and regulations, while the Moon and Jupiter may be considered guests visiting, or renters living in, a house which is not

---

* See, for example, *The Psychology of the Planets* by Francoise Gauquelin (San Diego, California: ACS Publications, Inc., 1982).

really theirs.

In other words, the ruler has more jurisdiction over the affairs of that house than any other planet in the chart, including those which may be there. I do not subscribe to the theory that a rising planet or one in high focus is the chart ruler. There are many different schools of thought about the planet judged to be the chart ruler and you can measure it in many different ways — harmonics, astrodynes, strength by sign, element or quality — but in keeping it simplistic, your chart ruler is the planet which rules your Ascendant. Where it is, you function best. Whatever house that ruling planet occupies in your particular chart is where you can function in a very positive and forceful way. This is, of course, modified by the planet in question. Uranus would not symbolize the same actions as the Sun, Venus or Saturn.

Regardless of whose chart you are looking at, you will get tremendous insight if you remember to look at the **ruling planet** and key in on it. I do a lot of quick interpretations. People come up to me after a class or lecture, stick a chart in front of me and say, "Tell me about this person." It may be their own chart or one of a friend or family member. I don't always have time to give them a whole chart reading. The first thing I do is look for the Ascendant ruler and comment about the house it is in. You really can't miss with this method, because where that planet is will be a very important area in the person's life.

If, for instance, the Ascendant ruler is in the 6th house, you know the person could be a capable, hard worker or could have a lot of health problems. Invariably, that placement works in one of these two ways. They may be dedicated to service in the work that they do, but you have a clue right away and can amplify from there, depending on the sign the planet is in, the aspects and other factors in the chart.

When there are challenging aspects to your chart ruler, you may have to deal with health problems related to the planet and the sign, but if you use the energies for work instead, you probably won't have time to be sick.

EMPTY HOUSES

House rulers play a vital part in the interpretation of **empty houses**. One of the things I run into with beginning students is: "I have an empty 5th house. Does that mean I will never have children?" Most all astrologers have been confronted with: "I don't have any planets in my 7th house. Am I ever going to marry?" I ran into that early in my career as a counselor. A lady called and made an appointment. When asked if there were any specific problems, she said, "Yes, I have been to another astrologer and he told me I'd never marry.'' She was about 26 years old and felt she was in danger of becoming an old maid. I asked what his reason was for telling her that and asked if she wanted to marry. She was anxious to get married and replied that he told her that because there were no planets in her 7th house, it was unlikely that she would ever wed. She became a client, also a student of astrology and has been married twice. The first marriage was not too happy and maybe this was what the astrologer saw and was trying to keep her from. Her second marriage is very happy and she has a darling baby girl.

There are empty houses in every chart, and everyone has at least two someplace because there are only 10 planets and 12 houses. Beginning astrologers often have a problem about what to say about those empty houses. If you make it a point to locate the ruler, you will find that gives considerable information about the affairs of the empty house.

DECANATES AND DWADS

There is a system I find invaluable when assessing these houses. That is to look at the **decanate and dwad** rulers of the houses. Decanates are a method of dividing the signs into three sections of 10° each. Dwads divide the signs into twelfths (each segment having 2½°). The decanate of the first 10° of any sign emphasizes the sign itself and is ruled by the ruler of the sign. The next 10° (decanate) is represented by the second sign of the element. The last 10° is indicated by the third sign of the element. The decanates of the sign Aries are Aries, Leo and Sagittarius. The first 10° are Aries and said to be ruled by Mars. The next 10° have a Leo quality and are ruled by the Sun. The last 10° (of the sign Aries) are the Sagittarius decanate and are ruled by Jupiter. Dwads start with the sign and proceed through all the signs in the zodiac in 2½° segments. The first dwad of Taurus (0° to 2½°) is Taurus, the second dwad of Taurus (2½° to 5°) is Gemini, and so on. This system is illustrated in Volume II of *The Only Way To...Learn Astrology* and in *12 Times 12*.

When you have an empty house with a middle or late degree on the cusp, after you look at the house and sign that the ruler of the cusp is in, check the decanate ruler for more information. And if you care to go further, look at the dwad ruler. For example, if 15° Gemini is on the cusp of the 4th house and the house is unoccupied by any planets, see where Mercury (the ruler of Gemini) is; but also bring in Venus because the Libra decanate is involved. You could check the placement of Jupiter as well because it rules that dwad.

For instance, in the example just cited, you might say that your parents were interested in your early education and you probably had, depending on the aspects to and placement of Mercury, good lines of communication with them. If Mercury is in Aquarius, your parents were probably fairly progressive. At least, you grew up in a home where you weren't made to toe the line traditionally. If Venus, the decanate ruler, is in Capricorn in the 12th house, it may indicate a tacit understanding and a deeply loving but reserved relationship. You realize it may have been a pretty free-and-easy household with a lot of intellectual conversation, but your parents made you shape up when you stepped out of line. You would not have picked up this information from Mercury in Aquarius ruling the 4th house. If Jupiter the dwad ruler were in Scorpio in the 9th house, religion or philosophy may have played a role in your relationship with your parents.

I do not feel that there is a hard-and-fast rule about which parent is in which house. The first astrology book I read said that my mother was the 4th house and my father the 10th; the second book said just the opposite. Two or three books down the line said that if you were a woman, your mother is the 10th and if you're a man, your father is the 10th. After doing much counseling and teaching, I would say to someone with a challenging Moon in the 4th house, "You had a hard time relating to your mother." The person would reply, "No, my mother and I get along fine. It's my father I have problems with." You see an afflicted Saturn in the 10th house square to the Sun and say, "Father problems?" The client replies, "No, my mother died when I was two and he was both mother and father to me." So much for the 10th house as the father and the 4th house as the mother.

The Sun relates to the father and the Moon to the mother, except when you talk to someone about their parents. Then I find them interchangeable and dependent upon many other factors in the chart and upon how far a person has evolved. If the client is dealing with the stress in their life pretty well, then you may have a hard time sorting out what represents the mother and which house and/or planet relates to the father. You have to ask the person, and this is very important. It is not necessary to "prove" astrology to anyone. If you do counseling, you must ask questions. It is not necessary for you to know all about a person beforehand. In fact, it's probably better if you don't because it is easier for you to be objective.

If you see something in the chart that indicates potential parental issues, say, "I see you might have had problems relating to a parent. Which one might it be?" Or, "It appears you felt a lot of emotional support from a parental figure. Who would you say it was?" This is a much better approach than psyching yourself into thinking that you know all about a person from their chart. You cannot possibly know everything about them.

INTERCEPTED HOUSES

With **intercepted houses**, it is necessary to give the interception a lot of attention. I believe these houses are the most important axis in the chart, whether or not they have planets posited in them. I feel it is important to use a wheel that gives actual house size. It takes a little longer to draw the chart that way, but it is quite graphically helpful in noting house size. Generally, the intercepted house has the largest area. You have the symbolism of at least three planets in each intercepted house: the planet that rules the sign on the cusp; the planet that rules the intercepted sign; the planet ruling the degrees of the third sign in the house. If you happen to have planets in the house, you can see the importance of that axis in the individual's life and psyche.

If 29° is on the cusp of a house, that house is ruled by the planet which rules that sign, but you do have to take into consideration the next sign and its ruler as having great meaning in reading the affairs of the house. This is particularly true of the 1st house, where you are dealing with personality, appearance and character. If you have 29° Aquarius rising and 30° of Pisces intercepted in the 1st house, many people will see you as a Pisces. If you have a planet there, the situation is even more complicated. The planet must be taken into consideration.

1ST HOUSE

The **1st house** and its ruler are significant in assessing your attitudes, behavior, and appearance; and the house that holds the ruler is an area where you usually function at your best.

2ND HOUSE

Wherever the **2nd house** ruler is in your horoscope is where you learn values. The 2nd house of the chart shows how you develop your value system, how you learn to evaluate yourself. It is the house of possessions, earning ability and personal freedom. It also denotes your inner and outer resources and talents and is the house where you can seek and find your freedom. In other words, it gets down to self-worth. It's how you earn your money, how and what you buy, what you spend, what's important to you; but above all, it is the house that shows how you learn what you value. Where the ruler is describes an area **where** you learn about these values. If the ruler of your 2nd house is in the 7th house, where are you going to learn this? From partnership or interaction with other people. But don't tie that 7th house only to partnership. It is all the people you deal with on a face-to-face basis. That can be friends, enemies, strangers, agents who work on your behalf. So if your 2nd house ruler is in the 7th house, other people will help you to develop your value system.

If your 2nd house ruler is in the 8th house, you may have to struggle for a large part of your life not to sublimate your value system to someone else's. This is much more applicable than if your 2nd house ruler is in the 7th house. You're influenced by other people when it is in the 7th, but with your 2nd house ruler in the 8th house, you tend to have trouble distinguishing whether you want to adopt their values or whether you want to stay with what you've developed yourself.

3RD HOUSE

The **3rd house** represents your need to communicate your ideas, to express verbally or in writing. It shows early education, how you relate to your environment, the way you get along with your siblings (if you have any). It also indicates short trips and all means of land transportation such as cars, trains and buses. When I look at the 3rd house my first thought is, "How does this person communicate?" I find that communication is the main province of this house. You can tell a lot about the personality and the person's projection of it from the 1st and 3rd houses. If you look to the houses that the rulers of these houses are in, you will add great depth to your analysis of the horoscope.

If you have the ruler of your 3rd house in the 10th, you have a great need to be heard, to voice your thoughts and ideas, and you may feel most comfortable doing it from a stage. This need for self-expression becomes a projection of your ego and usually catapults you into some sort of limelight. You come to public attention through what you say or write more often than because of what you do.

When the ruling planet has challenging aspects, notoriety may be what you seek; you may have difficulty getting the words out or you may stammer or stutter when it is necessary for you to speak in public. Of course, other factors in your chart would indicate this also. Communication blocks are sometimes related to harsh personal standards. The 10th house (like Saturn) can symbolize a tendency toward critical, exacting judgment which tends to focus on shortcomings rather than assets. You need to be practical and realistic without being too hard on yourself.

4TH HOUSE

The **4th house** has always been a stumbling block for me. I think every astrologer has a blind spot, and the 4th is the house where I have tripped and fallen. Over the years, I have concluded that it is much more than your parents and early life. It shows your psychological conditioning and what you base your attitudes on. Since life is basically an attitude, this becomes a very important house in the delineation of a chart. Typically it signifies the home you wish to establish for yourself. It represents your private life, one of your parents — usually the most nurturing one in your childhood. It is your foundation and shows the closing years of your life and the end of all matters.

You can tell a tremendous amount about a person's innermost attitudes and feelings — not the part of their personality that they show the world, like the 1st house, but how they really feel deeply within themselves — by careful analysis of the 4th house.

If you have the ruler of your 4th house in the 2nd, you may be extremely money conscious, but it may also signify that you earn (2nd) by working in the home (4th) or by dealing in commodities like real estate, agriculture, geology and related fields. Your attitude toward life can be based on what money buys, your ability to apply your talents, or your earning capacity. Generally, security (emotional and physical) is important to you.

5TH HOUSE

The **5th house** shows creativity and children; it is the house of love and romance, speculation and daring. Noel Tyl did a series of books several years ago and made a good case for the 5th as the house of sex. This is where romance starts; the 5th shows unbonded relationships, and these are often sexual, but I cannot agree that the 5th is the house of sex. I think it is more the fun you get out of life and, for that matter, sex. One area of the 5th house that is often neglected in chart reading is that it is the house of risk and danger. It is where you speculate; where you gamble, not just with money or property. It is where you speculate or gamble with your life. Many race-car drivers, athletes, aviators, people who work in risky professions (pipefitters, steeplejacks) have a heavily tenanted 5th house. Their vocational houses (2nd, 6th, 10th) may be tied to the 5th in some way.

The 5th house represents children, and theoretically Leos (the natural sign for this house) are supposed to love children. It doesn't always work that way. Either they love children or they don't want them around at all. Leos only love children who love **them**; they demand a response from those they love. Planets in the 5th act much the same way. I had several women in a class one time who each had nine or more children. I assumed they all had to have a strong 5th house or strong Leo. Three of the four were Aries, the other was a Capricorn and only one had planets in the 5th. Of course, other elements in the charts indicated their need for such large families.

If the ruler of your 5th house is in the 12th, your romantic encounters may be of the clandestine variety. Your pleasure may come from research into the past and your creativity may come from your need to be by yourself, in a field such as writing or genealogy. You may be a creative artist or performer; you may be very dramatic and good at sales, promotion and persuasion.

6TH HOUSE

The **6th house** to me is an easy one to delineate. People with planets in the 6th house are some of the most interesting ones I know. I feel that house placement is more significant than signs. It is people who have planets in the 6th house (especially the Sun) who have proven this to me. Without exception, in my experience, those with the Sun in the 6th house come across to others as Virgo. You have to know them a long time before you see their Sun sign qualities. People with planets in the 6th house often have health problems until they learn to use those planets in a working situation. They're often the people who have never worked. "I don't know how to go out and get a job." "My husband has always taken care of me." "Father supports me." "I dabble in the arts and that is my work." Most of them have health problems; some of them very serious problems.

The 6th house person needs to keep busy. The work they do can be volunteer work, but it must be something that makes them feel that they are contributing, that they are worthwhile, that they are somehow serving the community. As Isabel Hickey said, "This is the serve or suffer house."

If you have the ruler of the 6th in the 11th, you may find your friends in your place of business, financial support for a business effort may come through the government or an acquaintance, or you could work for a large organization.

7TH HOUSE

The **7th** is a relationship house and therefore describes your social activities as well as your attitude toward marital or business partnerships. It also shows anyone who acts in your behalf such as lawyers or agents. It is considered the house of your open enemies, the public and what you look for in others.

When the Sun is in the 7th house, you find a Libra-type person, regardless of the sign it is in. I have a friend whom I met when she came to a beginning astrology class many years ago. For the first two years I knew her, I never saw her without the two ladies she came to class with. They always arrived and left together. We became friendly and she would drop in to talk about astrology or to ask a question about something that was puzzling her. She always had someone with her: a friend, her husband or children, a neighbor or neighbor's child; someone was with her every time. She has a Taurus Sun and Scorpio rising and I wondered why she always had to be in the company of other people. Her Sun is in the 7th house.

I knew Libra rising people don't do anything by themselves if they can possibly help it. My husband has a Libra Ascendant, and when the kids were little he'd ask me to go to the store with him to pick up a magazine. If I was doing the laundry or dishes and declined, he'd ask the oldest child to go. He'd reply, "No, Dad. I have to do my homework." My husband would go to the next one. "I have a ball game, Dad. See you later." He'd work his way through all four kids and wind up taking the dog rather than go alone. Libra rising people rarely like to go anywhere or do anything by themselves. I know some independent Librans, but they do not have the Sun in the 7th house.

On the other hand, people who have a 12th house Sun prefer to do things by themselves. Even more so than those with the Sun in the 1st. People with the Sun in the 12th are often not as shy as you may be led to believe. It depends on the sign. Aries, Leo or Sagittarius Sun in the 12th house is usually not inhibited, but they may be a loner. They don't mind doing things by themselves, as opposed to the 7th house Sun person who needs companionship to feel complete. Anyone with many planets in the 7th house needs to find various partners and is able to have two or three partners at the same time. I don't mean bigamy. Business partnerships could be the answer. People with strong 7th house emphasis, ruler of the 1st, 6th or 7th in the 7th, all may well be involved in partnerships. This can be marital partnership or someone they go skiing with. They only see that person when they go skiing.

When I began my study of astrology, two of my sons were of draft age and the Vietnam War was raging. One son came home and announced that he had enlisted in the service. I rushed to my friend's house with his chart in hand and said, "What house do I look at for him going into the service?" She replied that she was taught to look at the 6th house for service rendered. There were aspects to his 6th house by progression and transit and I was very nervous. I really didn't want him to go into the service as my best friend's son had just been killed in 'Nam. I watched the progressions and transits operate and he didn't leave. Instead, he went to work. He was waiting to be called for his physical; he had applied for a specific branch of the service, a photography unit. They said they wouldn't take him unless they could place him there. The aspects passed, and though I was greatly relieved when he didn't get his assignment, I thought astrology didn't work. A few months later I ran across an article in an old astrology magazine. Someone had written a letter to the editor and said that when her son had gone to war in World War II, there had been aspects to the 7th house involved. She said she had gone to a famous astrologer and he said the 7th house depicted war and before you went off to war, you had to have aspects involving the 7th. The 7th house is the service you give your country in time of war. In subsequent study, I have found this to be true.

If the ruler of your 7th is in your 1st house, you probably identify strongly with your partner. Certainly, partnership is important to you and often you have the need to dominate the partnership. Whether you will or not depends upon the planet, the sign and the aspects. But basically you are a leader rather than a follower and function best in that role.

8TH HOUSE

My earliest recollections of the **8th house** always referred to sex, death and taxes. I wasn't particularly interested in taxes, and sex wasn't one of the things we talked about much (times sure have changed). I certainly wasn't going to tell people about when or where or how they were going to die, so I sort of skipped over the 8th house when I was doing charts. I'd tell them they had a healthy attitude toward sex and hopefully would live a long time. I really had a hard time talking about the 8th house, not because I am inhibited, but because I didn't know what to say. Until I had done many charts of people with an active 8th house, my knowledge was limited.

Most of the people I know who have a strong 8th house are not the sexy people they've been depicted as. They may be sexy, but it is not because of their 8th house planets. They are very practical. They take on a Scorpio attitude: incisive, into details and follow-through. These are the people who, no matter how badly life treats them, land on their feet. They are survivors. It may be the Plutonian quality of regeneration. It sounds nice to say that the 8th house is regenerative and reforming, but what do those words mean? Practical application means these are the survivors: those who endure trauma, seemingly insurmountable problems, near death, but they are the ones who bounce back.

A very dear friend has her Ascendant ruler in the 8th house. She is not a very outdoorsy person, but was persuaded to take a rafting trip down the Colorado River. The raft was overcrowded. The weather turned bad. The raft overturned and she was trapped underneath and swept several miles down the river. No one in the party expected her to survive, but she did. The trauma was great and she had injuries, but she pulled through.

Another thing to remember about the 8th house is that it is a financial house. Many people with 8th house emphasis are in the money fields. They have the need to do something with other people's money. They may do it very well, depending on aspects and attitude. Saturn in the 8th often indicates that you are obligated to handle another's finances, not necessarily because you want to, but you may become executor of a will, for example. You would function well as the treasurer of a large organization because you have such a strong feeling of responsibility toward other people and their money.

The 2nd house comes in by polarity. Wherever Saturn is in the chart, a person tends to overcompensate. Sometimes the person with Saturn in the 8th house is extremely active sexually, with the need to prove the self through sex. With Saturn in either the 2nd or the 8th house, I have rarely observed the person to have money problems. Saturn in the 2nd will have money because they are willing to work hard for it, go out there and earn it; because somehow they fear poverty and need the security of money in the bank. A classic example is Jacqueline Onassis, who has Saturn right on the cusp of the 2nd house; she never felt she had enough money. Most of us could live very well on a tenth of what she has, but she has a difficult time because of the principle of overcompensation. Saturn in the 8th house has similar themes. Money doesn't come easily, but once you earn it, you know how to hang on to it and make it grow, often on the advice of others.

The Sun in the 2nd house automatically gravitates toward moneymaking ideas. Jupiter is the planet in the 2nd house that doesn't usually give a hoot about finances. You could care less about whether or not you have money, but are pretty lucky in obtaining it. If you don't have it, you manage, and if you do have it, you spend it. Jupiter in the 2nd does not guarantee a potful of money. Saturn does. By hook or by crook, you are going to have money in the bank because this is vital to you. You value material security. Jupiter indicates faith ("I can always get more.") or a casual, carefree attitude, so you may have money or you may not, depending on aspects and other factors in the horoscope.

Since the 8th house signifies the financial, moral, spiritual and physical support you receive from others, if the ruler of the 8th is in the 9th and has challenging aspects, you may not be able to complete your higher education (9th) because of lack of financial backing (8th) or because in your overly optimistic appraisal you did not lay the proper foundation. This may prevent you from utilizing your abilities to handle other people's resources.

9TH HOUSE

The **9th** is one of the most interesting houses in the chart. It encompasses so much territory. The 9th house, everything else aside, is aspiration: what you dream about — what you hope to do for yourself, not necessarily out in the world, but what is going to make you personally happy. It represents the philosophies you gain through the experience of living life. It shows what you learn to project, to appreciate, to want; and if you fulfill your 9th house promise, you're doing a good job of living your life through your chart.

Traditionally, the 9th house represents your higher mind, philosophy and aspirations, religious attitude, dealing with the law, long-distance travel and any foreign transactions, as well as your higher education, grandchildren and in-laws.

Where the ruler of the 9th house is will indicate how you work through the 9th house. If, for instance, it is in the 12th, it is helpful if you meditate to get in touch with your inner self, to sort out your ideals, philosophies and motives. You may need a few hours alone each day to unwind and get your life into perspective. People with planets in the 12th house need time to themselves every day to recharge their batteries. A lot of folks do not realize this about themselves and wonder why they're nervous, shattered wrecks. Planets in the 12th house indicate a real need to withdraw and tune into the Universe (God) through art, nature, music, prayer or beauty.

10TH HOUSE

The **10th house** relates to achievement and recognition, so it is where you try particularly hard to prove yourself. It shows your profession, status and reputation — and, psychologically, your real ego needs. It indicates the opposite parent from the 4th house, the one who carries the most authority, and in later years it stands for anyone who represents that authoritarian pattern, such as your boss, the government, law, etc.

Your 10th house is your broadcasting station. The 1st house symbolizes your personality: how you relate to people on a one-to-one basis. When you shake hands, the person is seeing your 1st house and the planets in it. It is how you express on an immediate level. But if you have occasion to stand up in front of a crowd of people, to lecture, at the PTA, in church, any place that might be considered "on stage," you are projecting through your 10th house much more than your 1st. You are all the parts of your chart, but what others see when you are on your best behavior is your 10th house. The 10th is the highest you can reach on a practical level. The 9th is what you aspire to on a personal, moral, philosophical level, but the 10th is what you can achieve in a worldly way.

The 10th house is where we are all headed as far as career or profession is concerned. When you talk about a job, you are talking about the 6th house. A career or profession is the 10th. A lot of people never get into a career, but they still have a 10th house. This house shows your achievement in your particular sphere. Many women of my acquaintance have very active 10th houses, yet they have no career except that of homemaking and child rearing which are really vital endeavors. They tend to live their lives through partners and children. In such cases, when the Sun is in the 10th house, I also look to the Earth which is exactly opposite the Sun by degree, sign and minute. The Earth indicates where your mission in life is. If you have a 10th house Sun, Earth is in the 4th, then perhaps your mission is in your home, applying your psychological attitudes and using your fundamental understanding to become a better person. You are often the foundation of the family structure, providing your offspring with a good background; you're supportive and helpful to your partner.

The Sun in the 10th house individual can also make a career out of creativity, including having children. So can the Moon there, becoming the "professional mother" — nurse, nanny, housekeeper, etc.

If the ruler of your 10th is in the 4th house, your profession may be linked to your home, such as writing, art or any other work that can be managed from the home environment. Often you will embrace a career that is earth or land connected, such as farming, archeology, geology or real estate. You could also work with one or both of your parents or you may take over their business.

11TH HOUSE

The **11th house** shows how you relate to people in a group situation. Strong 11th houses are often loners. Aquarians and those with the Sun in the 11th house are totally individualistic. They do their own thing, regardless of rules and regulations. They may do it quietly, unobtrusively, or with fanfare, like Angela Davis who made a lot of waves in the 1960s. Whenever you refer to a house, you also talk about the sign that naturally goes with it.

The 11th house represents social and mental relationships, those you select for shared interests — in other words, your friends. It shows the results of your ambition (it follows the 10th); it describes the goals and aims you hope to reach through your career or business.

The organizers and joiners do not necessarily have Aquarius or 11th house planets, although they can. My coauthor and friend Marion D. March is a prime example. She is a great organization person. She's an Aquarian, but has a 3rd house Sun, so she is an Aquarian who needs to communicate, to talk to others. Her Sagittarian Ascendant denotes more outgoing qualities, and Jupiter that rules the Ascendant is in the 11th house. Here is a case where the chart ruler in the 11th added to everything else in the chart indicates organizational qualities. She also belonged to a lot of groups — youth groups, educational groups, welfare groups, etc.

Uranus indicates a person's own need for independence, uniqueness and freedom. If we deny these feelings, we unconsciously attract people and events that will upset us, change things and give us the space we are unaware of needing. When things seem to get out of control, it may be our own inner drive not to be bored that is operating. If we learn to express positively, there need be no problems with Uranus or the 11th house. Often planets in the 11th house take on some Uranian coloration and therefore act differently than what you might expect.

With the ruler of your 11th house in the 5th, your friends play an important role in your life, and often your social life is active and sometimes hectic. A daughter- or son-in-law may become very close to you and share your pleasures.

12TH HOUSE

The **12th house** is the most interesting one of all and is usually badly maligned. The "dustbin" of the zodiac is not an apt description, nor a fair one. If you are using the energies of your chart correctly, you are drawing strength from your 12th house. The sign on the cusp depicts the kind of strength you have, and wherever the planet is that rules that sign shows where the strength is coming from. The position of the ruler of the 12th house indicates where you can fall back and gain inner strength. If, for instance, it is in the 3rd house, brothers and sisters may prove to be supportive of you.

Planets in the 12th house are the most rewarding when they are used properly because they indicate a need for you to look into yourself, including through prayer and meditation. You feel a compulsion to go inside and get answers instead of looking to everybody else or to external conditions for direction. When you use your 12th house correctly, you are living your life properly. Don't hide there. Make your faith work for you.

SATURN: TEACHER, TASKMASTER AND FRIEND

by Marion D. March

Why do we fear Saturn? Why do we tremble when someone mentions that Saturn is going to conjunct our Midheaven or Ascendant? What is it about this large planet that is not one of the personal planets, yet is such a strong key to our childhood, our development, our life?

Maybe we need to take some time to understand the innate and archetypal principles involved, and as we understand them, we can better grasp the meaning of the cyclic movement of Saturn through the horoscope.

Saturn is the second largest (after Jupiter) of all the planets in our solar system. It used to be considered the furthest out until the discovery of Uranus in 1781, Neptune in 1846 and Pluto in 1930.

Mythology

In mythology Saturnus is the Roman counterpart of the Greek god Cronus, the god of time. Son of Uranus and Gaea, the Earth goddess, he married Rhea by whom he had many children. Among them were such familiar names as Poseidon (Neptune), Hades (Pluto) and Zeus (Jupiter). Unfortunately Saturn had a terrible habit of eating his own children, mostly out of fear of being dethroned by them just as he had dispossessed his father Uranus. His wife Rhea therefore hid some of the children and sure enough, one of them, Zeus, grew up secretly in a cave on Mount Ida in Greece. When he became an adult, he efficiently got rid of his father to become the undisputed king of the heavens.

Maybe that is one of the reasons we are so afraid of Saturn —
we still see him as the "child eater;" but maybe we also feel Saturn's
fear of "dethronement" and this inner insecurity makes us overreact.
In olden days Saturn was considered totally malefic, evil and destruc-
tive. Modern astrological interpretations are pretty far removed from
the mythological and long-ago ones. Life has changed since the ancients
interpreted the skies for us.

Meanings

Our key words for Saturn today are: form, discipline, responsibility,
the urge for security and safety, organization, ambition, career capacity,
limitations, sorrow and delay. Saturn rules theory and scientific law,
older persons, depth, patience, timing, tradition, conventionality, orthodoxy and productive use of time. Saturn represents the principles
of truth, of contraction, of solidification, of wisdom and of aging. Its
action is slow and lasting.

Saturn rules the sign Capricorn and we blend some of the Capri-
cornian qualities with those of Saturn: cautious, scrupulous,
businesslike, practical, serious, economical and hardworking. Of the
more negative tendencies we add egotistic, domineering, unforgiving,
brooding, inhibited and status seeking.

Saturn is also the natural ruler of the 10th house of honor, reputation, standing in the community, status, fame, business and social activities, and most of all — our ego. It shows how the world sees and
evaluates us, yet do we know how to evaluate ourselves?

Overcompensation

In chart delineation we usually say: wherever Saturn falls in the chart
is where we feel least secure and tend to overcompensate. Why do we
feel insecure? Possibly because we see Cronus, the god of time,
translated into our "Father Time" as the reaper who with his sickle
cuts down our earthly life. Thus Saturn represents the first law of
manifestation, namely the law of limitation. Our life on Earth is limited
and eventually has to end in the death of the body, and that scares us.
But is limitation so bad? Would we really always like the Jupiterian
principle of "the sky is the limit"? If we have a tumor, would we prefer
the Jupiterian expansion or the Saturnian limitation and restriction?

In anatomy, Saturn rules the skin and skeletal system. If we had
no skin to limit our bones, where would we be with bones dancing
around and popping out every which way? So when we think in very

practical (Saturnian) terms, how bad are certain limitations?

Let's approach Saturn from the psychological angle. Why do we overcompensate wherever Saturn is placed or rules? Because we are not sure of ourselves in those areas. What makes us insecure, psychologically speaking? Saturn's principles are truth, responsibility (mainly taking responsibility for our own actions) and pragmatism. Saturn indicates the knowledge that, as the great poet John Greenleaf Whittier said:

> The tissue of the Life to be,
> We weave with colors all our own,
> And in the field of Destiny
> We reap as we have sown.

Whittier paraphrased the familiar biblical saying: "Whatsoever a man soweth, that shall he also reap." What a tremendous responsibility that places on us. That means I myself can shape a part of my destiny. I am responsible for my actions! But it also means that I cannot blame anyone else, and this is hard to swallow. It is much easier to say, "Fate is against me," "My parents are to blame," or my race, society, my neighborhood holds me back (or even "It's Saturn's fault!") — anybody but me.

If we believe in reincarnation, we may even go a step further and say that we decide when to be born, and in the overall picture we are predestined as to when we die; we may even come here in order to learn certain lessons of life and thus fulfill another cog in our pursuit of breaking the eternal cycle of *karma* and *dharma*, and becoming one with the Universe.

Consequences

In esoteric astrology Saturn is the "Lord of *Karma*." Whatever stage of evolvement we have reached before, determines the form we take the next time around. Whatever lesson we did not learn, we try to master the next time. That is the meaning of *karma*: cause and effect, action and reaction, what we sow we will reap. Whether esoteric or mundane, psychological, humanistic or any other approach to astrology, Saturn's meaning is the same — never punitive, not good or bad, just — you are your own judge! And that is another problematical area. Who really wants to judge oneself? And judge truthfully and honestly as Saturn demands? That's a tall, tall order.

What then is our normal and human reaction? We put on this great front of "I don't care" or "I am the Rock of Gibraltar and nothing can crumble me.'' Are we going to admit that we are not really strong? That would leave us wide open and terribly vulnerable. Do I want to be hurt? Do you? Of course not! So probably we will hide our fears behind bravura, our feelings and emotions behind coldness or an arrogant air of superiority — all reactions we have seen time and time again when analyzing the houses Saturn is in or rules.

Now let us dig a little deeper. Saturn represents the principle of truth. What kind of truth? Earthly truth! Saturn says: Here we are on this Earth with two legs, two arms, two eyes and five senses. We may wish to hide in the 12th house and strive for spiritual evolvement, for ESP or intuition or a sixth sense, but Saturn says: My friend, hiding is going to get you nowhere; learn to use your five senses and face yourself as well as life.

We may utilize Uranus by dreaming of escapades into the future or by giving ourselves to the cause of humanity. But Saturn the taskmaster says: First you must learn who you are before you can teach or help one other human being, much less humanity. You cannot look into the future until you understand the past, and most certainly the present.

Of course it must be glorious to rise from the ashes like the phoenix, to transform or transmute into something we are not, as Pluto strives to do, but Saturn the teacher says: You can't transform until you are formed. Don't run away from life, live it first!

Facing Facts

Uranus, Neptune and Pluto may be considered higher and more evolved than Saturn, since they are further away from Earth, transcendental in name and abstract in meaning, but Saturn is the ruler of the 10th house, the highest possible place in the chart. Saturn is what we need to reach for in this Earth incarnation. And that is the hardest lesson and of course another reason for our feelings of insecurity. To strive for truth, practical reality and perfection is much harder than to strive for dreams, ideas, concepts and theories which cannot be assessed by earthly or concrete measurements.

Saturn is a taskmaster, no doubt about it, because it symbolizes our inner demands for conscientious effort and serious application. This 10th house Saturn, of course, represents our ego and here we experience our greatest conflicts or insecurities. What are our real ego needs? Dare we admit to them and focus in on them, or do we hide behind platitudes and phony fronts because this is what we think is expected of us? Can the ego focus in on truth and reality when the word ego itself denies objectivity?

Ego is self — is my reality. Saturn says truth and reality. But whose truth and whose reality? Absolute truth? Absolute reality? That cannot exist within our earthly five-sense boundaries. The word absolute implies perfection and purity which can only be characteristic of something free from any restraint, including the restraint of senses or dimensions. But Saturn is composed of restraints — form is one of its purposes, so it cannot be absolute truth or reality. Instead it must be **my** truth and **my** reality in this world of ours called Earth. So in a mundane sense Saturn represents social truths and realities by setting limits, creating structure and enacting laws.

Once we comprehend Saturn's true nature and are ready to understand our own limitations, we are ready to accept ourselves in relationship to our world. Self-awareness is the first step to understanding our ego and its needs and taking concrete measures to meet these needs. As we grasp the principle, we are ready to climb the next rung on the ladder.

Where do most of us get lost or hung up? We fail to see that there are as many realities as there are people, and instead of taking responsibility for our own actions and living up to our own reality, we create an illusion of the kind of reality we think others want from us. My father (Saturn), my church (Saturn), my teacher (Saturn), want such and such from me. The government (Saturn), the authorities (Saturn), my career, my community and so on *ad infinitum*, all have supposed demands on me. Thus structure becomes rigidity; discipline becomes bigotry; adherence to principle turns to stubbornness; responsibility to inhibition; hard work to status seeking; and the laws of necessity become fatalism.

Once we understand these Saturnian principles, we can apply them to the natal and progressed horoscope, to synastry, to anything astrological or psychological, to life and to death. In order to translate the Saturnian reality into a recognizable reality, we also have to add time — not absolute time where yesterday, today and tomorrow may all be the same or intermingled, but Earth time — namely the clock. The clock has the same meaning for all people on Earth. By it we measure hours, days, years, birth and death.

Saturn Cycles

In Earth time Saturn takes approximately 29 years to complete its cycle through the zodiac. If you were born in February 1934 and Saturn was at 20° Aquarius at birth, in April 1963, by age 29 + , it will have traversed the entire horoscope and be back at 20° Aquarius. It will be there again in February 1993 when you are about 59 years old, and maybe even a third time at age 88 to 89. These Saturn "returns," as they are astrologically called, have a meaning in time and in human development.

Since the cycle is close to 29 years, it is in line with the motion of the Moon which needs between 28 and 29 days to return to its original position. Thus the Moon — archetype of the female or mother principle of nurturing, of the beginning or the womb or the 4th house — moves at the same symbolic (1 day = 1 year) rate as Saturn — archetype of the male or father principle of authority, of taking form and reaching out to the 10th house. Since our "beginning" and our "pinnacle" move at the same speed, we can say that it takes these planets around 7 + years to pass over or transit each quarter (the four angles) of the chart.

Any cycle of growth, astrologically speaking, has to start in the 1st house of physical beginnings. So the first 7 + years, Saturn would travel from the 1st house to the *Imum Coeli* (4th house), and this would be considered the first spurt of learning; the next 7 + years as Saturn rises to reach the Descendant or 7th house, the learning would deepen and knowledge should expand. From the 7th to the Midheaven (10th house), we should put all the learning to good use or into practice, so that when Saturn culminates at the MC, we are able to sit back and relax the next 7 + years, kind of rest on our laurels or collect the rewards of our hard work and study.

Translating this into years — birth to age 7 — we have lots of learning to do, to walk, to talk, to think, to be. From age 7 + to 14½ we go to school and not only learn the lessons of life, but those of the three R's. In other words, we deepen our perception of life. At age 14½ we are ready to go to secondary school and in many countries we have finished school and now face life through work, utilizing that which we have learned. At age 21 + to 29 we should be established in some work or way of life which enables us to continue doing the same thing without too much strain until we reach the Saturn conjunction and start the cycle all over again.

If we translate this into astrological houses, we would say that the 1st house represents birth to approximately 2 years and 5 months. Our physical body is forming, we learn to exist. The key word for Aries is "I am." We are beginning (1st house), we are pioneering into the first movement (to sit up, to crawl) and we are using the instinctive Martian energy of action.

The 2nd house teaches us values and dealing with possessions. Whereas the first house is strictly "me," the 2nd already encompasses "mine" or that which belongs to me — my toys, which I may not wish to share.

Just under age 5 we are ready to recognize some of the 3rd house concepts of "here," "in my neighborhood." We are prepared for kindergarten or early schooling, know how to function in our immediate environment, are ready to communicate and even to use reason.

By age 7 + we take a good look at our roots, we feel the first true understanding of "my home" or my private refuge against the outside world. As we reach the 4th house we already spend most of our days at school and can grasp the meaning of the security of our own four walls, as well as the nurturing and protective qualities of our parents.

Coincidentally, we now experience our first square — a momentous event, because it makes us realize that if we do want to be "me" and enjoy what is "mine" in "my neighborhood," we also need a place in the home to call "my room" or "my corner;" it cannot be all Mommy's or Daddy's — so we exercise our first defense mechanism and fight for a niche of our own. This will be particularly important if the previous 2 + years of the 3rd house included establishing a relationship with siblings.

By 9¾ we have reached the 5th house of love given — often to a teacher, sometimes a schoolmate or a movie idol or sports hero. This is also the natural house of the Sun. Here the young boy wakes up to recognize his father in a rather personalized way, like a youth group leader or little League coach. The daughter begins to see a sexual difference between mother and father for the first time, and when a boy offers to carry her school books, it is not only because they are heavy.

By age 12 + and the 6th house, we have to own up to our habits, especially those of work and at school. People expect chores from us like helping in the house and garden. Maybe we babysit or have a paper route or sell lemonade. In some countries this is the crucial time to decide if we will enroll in a school of academic learning to enter college at a later date, or if we will eventually perform some artisan or service-oriented line of work. In certain countries this is the time to enter a midschool or secondary school (like junior high in California).

By age 14½ we have gone halfway. We are now ready to leave the "me" and "mine" world and enter the realm of the 7th house by recognizing that "no man is an island." We may only be teenagers, but we now are aware of one-to-one relationships. In some Far East countries (such as India) this is the time for marriage. In all countries girls have started or are starting to menstruate (between 12 and 15 is the norm), so they as well as others realize they are not innocent children anymore.

The Venusian part of Libra, natural sign of the 7th house, beckons to both sexes. Since we are halfway in the cycle, we should also have learned enough to put some of it into practice. In many countries, school is only compulsory to age 14 or through the 8th grade. At this point the youngster ventures out into the bigger or outside world, away from the protective core of relatives and neighbors: in some cases to become an apprentice, in some cases to start work. The 1st house "me" meets the 7th house "you" and by becoming aware of (the positive key word for an opposition) the other, namely "you," we become more aware of who we are, what we really need and what our next action should be.

As we enter the 8th house, we have reached age 17. What was just "mine" in the 2nd house, is now "yours" in the 8th. This involvement with others used to signify the first real sexual experience, especially for the males — we are dealing with Scorpio. It often coincides with the first time we seek support from the outside world. Quite often it is the first inkling of our mortality. Someone in our environment may have died previously, but this seems to be the first time we really think about death, the finality of life as we know it and the possibility of life after death. Real sexual awakening and transcendental awakening often go hand in hand, as if Scorpio tries to prove that it is worthy of its three symbols: the scorpion, the eagle and the phoenix.

When we are nearly 19½, we enter the 9th house. We may have started college (higher education/9th house) at age 18 or, like so many young people do, taken a sabbatical and only started at 19. In Europe we may just have passed our "matura" or some other exams to get ready for University entrance. We are now definitely ready for the Jupiterian and Sagittarian stages of idealism. Whether enrolled in a university or working as a boxboy in a market, as an apprentice waiter or a rookie salesperson, this is the time of high aspirations, deep philosophies and endless debates over life, love and the pursuit of happiness. The "here" and "my neighborhood" of the 3rd house becomes "there" and even "over there" as all confines fall away.

We have now had over 7 years to put much of our earlier learning into practice and as we enter the 10th house at age 22, we should be ready for our first step into a real career or profession. In many cases we may just be graduating from a four-year college and look forward to a new standing in the community. Even if we are in a lengthy learning situation which requires the equivalent of a Master or Ph.D. degree, we are now a postgraduate and as such have a new status. The very private, sheltered and protected 4th has become the much more public 10th. With it come new responsibilities and of course the real Saturnian limitations, namely, the authorities, those in charge, the bosses and superiors who tell us what to do when.

In the 4th we had to fight for our existence as a person and not just as an extension of our parents — now in the 10th house we encounter the second Saturn square, and this time we have to establish our right to exist and survive in the world. The female, nurturing principle of the 4th has become the male principle in the 10th, demanding responsibility and reality, and setting its own limitations as it makes its demands.

In certain life situations, if we manage the square in a positive way, we can then sit back and for 7+ years reap the rewards of the seeds sown. In the 22 to 29 years' life span, we do not so much change activities as we try to work our way up the ladder. If we are married, we may be busy raising a family and establishing the principles learned previously.

But there are some subtle changes. As we get to the 11th house at age 24+, we reach out to friends and new social circles. If we are homemakers, we may join a neighborhood or school group, or we may just make new friends at our place of work. We now seem ready to develop our own associations rather than depend on relatives or our parental circle. Even at school and college we were tied to a rather limited group of peers, but now the world is our oyster and the choice is ours. This gives us a great feeling of independence, the Uranian principle of the 11th house, especially the first time around.

By age 26½ we are preparing to close the first cycle or our life. The Moon, calculated on a "day for a year" progressed motion, and Saturn, on a "day for a day" realistic transit motion, are slowly winding down to meet and establish our first real "maturity crisis." Before we are ready to start our next or second stage, we need time to think and take stock. The privacy of the 12th house affords us that luxury, and we best take time to decide on our future.

Do we know what we want to do next? Do we wish to make major or minor changes? Are we happy or satisfied with our achievements so far? This Neptune/Pisces house says: Time to tune in to the real me; to realize my hidden strengths and weaknesses, and sort out my feelings so as to be ready for a New Moon and a Saturn return by age 29. It is at this point that Saturn the stern one usually becomes Saturn our friend. As one of my students said: "Saturn is a real friend, it never lets you go until it knows you have learned the lesson."

This then is the flat chart or natural wheel rate of development. Of course Saturn does not start at the Ascendant for every person born, nor are all houses even in width. Saturn may spend less than two years in one house and more than four in another. Therefore certain stages of life may develop faster and others may need additional time to mature. That's the glory of astrology — each chart is unique and enables each of us to grow at a pace uniquely ours. And that's that glory of Saturn, our friend, who helps us accept the reality of it all.

INSIGHT ON INTERCEPTIONS
by Joan McEvers

Unless the astrologer uses the Equal House system, there comes a time when you run across interceptions in the horoscope. Interceptions exist because the curve of the Earth's surface causes a distortion in house sizes as we move north or south of the Equator. As this happens, some signs are found fully contained within a house, i.e., not appearing on either cusp. The farther north or south someone is born, the more chance there is of this happening. Often at latitudes of more than 50° north or south, two or more signs may be intercepted.

Proponents of the Equal House system claim that this fact invalidates most house systems including Koch and Placidus. After examining charts cast for various house systems, I feel there is great validity to interceptions. When they occur in the chart, they should not be ignored in delineation. There is much to be discovered in analyzing them carefully.

In one of the first classes I taught, there was a student who was born in Point Barrow, Alaska, which is 71N22. After redoing the math on the chart four times, I was still sure I had made a mistake. She had three signs intercepted in the 1st house and three in the 7th, therefore I was positive I had calculated the chart incorrectly. After rechecking the math and realizing that it was correct, I delineated the chart. I found to my (then) surprise that she had lived out the life shown by her unusual (to me) chart. People born far north or south of the Equator do not live the same type of lives as those of us born in more temperate climes; this is often indicated by the distortion of the houses in their horoscopes.

As deVore states, "The affairs of an intercepted house are generally more complicated and the planets therein are of more than average importance." Yes, this intercepted house axis is very complex. Often it is the largest axis, many times containing 40 or more degrees per house.

Even if the intercepted houses are unoccupied, there are at least three planetary keys to each house: the planet that rules the cusp, the planet that rules the intercepted sign and the planet that rules the other sign in the house. Thus, if there happen to be planets in the houses, this can be the most activated and complicated axis in the chart.

James Joyce
February 2, 1882
6:00 AM GMT
Dublin, Eire
53N20 6W15

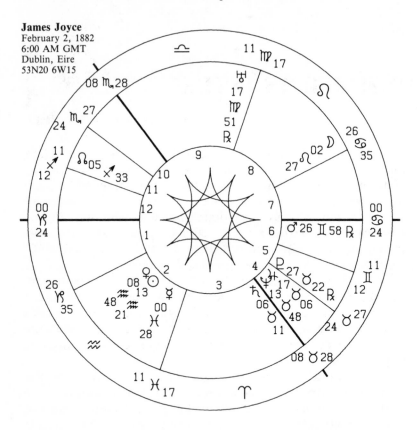

Source: Lockhart quotes Storme (C)

James Joyce

Consider the intercepted houses as the place to begin reading the horoscope. It is a focal point and you can gain great insight into the native's character, personality and abilities from a careful perusal of these two houses. Irish author James Joyce is a wonderful example. With Capricorn on the cusp of the 2nd house, Aquarius intercepted and 11° of Pisces also there, Saturn, Uranus and Neptune all offer insight into his value system which was such an important part of his communication. Venus, the Sun and Mercury are all in this house; Venus and the Sun both intercepted in Aquarius. Mercury is in Pisces. His 8th house has Cancer on the cusp, Leo is intercepted and Virgo is also there. The Moon is intercepted in the house in Leo. As we can see from analyzing this axis, much of the chart is focused on his perception of his values in relation to those of other people and his efforts to bring about that synthesis. The 2nd house/8th house axis also emphasizes the issues of sensuality (food, drink, physical indulgences) and the handling of money and material resources which were important issues in his life and writing.

Joyce was born in Dublin, Ireland, which is 53° north and he has a second pair of intercepted houses: the 3rd and 9th. We find this often in the charts of writers. He has the rulership of Neptune, Mars and Venus in the 3rd house, as well as Saturn which is placed there. Since this is the house that relates to communication, Neptune represents his imagination; Mars — the directness of his language; Venus — his concern with sensuality and values; and Saturn — his dedication to his job. With Mercury, Venus and Pluto involved with his 9th house, it is easy to see why writing was an all-consuming passion that occupied his every waking moment. Uranus there symbolizes his need to publish something totally new and different, and the trine from Uranus to Neptune and Jupiter indicates the flow, if not the ease, of his literary output.

Joyce was a slow, painstaking writer whose lifetime output was slight in comparison with other authors of his day, but analysis of his works (particularly the novel *Ulysses*) is an ongoing work for dedicated "Joyceophiles." With the Sun intercepted, it is often necessary for the person to find a special field in life to stand alone. Joyce did this with the uniqueness of his writing. He created a whole new language compounded of most of the world's ancient and modern tongues for his brilliant novel *Finnegan's Wake*. With Venus intercepted, a person often seeks a creative outlet to release the feeling that love limits. His relationship with Nora Barnacle was of a limiting variety, though through reading his love letters to her, we realize how deeply he cared for her. An intercepted Moon indicates emotional intensification and perhaps, in this case, it symbolizes the dedication of those who still celebrate Joyce's *Ulysses* by participating in marathon readings each June 16, the anniversary of the day when the action took place in the novel.

Linked Houses

A very important point, often overlooked in reading a chart, is that when there are intercepted signs, two pairs of adjacent cusps share the same sign. The activities of the two houses that share the same sign are linked together in some way. Often there is a 12th or 2nd house theme present. In the system of derivative houses, the earlier of adjacent houses is the 12th house to the later, and the later of adjacent houses is the 2nd house to the earlier one. For example, when the 3rd and 4th houses are linked together, there may be a sister or brother who takes the place of a parent; it may even be an aunt or uncle, but there is a pseudoparent — a very 12th house sort of feeling. Many times, a parent will pay for short trips, cars, etc. This is the 2nd house motivation, help or support through the 4th.

1ST AND 2ND HOUSES

If it is the 1st and 2nd houses tied together, perhaps the native earns his own way in life like union leader Walter Reuther. Generally, control of one's own resources and possessions is central to the identity and nature. Material comfort, sensuality and pleasure may be very important to the individual. Such people are likely to determine their own values.

2ND AND 3RD HOUSES

If it is the 2nd and 3rd that share the same sign, the person's sources of income may involve the communication or transportation fields. A lot of writers have this, including Margery Allingham, A. J. Cronin and James Hilton. Family values are likely, whether this individual is influenced by a sibling or provides the influence on the values adopted by siblings. Going into business with brothers, sisters and/or other collateral relatives (aunts, uncles) is also possible.

3RD AND 4TH HOUSES

If the 3rd and 4th houses are linked, there is a parent/sibling interchange. Potentials include a sibling taking the place of a parent, this person playing a parental role to siblings, and a parent who acts like a sibling. A brother or sister may also share a home with the native or there may be much moving around in early childhood. Rock star Peter Frampton made many home changes in his early life. Communication and the expression of ideas may flow more easily at home; words and intellect may be used for emotional support and security.

4TH AND 5TH HOUSES

When the 4th and 5th house cusps share the same sign, we may find the person whose children (5th) often come back home (4th) to live, or the creative homemaker who knits, sews and even lays bricks. Again, this may indicate the artist or author who works at home. Joyce has the 4th and 5th houses linked by the sign Taurus, reaffirming his need to project his value system and sensuousness through the creative work he did in his home.

5TH AND 6TH HOUSES

If the 5th house is linked to the 6th, the work is likely to involve sports, creativity, charisma, entertainment or some opportunity to be on stage and noticed by other people. *Kung fu* master Bruce Lee is a good example of the sports and entertainment connection. This is also a common combination for people who coach or manage a team of some kind, as well as teachers. Many people who donate service to children's organizations such as Cub Scouts, Bluebirds, Little League, etc., have this placement. Family businesses are also possible; one can work with one's own children as well as other people's children.

6TH AND 7TH HOUSES

When the 6th and 7th houses are tied together, the work is likely to involve other people in some way. This can range from working with the public, especially in fields such as law and counseling, to literally working with a marital partner or a business partner (rather than on one's own). Of course, much depends on what sign is on the two cusps and what is going on in the rest of the chart. Lauren Bacall, who has Capricorn on the cusps of the 6th and 7th houses, worked with and then married Humphrey Bogart, who had a Capricorn Sun. People who combine business with the pleasure of a relationship just need to be sure that they do not allow the business attitude (careful, analytical, flaw-finding) to spill over into the emotional side of their relationships.

7TH AND 8TH HOUSES

If the 7th and 8th houses are linked, it could indicate that the native is inclined to form business partnerships. Joint resources are likely to be a focus in the relationship, and inheritance from a partner is possible. Politics is a potential field of success since it involves support (8th) of the public (7th). Long-time mayor of New York John Lindsay has Gemini on the 7th and 8th, and the public was very vocal both with their support and with the denial of support for him.

8TH AND 9TH HOUSES

With the 8th and 9th tied together, the ideals, philosophy and search for meaning are linked with depth, sex, transformation and looking beneath the surface. This can include an affinity for the psychic, mystic or occult (Rod Serling). It can be writing or publishing in the financial or mystery fields (Arthur Conan Doyle) or explicit sex novels. Teaching about any of these areas is also possible. The mind may be drawn to investigate all kinds of hidden things: archaeology, the idealistic detective, the inspirational worker in a hospice, the tracer of insurance fraud, etc.

9TH AND 10TH HOUSES

When the 9th and 10th are linked, the career may involve idealism, religion, philosophy, the law, education or spiritual values. Extensive travel for business is also possible (Bob Hope), or a foreign-born parent may be helpful in the career. The ultimate beliefs (9th), whether religious, scientific or spiritual, are likely to be conventional and traditional (10th).

10TH AND 11TH HOUSES

If you find the 10th and 11th sharing the same sign, an executive or leadership role involving groups or causes is a possibility. Government work (Caspar Weinberger) and politics are also likely choices. Since "who you know" is important, it should be no surprise that friends and social relationships often contribute to and advance the career of the person with this blend. The military also is a popular choice.

11TH AND 12TH HOUSES

When the 11th and 12th houses are tied together, humanitarianism and idealism tend to reinforce one another. Thus, the individual is often drawn to social work or the charitable fields. There is a need to withdraw and have time to the self. Or, frustrated idealism and unactualized needs for independence may unconsciously lead to confinement of some kind. Many times the goals are connected with a need for privacy as well as an ability to help others and thus could indicate a person who works as a psychologist, counselor or astrologer. Death-and-dying author Elisabeth Kubler-Ross has this placement and she questioned and interviewed many people (11th house) over the years about their 12th house experiences.

12TH AND 1ST HOUSES

If the 12th and 1st are linked by sign, the native often may have a Piscean (idealistic, dreamy, imaginative, artistic) overlay to the basic self-expression. Many actors and actresses have this placement, indicating perhaps that they can project the inner self through the personality.

(Anne Bancroft, Faye Dunaway, Tony Curtis, Ellen Burstyn, Derek Jacobi). Where basic faith is present, there is great inner strength to call on. (Such people believe that God is truly on their side.) Where faith is lacking, introversion, shyness, misplaced ideals or a personal fantasy world can create problems. Clear definition and assertive pursuit of the native's highest goals is the best bet.

Placement of Ruler of Interception

It is very important to note where the planet is that rules the intercepted sign. The house and sign this significator is in will give a great deal of information about how the affairs relating to the interception will work out. In James Joyce's chart, Aquarius is intercepted in the 2nd house, and the ruler Uranus is in Virgo in the 9th house. His novel *Ulysses* was considered contraband material because of the content and language and was brought out in a very limited edition. Therefore, his income (2nd house) was quite limited until 1934 after a famous court decision by Judge Woolsey declared that *Ulysses* was not obscene. Uranus, ruling the intercepted sign, placed in the legal 9th house and trine Neptune, ruler of the 3rd house of writing, indicates the legal struggle and the final positive outcome.

The Sun rules the intercepted sign in Joyce's 8th house and is intercepted itself in the 2nd. He was plagued all his life by financial problems in spite of the fact that the Sun was conjunct Venus. He expressed the material focus of that conjunction through indulgence in drinking rather than making money. Mars, the ruler of the intercepted sign in the 3rd house, is in the 6th, trine Mercury, indicating his ability to work (6th) at communication (Mercury). Venus, ruler of the 9th house interception, is in the 2nd house; it squares Saturn. Once he left his birthplace Ireland, he never returned, though he always had a concern for what was happening there and was eager for local news. But he felt the Irish culture and the Catholic Church had a suffocating effect upon his art.

House

Another consideration in looking at intercepted signs is that the interception seems to work itself out easier when the signs that are intercepted relate to the houses. For instance, someone who has Aries/Libra intercepted in the 1st and 7th houses has less trouble finding a way to work out the concentration of the interception than one who has it across another house axis.

In working with many charts, I have not found that our reactions to issues shown by planets in interception are weak. In fact, to the contrary, such reactions seem to be emphasized in the life as though the planet by being intercepted symbolizes strength. There is a popular theory that the energy of a planet in interception is held back and does not operate potently. In some cases this is true; but once the person learns to use the force depicted by that planet, it can become the most powerful motivation in the chart. The characteristics of an intercepted planet seem to operate subtly in the life, until the planet moves out of interception by secondary progression. Then the energy seems to be limitless, like a person who has been pent up in a hospital or jail and is released. There is a need to express directly and openly. When the Sun, Moon or Ascendant ruler is intercepted, there may seem to be a delay in getting the life started, but once the energy is released, there is no holding these people back.

There seems to be more of a correlation with the houses that are intercepted rather than with the signs. People who do something outstanding to become noticed often have an intercepted **1st/7th house axis**. Some examples are: Evangeline Adams, the astrologer who proved her case in court with Aries/Libra; George Steinbrenner, vociferous owner of the New York Yankees, has Leo/Aquarius intercepted in the 1st/7th; Billy Mitchell, the outspoken aviator and author, had Virgo/Pisces as did Karl Marx, the founder of modern socialism. All of these people were straightforward, free-speaking individualists, which would seem to belie the theory that interceptions in the 1st/7th axis indicate people who bottle up their assertiveness.

Many creative people — composers, artists, sculptors — have the **2nd/8th house** intercepted such as Renoir and Massenet with Aries/Libra; Braque with Taurus/Scorpio; Grandma Moses and Rodin with Virgo/Pisces.

The **3rd/9th axis** is highlighted by interception in many writers' charts: science-fiction author Ray Bradbury and war correspondent Ernie Pyle with Aries/Libra; mystery writer Ross MacDonald has Cancer/Capricorn intercepted here; Simone de Beauvoir, Emily Bronte and Edna Ferber all have Leo/Aquarius interceptions; Lewis Carroll and Hans Christian Anderson share Virgo/Pisces interceptions.

Politicians and statesmen often have the **4th/10th axis** intercepted. Joseph Goebbels, Jawaharal Nehru and Lord Louis Mountbatten all share Taurus/Scorpio interceptions across the meridian houses; Morris Udall has Aries/Libra and Canada's Joe Clark has Cancer/Capricorn.

The **5th/11th axis** intercepted provides us with a wide range of people to choose from: actors, entertainers, sports figures, those with a musical bent. To name a few: actor Jason Robards with Virgo/Pisces; composers Richard Rodgers and Giuseppe Verdi and opera star Cesare Siepe with Aries/Libra; actor Ken Howard with Taurus/Scorpio; singer Jeannette MacDonald with Gemini/Sagittarius.

There are a wide variety of people with the **6th/12th house** intercepted. Some of them have an interest in politics: Romana Banuelos, US Treasurer, with Aries/Libra; Adlai Stevenson with Taurus/Scorpio; Peter the Great of Russia with Virgo/Pisces. Billy Graham the evangelist has the interception in Virgo/Pisces. Many are interested in sports: golfer Cary Middlecoff, skater Karen Magnuson and pitching great Sandy Koufax with Virgo/Pisces. Surprisingly many sports figures had the Virgo/Pisces signs intercepted in many different areas of the chart. For instance: basketball star Wilt Chamberlain and runner Herb Elliot in the 4th/10th; tennis player Vitas Gerulaitas, track great Bob Hayes and baseball whiz Joe Morgan in the 5th/11th; golfer Tony Jacklin in the 3rd/9th; basketball player Jerry Lucas in the 2nd/8th. Virgo and Pisces are often highlighted in charts of athletes, perhaps due to the dedication (Virgo) required to succeed in this field and also the pedal mobility (Pisces) needed to be outstanding in sports.

Interaction of Rulers

Interceptions need to be carefully analyzed in a number of different ways in the chart. Another consideration is how the rulers of the three signs involved with the intercepted house relate to each other, or even if they do. In Joyce's chart, Saturn, Uranus and Neptune all have some rulership of the 2nd house. Since Neptune and Uranus trine each other and Saturn and Neptune conjunct, some of the affairs of that house ran smoothly, but because there was no aspect between Saturn and Uranus, the situations symbolized by those planets needed attention. Financial problems always plagued Joyce and he often lived in terrible poverty, complicated by his heavy drinking, deteriorating eyesight and the mental illness of his daughter. The Moon, Sun and Mercury all have jurisdiction of the 8th house. Because the Moon inconjuncts Mercury, he had to make adjustments in the areas concerning his values (2nd), needs (Moon) and the demands made upon him by other people (8th), especially his wife (Moon). Since both the Sun and Mercury are in the same house (2nd), they have some relationship to each other and so work well together.

Neptune, Mars and Venus all have rulership of the intercepted 3rd house. Venus squares Neptune indicating creative vision poured into his work. However, there is no aspect between either Mars/Venus or Mars/Neptune, suggesting that his inspirational drive was hard to come by. Because of the great amount of time it took for him to complete his works, this observation seems to be verified. Mercury, Venus and Pluto are all involved in rulership of the intercepted 9th house. There are no aspects from Mercury to Venus, nor from Venus to Pluto, but the square from Mercury to Pluto indicates the mental probity so necessary to a writer.

A DIFFERENT APPROACH TO VOCATIONAL APTITUDES
by Marion D. March

There are two questions every astrologer hears again and again and again. One is "Should I marry John or Joe or...?" — which the art of chart synastry answers fairly well. The other is "What are my vocational talents or aptitudes?" Often the question becomes very involved: "I would just love to be a playwright, but I really want to own a large home. Can I be sure there'll be enough money for that through writing?" or "Please help me, I want to be an athlete but I never seem to find the time to really practice as I should."

Can astrology answer such questions? Yes and no. We do see vocational aptitudes that can help a person find a direction; but no, we cannot know if someone will be a poor playwright or a rich whatever — nor can we predict if the individual will be a rich playwright. All we can establish is dramatic writing talent, the ability to make money, the will or ambition to succeed. We do not know where the free will may lead that person at a given moment in time, nor what the priorities of the moment may be.

Can astrology help somebody who wants to be an athlete but is too undisciplined to practice? We can see physical aptitudes leading to athletic ability as well as inertia or difficulties in organizing or sticking to structure — but we do not know if the questioner really wants to buckle down enough to challenge the weak points and utilize the positive energies.

Traditional Areas

There are usually three areas considered as keys to the vocational potential — namely, the 2nd, the 6th and the 10th houses. These 3 houses should be looked at, but with discretion and the realization that other important areas of the chart must also be studied.

The 10th is a key house, since it not only indicates the possible career, but, more importantly, it is the highest we can reach for and shows our ego needs. If we do not fulfill some of our true needs, we cannot feel satisfied. The 10th house also reflects the recognition we may receive from the community or world and if such recognition is important to our needs or well-being. When I say the 10th house (or any other house) I am referring to the sign on the cusp, in what sign and house the ruler of that cusp is located, and what aspects the ruler makes in the chart — also, are there planets in the house and how are they integrated with the rest of the chart. Since it is always easier to follow an actual example, here is the chart of tennis champion Chris Evert Lloyd.

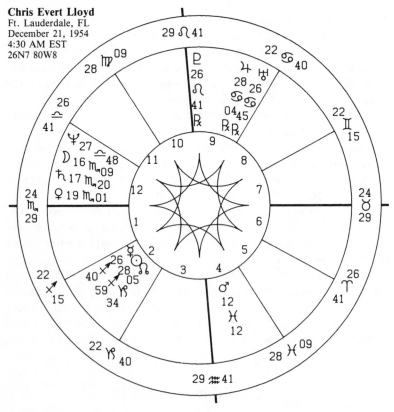

Chris Evert Lloyd
Ft. Lauderdale, FL
December 21, 1954
4:30 AM EST
26N7 80W8

Source: *Profiles of Women* (C)

Chris Evert Lloyd

Her 10th house cusp at 29° Leo indicates that she feels a need to shine in all career matters. Since the cusp is at 29°, considered a critical degree as it is ready to switch into another sign very soon, Chris may feel an urgency to achieve, pressing her into action at an earlier age than other people with a Leo Midheaven. The Sun at nearly 29° Sagittarius is in the 2nd house, symbolizing a wish to find security through some tangible means, like money! (This need is doubly emphasized since there are no planets in earth signs, and there is a tendency to overcompensate in areas where we have an innate lack.) Sagittarians prefer to be outdoors, able to move around or travel, all possibilities in a sport like tennis. The Sun trines the MC (10th house cusp) and denotes that Chris may find it fairly easy to achieve her highest goals.

The Sun conjunct Mercury indicates that her thinking or mental functions can go hand in hand with her inner individuality, which may tend to make her a bit egocentric. The Sun inconjunct (quincunx) its own ruler Jupiter and Uranus, from the 2nd to the 9th house, shows a need to avoid certain excesses, a tendency toward arrogance, and the fact that self-discipline would be a very positive outlet of the energies (Saturn trine Mars verifies this), and a need to learn to curb her impatience and restlessness as well as a subtle need to rebel.

Pluto is just behind the MC (a most important position for a planet according to the massive research of Michel and Francoise Gauquelin). The research of Michel and Francoise Gauquelin has indicated that planets **behind** the angles, in the mutable houses — especially the 9th and 12th — are particularly important keys to the basic character and also to vocations.* Pluto trine the Sun indicates that Chris could be extremely ambitious and need a career where she can prove herself. Her ability to do so seems given. The Sun sextile Neptune suggests a sensitive nature, an idealist with both imagination and opportunity, but it also demonstrates that Chris may be very thin-skinned, easily hurt even when no harm is intended. With this brief delineation we already get some insight into the dos and don'ts of this chart.

---

* The Gauquelins found Mars in those positions, in odds many times against chance, in the charts of top-notch athletes, surgeons and military men. Saturn fell in those positions in the charts of scientists. The Moon graced those areas for writers, while Jupiter occupied those sites with actors and politicians. For further information, see *The Psychology of the Planets* by Francoise Gauquelin or *Cosmic Clocks* by Michel Gauquelin.

Christian Dior

Dress designer Christian Dior also had a Leo Midheaven and he needed public acclaim; but his Sun was in Aquarius in the 3rd house, opposition the Moon, and both luminaries squared Mars forming a strong T-square. He was motivated in a totally different way than Chris.

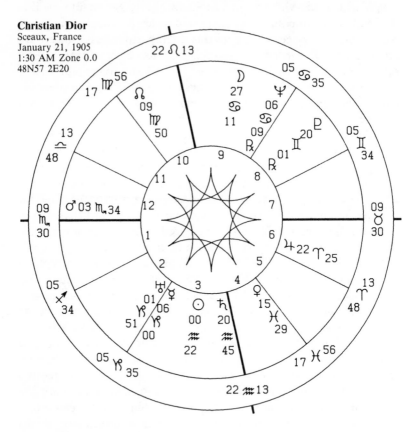

Christian Dior
Sceaux, France
January 21, 1905
1:30 AM Zone 0.0
48N57 2E20

Source: Penfield quotes Tager — Germany Archives (C)

Of the other two houses usually considered in vocational analysis, the 2nd house does not really point to aptitudes or talents. At best it indicates our ability to earn money and the satisfaction we get from our efforts; it only assumes great importance if we are very insecure and feel that money can buy security. Therefore this house, in my opinion, suggests secondary rather then primary needs and rates pretty far down the line in importance.

The 6th house is even less necessary in an occupational search, since it outlines the kind of work we could do and how well we might do it, rather than pinpointing our talents or abilities. We may be very creative and wish to become an artist, but while learning our trade, in order to buy groceries or pay the rent, we may do some office work; this would show in the 6th house. Our ability to paint need not.

What does tie the 2nd, 6th and 10th houses together is the fact that all three are the houses of substance (earth) and indicate our tangible endeavors. Therefore the element on the cusp of these houses can give an idea as to the field of interest. The fire signs usually like action, and evince enthusiasm and leadership (Chris has fire signs on the 2nd, 6th and 10th houses), whereas earth signs prefer productive and practical goals. Air needs to communicate and utilize the intellectual resources while water likes to use its intuitive and sensitive nature in a nurturing and caring way.

The Ascendant

On the other hand, the Ascendant is a very important indicator. Just as the 10th house, it is an angle and as such denotes where the action is. It also describes our outer personality, the face we like to show the world. If our Ascendant shows a demand for glamor, ditchdigging may not be our calling. If we have an aggressive nature denoted by the Ascendant, we may not do well in a subordinate position, while a very sensitive one may have trouble coping in public positions that expose us to media criticism or opinions. All such facts must be considered.

Chris Evert has Scorpio rising and her chart ruler, Pluto, is conjunct the MC (another confirmation that she rarely wants to take a back seat and needs to succeed). Her Scorpio nature is intense and emotional; she can fight for what she wants and stubbornly see things through (4 planets in fixed signs and fixed angles). Scorpios like to experience life in its totality, and with the chart ruler in Leo, her energies can be expressed with exuberance, vim and vigor. Sitting behind a desk would not fulfill her needs.

Dior also had Scorpio rising, but his Pluto was in Gemini in the 8th house, square Venus, trine Saturn exactly and sextile Jupiter and the MC. He was a very intense and emotional personality, but he preferred to play a partly sexual, partly intellectual role. With the chart ruler in the 8th house, he was looking for public support.

We should also examine the 5th house to see if a creative effort is important to the individual. Evert Lloyd has Pisces on the cusp and Neptune is in Libra in the 12th house. Her creativity could give her inner pleasure (or she might have secret love affairs). We will discuss the importance of Neptune in her chart later.

Leontyne Price

Opera singer Leontyne Price has Gemini on her 5th house cusp and Mercury is in Pisces in her 1st house. To express her creativity and to personalize it is most important to her, particularly with Mercury at 0°, a critical (beginning) degree. Pisces' ruler, Neptune, is in opposition in the public 7th house. Pisces (as well as Taurus) is considered the sign of a beautiful voice.

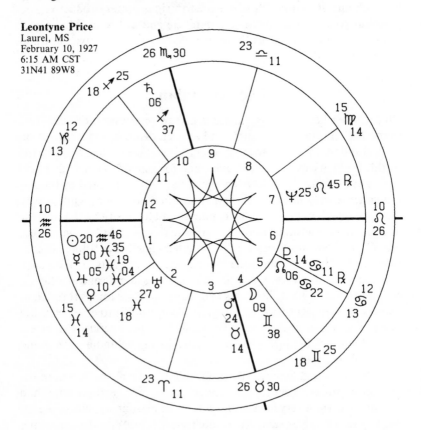

Leontyne Price
Laurel, MS
February 10, 1927
6:15 AM CST
31N41 89W8

Source: *Profiles of Women* (A)

Christian Dior, like Chris Evert Lloyd, had Pisces on the 5th house cusp. His Neptune was in Cancer (women and the public) in the 9th house, exactly opposite Mercury. It was good for him to publicize (9th/3rd/Mercury) his creativity on a large scale in some fashion involving beauty.

Jupiter's Role

In vocational interpretation it becomes important to understand what Jupiter, Sagittarius and the 9th house really symbolize. Of course religion, philosophy and long trips — the classic delineations — are included. But let's not forget salesmanship, missionary zeal, publishing, publicity, the law, higher education or adult education. Let's remember that Sagittarius as well as Jupiter has ideas and ideals and that Jupiter always wants to grow and expand; but most of all, we need to realize that the 9th house denotes our vision. Dior with Neptune and the Moon in his 9th house had grand visions as to how he wanted to use his creative talents.

Chris with Jupiter, Uranus and Pluto in the 9th house would hardly be satisfied with Junior League tennis or, for that matter, anything on a small scale. It is this 9th house vision that can make the difference between a pedestrian or exalted occupation, between the butcher and the surgeon, a billing clerk and a mathematician, a dressmaker or *haute couture* designer.

Configurations can also be the key to understanding the individual's needs and motivations. The T-square and grand cross indicate action. A stellium depicts concentrated efforts, therefore the sign and houses involved must be carefully considered and blended in.

Pisces' Veil

Chris Evert Lloyd has a stellium in Scorpio just behind the Ascendant, emphasizing many of the Scorpio qualities mentioned in connection with the Ascendant, but also stressing some Neptunian/Piscean (12th house) qualities. Neptune and Pisces can be very misleading and their elusive qualities are hard to define. They are most often prominent in the arts for talent, imagination and creativity, they are important in psychology and related fields for intuition and perception, and in religion for illumination and spirituality. But they are also very significant in sports and dancing where they can denote agility and coordination of the feet, which would be the case in Chris's chart.

Leontyne Price has strong Neptune/Pisces qualities in her chart. Neptune is angular in the 7th house and involved in a very important grand cross (opposition Sun and Mercury, square Mars and MC). She has a stellium in Pisces, part of which (Jupiter and Venus) are involved in squares to Saturn and the Moon, forming a T-square.

Angles and Aspects

Angular planets need to be considered, since they too may point to action. Chris's Mars in Pisces in the 4th house symbolizes her need to be active and the ease (trines to the Moon, Venus and Saturn) with which she could act. The trine to Saturn is considered a classic aspect for good timing.

Dior's Venus was angular and denoted action involving women or Venusian products, but he encountered many challenges along the way (Venus square chart ruler Pluto).

Aspects to the luminaries can be indicative of a person's needs, especially those to the Moon which show emotional reactions. The Moon's conjunction to Saturn reinforces Chris's need to prove herself, not only to the world, but also to her parents. This conjunction (Moon/emotions with Saturn/denials) could indicate childhood feelings of a parent who did not give her all the affection and tenderness she craved, or that it was hard to live up to that parent's expectations, which made her try doubly hard from childhood on.

Since aspects integrate the chart by linking one planet with another, they are always important in any delineation, including one for vocational aptitudes. In fact, according to some astrologers, the closest square can denote occupational talents. In the Evert Lloyd chart, it is Neptune which squares Jupiter and Uranus in a very tight orb, indicating a possible lack of caution and innate optimism, but the three planets involved are too impersonal to give vocational guidance. At best they suggest a rich imagination and confirm some factors noticed earlier, such as her need to do everything on a large scale (Jupiter, the great exaggerator).

Professions

At this point we have a pretty good idea of Chris Evert Lloyd's needs. We know that Chris has a strong ego, the need and will to succeed, good timing and physical stamina (Sun trine Pluto). She is action oriented, needs money to feel secure and likes to move around or travel. She would prefer to be her own boss. But which specific vocations do these traits involve? The next step then is to analyze what some professions entail.

THE ARTS

Artists generally have a strong Venus and Neptune, an involved Uranus for unique ideas and a creative 5th house. But remember that the Venus/Taurus type prefers the tactile and sensual approach (ceramics, sculpture and of course the voice) while the Venus/Libra type is color conscious, prefers beauty and is aesthetically motivated.

In **music** for instrumentalist and composers we look for strong Virgo tendencies (for precision) and a prominent Saturn (for discipline). Conductors, who are leaders in the true sense of the word, would have lots of Aries and active angles. Singers require not only some of the Taurus or Pisces emphasis previously discussed, but also a strong Sun; Leontyne Price's Sun is angular and involved in a grand cross. Some aspect linking Venus with Saturn can indicate the necessary discipline. (Price has the square.)

Writers should have Mercury, Gemini, 3rd house, and Virgo importantly placed in the chart. But we also expect some 12th or 4th house involvement, since they write alone or in their home. (Remember, the Gauquelins found highly successful writers had the Moon in the 9th or 12th houses or just 10° into the 10th or 1st.) Here again you need to differentiate between the journalist who may be out on the road to get the story and writes it in a noisy pressroom (Mercury/Gemini/3rd), the factual writer (strong Virgo and Saturn), the fiction writer (more Neptune) or the mystery writer (more Scorpio/Pluto/8th), to cite a few.

ATHLETES

Athletes are often denoted by strong Aries or Mars. (The Gauquelins found Mars in the 9th or 12th houses or 10° into the 1st or 10th among highly successful athletes.) Athletes also need Saturn to indicate discipline and Mars to Saturn aspects for timing. As previously mentioned, the Neptune/Pisces element is often involved for agility and of course in such sports as ice-skating it assumes great importance. Jupiter and Sagittarius often represent certain sports that involve nature or the great big outdoors (hiking, hunting, archery) but as with Neptune, Jupiter is tricky and can stand for many things. Very important for most athletic feats is an angular Pluto (endurance) and a strong Sun for recognition and the will to win. (Chris Evert Lloyd has all these traits.)

BUSINESS

Here, of course, we look for the wish to make money (2nd/Taurus/Scorpio), plus executive ability, leadership and ambition (mostly Saturn/Capricorn and 10th). Certain business people will need a prominent Mercury to communicate with the people at work and a good Venus to radiate ease and warmth. Such professions as **banking, brokerage, investments**, etc., need 8th house involvement (other people's monies and support).

For **bookkeepers** or CPAs, more Mercury/Virgo and 6th house is necessary (routine, details and figures). **Salespeople**, on the other hand, usually have strong Sagittarius and Jupiter in their charts, Jupiter and Mercury involvements for selling, Mercury and Gemini to communicate and for the top sellers, Jupiter/Neptune (the super storyteller) or Mercury/Neptune (the type that can sell ice to an Eskimo) in aspect to each other.

LEGAL
There are many types of law and each has different requirements. **Criminal Lawyers** need a combative 7th house (one-to-one struggle) strong Sun/Leo and Moon, since they stand in front of the jury and emote in passionate terms. They also need some Venus/Libra and or Jupiter/Sagittarius involvement to even become interested in the field of law.

Judges or **justices**, of course, start out with Venus/Libra, but for them the Jupiter/Sagittarius emphasis is very important and to become interested in their specialty, they seem to have less fire than the criminal lawyer but more earth in order to make practical decisions and more water (intuition and sensitivity). In many of the charts I have worked with, Pluto and Saturn are integrated through configurations and often angular. **Corporate Lawyers** will resemble businessmen in many respects, except that they too need strong Libra or Jupiter/Sagittarius involvement to even enter law school.

RELIGION
Religious people mostly have a strong Sagittarius/9th house emphasis, with some Saturn involvement for discipline. **Spirituality** can be found through a strong Neptune/Pisces orientation. **Traditional religion** is symbolized by Saturn/Capricorn as well as Jupiter/Sagittarius, whereas **unorthodox religions** have prominent Uranus/Aquarius features. **Metaphysical tendencies** are shown by an 8th house, Scorpio or Pluto emphasis. The real saint or seers, by the way, have heavy earth in the chart — they seem to see reality (earth) in its most evolved or realistic terms.

MEDICINE
Here again we must decide what kind of medicine is practiced. **Hospital**

workers generally have some 12th house/Pisces/Neptune emphasis. But if they are **nurses** and give service, Virgo and the 6th house need to be brought into the picture. **Medical technicians** usually evince strong Aquarian and 11th house involvements while **medical research** shows prominence for Pluto, Scorpio or the 8th house. Doctors fall into many of the above categories — more Pluto/Scorpio/8th house and Mars for the **surgeon**, more 5th house/Leo for the **pediatrician** as well as the **heart specialist**, etc. All medical personnel need strong Mercury in the horoscope.

I could go on forever, but you probably got the idea...Just a few interesting tidbits I found in working with, researching and teaching vocational aptitudes:

POLITICIANS

Politicians should have a strong 8th house to get support from others, an important Sun for a big ego and the need to shine plus a prominent Pluto for power and a wish to manipulate. An importantly placed Mercury demonstrating ease of communication can also be very helpful.

ACTORS

Actors may have their Sun or Leo in high focus, but what they really need is emphasis on Neptune, Pisces and the 12th house, since most of them hide behind the role they play, rather than reveal their true nature. Neptune shows glamor, magnetism and charisma. It also plays a big role in movies and television, since it rules film and emphasizes creativity, especially when in aspect to Venus. The Gauquelins found Jupiter often in the 9th or 12th houses for actors and politicians.

ASTRONAUTS

Astronauts all seem to share a strong Saturn (they most certainly must be disciplined) and a prominent Uranus (for daring, inventiveness and imagination rather than rebellion, since Saturn is so evident). Of the 25 charts I examined, all show much fire and have a predominant Mars in the chart (indicating energy and action). Air and the 11th house also are emphasized, probably because they work as part of a large group with air and space.

ASTROLOGERS

Astrologers share a prominent Neptune/12th house for perception and intuition, strong Uranus in aspect to the luminaries (they are unique and individualistic). Most of them have very challenged Mercuries, mental Moons, and both luminaries are somehow emphasized. This was from a sample of approximately 50 astrologers.

Summary

Look at the three charts presented here and see how they relate to the above information, as well as any other charts you have. My students really learned when I presented them with six or seven charts of criminal lawyers or dress designers or opera singers and asked them to find what these people seemed to have in common. Try it and good luck.

FAMILY PATTERNS: HOW TO FIND HEREDITY IN THE CHART

by Joan McEvers

For many years I have done charts of my students and their families. Early in my teaching career I had a student who was an Aquarian with a Gemini Ascendant. Her husband was a Pisces with Libra rising. Their little boy who was then about a year old had his Sun in Gemini right on his mother's Ascendant, Libra rising and his Pisces Moon was exactly conjunct his dad's Sun. In observing the charts in class, I commented on how well the little boy fit into their family with the close ties to both parents' charts. Her answer surprised me. She said, "I'm amazed, because he is adopted." She went on to explain that from the moment they brought him home, shortly after his birth, they had both felt very close to him and had almost forgotten that this baby hadn't been born to them. At that time, I didn't realize the significance of this incident, but I've had many occasions since to consider it.

People Outside the Family Patterns

I have read that when a child comes into a family with no Sun, Moon or Ascendant link with either parent, this child is one who came into the family structure for the purpose of learning from or teaching some kind of lesson to the others. It usually works both ways, and though it may seem to be a struggle sometimes, both the child and the parents can benefit from the relationship. Conversely, the child who has links with one or both parents will harmonize into the family structure with little stress.

If one believes in the theory of reincarnation, the belief is that this particular child has been with the parents in a past life and fulfills the heredity pattern. The one who doesn't share the placements is new to the grouping and the group must work at fitting together.

In one family of my acquaintance — father, mother, three sons and a daughter — they all share Sun, Moon and Ascendant links, except for the second-oldest boy. Son #1 has Sun in Pisces where mother's Moon is and his Moon is in Capricorn like his father. Son #3 has Sun in Capricorn like father's Moon and the daughter has Libra rising, the same as her father. Son #2 has nothing in common with either parent and only a slight tie with the sister: both have the Moon in Aquarius.

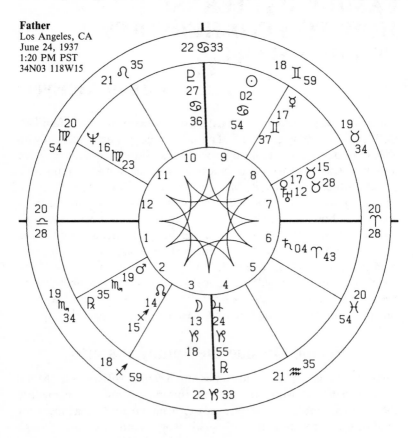

Father
Los Angeles, CA
June 24, 1937
1:20 PM PST
34N03 118W15

The second son is the child who has been most difficult for both parents to understand and they have felt much consternation, frustration and unhappiness over his actions. The other children in this family are well behaved and function well within the family circle. This child has always been the odd one — the one who is unconventional and disruptive, who does not fit the family pattern. Over the years, with much attention and careful handling and a lot of counseling, they have learned much from this boy, and he has learned from them. There has always been a strong bond between him and his sister. These children are grown now and this young man still feels like the odd one out. His brothers and young sister all work, are good students, and have good relationships with the parents and each other. He is a high school dropout, into drugs, unable to find steady work and has literally dropped out of society. I do not mean to imply that his lack of contact with his parents' charts is totally responsible for his behavior, but I do feel that the lack of rapport with the family structure is partly accountable for his lack of direction and self-esteem.

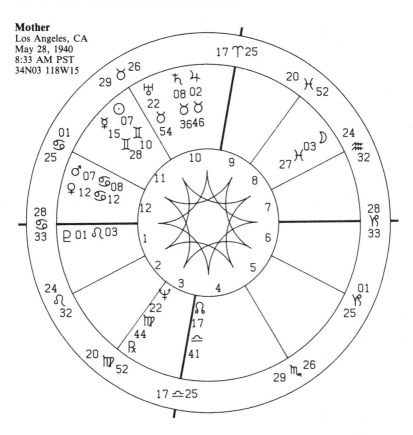

Mother
Los Angeles, CA
May 28, 1940
8:33 AM PST
34N03 118W15

It is easy to scapegoat a child who is "different," who does not follow the rules a family establishes and believes to be "normal." There is an extra burden for understanding with such a child, both for the child to the parents and for the parents to the child. When people are exposed to alternative patterns, they can either learn and grow or reject and condemn.

Son #1
Santa Monica, CA
March 5, 1959
8:21 AM PST
34N01 118W29

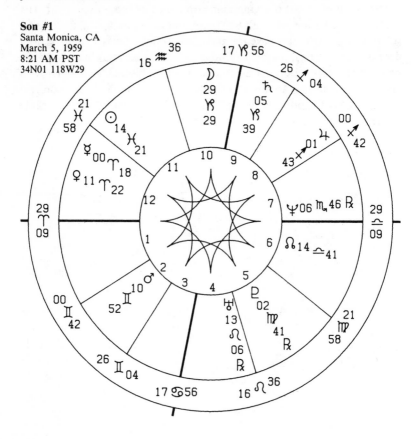

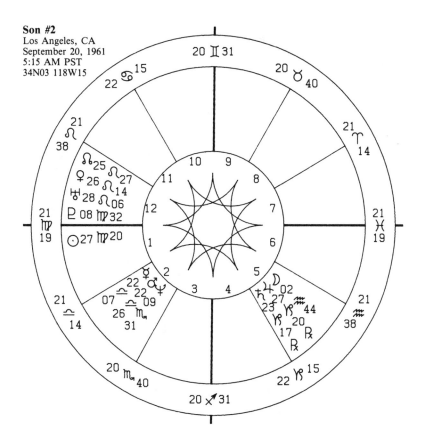

Son #2
Los Angeles, CA
September 20, 1961
5:15 AM PST
34N03 118W15

Son #3
Los Angeles, CA
January 4, 1964
1:30 PM PST
34N03 118W15

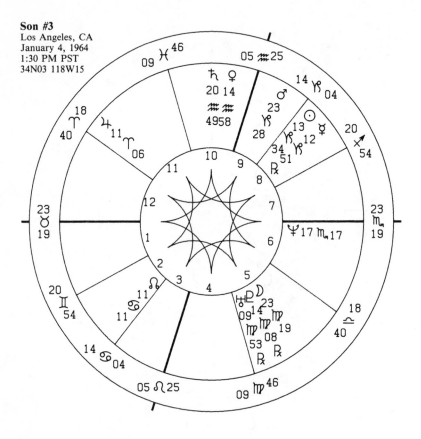

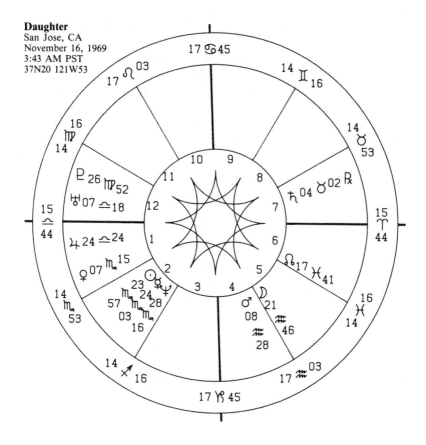

Daughter
San Jose, CA
November 16, 1969
3:43 AM PST
37N20 121W53

Repeated Signs

In another family, the father, mother and son all have Gemini Ascendants. They are always ready to leap into the car, or a plane or bus and take off at a moment's notice. They cannot understand why the daughter of the family doesn't share their enthusiasm for travel. She has a Taurus Ascendant and would rather stay home and bake cookies.

Needless to say, it is not just the Sun, Moon and Ascendant that give the key to family chart patterns. All of the planets in the comparison give us vital clues in parent-child relationships. If you have ever studied family birth charts, you must have noticed how often they interlink. The same signs appear frequently. You will find that generation after generation will repeat mutable signs, for instance. Another group will show mostly water and air, while a third family will have fixed or cardinal signs predominant.

In the charts of one family in my files, fire and air signs prevail. The father has an Aries Sun, Libra Ascendant and Gemini Moon. His mother has an Aries Moon, his father a Libra Moon. His maternal grandfather and his son share the same Aries birth date and this son has a Moon in Libra. His grandmother and his daughter were born on the same day and have the Sun in Gemini and Moon in Leo. His adopted sons are both Leos: one has a Moon in Aries and Libra rising; the other has a stellium in Libra conjunct his Ascendant. His wife is Aquarius with a Moon in Leo and her mother was a Gemini.

Aspect Themes

Very often the same aspect pattern turns up in family charts. In one family, the mother has Moon opposed to Mercury and Sun square Mars. The father also has Sun square Mars. Need I say this has been a rather stormy marriage. All seven children have either the Moon/Mercury or Mars/Sun aspect, one has both and even the first grandchild has Sun square Mars. A volatile family, but they have great rapport and understanding. They are also very active, talented, musical and accomplished.

As a general rule, the horoscopes of two family members will be found to have more in common than the charts of two unrelated people. Johannes Kepler, the great astronomer/astrologer of the seventeenth century was among the first to notice and mention the similarity of family member charts.

House/Sign Relationships

Many times you will notice how much a child acts like a particular parent or grandparent and check to see if they have signs in common only to discover that they have the Sun in different signs but with the same house position. Or they will react the same on the emotional level, even though their Moons are in different signs. Again, check the lunar house placement. In one family grouping, the father, daughter and one daughter-in-law all have the Sun in the 6th house. The mother, one son and another daughter-in-law have the Moon there. In this same family two of the sons have the Sun in the 2nd house; so do two of the grandchildren. The other grandchild has the Moon in the 2nd.

Child's Sun in Parent's House

It is most interesting to note where your child's Sun falls in your chart.

If it is in your **1st house,** this is the child most like you in personality and outlook. This is true even though your Suns are not in the same sign. Your Ascendant is the expression of your personality and if your child's Sun is in that sign and in your 1st house, there will be a similarity of expression and ideas and you will find it easy to relate to this child. If you like yourself, you like the child. If you don't like yourself, you won't like the child. Much, of course, depends on aspects and other chart placements, but as a rule of thumb, this applies quite well.

If you are fortunate enough that your child's Sun falls into your **2nd house,** you may be assured of material support. This child is well able to express your values in life, sees material things from the same view as you, and will most likely be willing to help you if and when you ever need help.

The **3rd house** child is the one who usually communicates well with you and will be willing to confide problems and seek your advice. This could be the child who likes to go shopping and visiting with you and whose company you enjoy while traveling. This is the one most likely to keep in touch after leaving home and is also the one who maintains the family network, calling and writing brothers and sisters.

The **4th house** child can be a great blessing, as this is the one who usually stays close to home and is the last to leave, which is fine unless it is your oldest child. After leaving, this one will always return, not necessarily to stay, but for long visits. This is the child you can depend on for help and who will usually take great pride in the family home, so therefore will do chores willingly. This position is much like the person who has Saturn in the 4th house: there is a strong family tie. The problem here may be **too** strong a parental link: the mama's boy or the old maid.

The child who has his or her Sun in the parents' **5th house** is often the favorite or fair-haired child. Since the parent finds this child so entertaining and loving, she or he can sometimes get away with murder. We have all observed this phenomenon — mother's or father's little darling who can do no wrong in their eyes. Do a little astrological checking and you'll see why.

Since the **6th house** has to do with work, health and service, this is the child most willing to help all family members. They will wait on both parents as a matter of accepted responsibility and will be sympathetic and understanding of your sorrows, needs and health problems. This is the child you can depend on to do your shopping, drive you to the doctor, take you to church, even do your laundry if necessary. Try not to turn this child into a servant; it is easy to take advantage of anyone who has their Sun in your 6th house.

The **7th house** in your chart represents your partner, so the child whose Sun is here will be most like your mate, at least in your eyes. This is also the one you can best deal with on a one-to-one basis. Usually there is a marked physical resemblance and this can indicate the favorite child of the partner. Interestingly enough, your partner may not view the child this way, but since your horoscope is **your** perception of the world, this is how you view it.

The **8th house** child often is the one who inherits the parent's material wealth. This can also be the one who will take over the parent's business or follow in the parent's footsteps vocationally. Many times this is the child who is born shortly after the death of an older person in the family, such as a grandparent. This also reflects the Scorpio link, since the 8th is Scorpio's natural house.

The **9th house** is the 5th from the 5th and designates the pleasure you derive from parenthood. The child whose Sun falls in your 9th house pleases and amuses with bright sayings and you may often quote them and tell stories about their precocious behavior. This is the child who most epitomizes your philosophy and who may be very supportive of your ideas and ideals. This can also be the child who travels far from home and who may not keep in touch with the family.

The **10th house** child is the one most likely to realize your fondest ambitions, who may also bring the family name before the public. This is the one who has great respect for and pride in the family background. Often this, as well as the one with the Sun in your 8th house, can be the child who follows in your footsteps careerwise or the one who takes over the family business. In your eyes this may be the most responsible of your children.

The child whose Sun falls in your **11th house** is usually your friend. This is the one who holds the family together, who organizes the get-togethers and family reunions. Your friends will also enjoy this child and there seems to be no age barrier between you.

Since the **12th house** suggests a quiet retreat, many times this is the child who remains in the background, who quietly goes about their business and is most compassionate in a remote sort of way. This can also be the child who brings sorrow into your life. How and why may be determined by the aspects the child's Sun makes to the rest of your chart. This could also be the one who stimulates your idealism, healing spirit and need for beauty.

Attitudes Towards Children

As a parent, your attitude toward your children is indicated by the planets in and ruling your 5th house, the house of children. The **Sun** in or ruling the 5th usually implies strong love and attachment to your children. It does not, however, promise a large family. Your children are often the focus of your life, and your relationship, at its best, is open and generous.

If the **Moon** rules the 5th house, or is placed there, you may have a very maternal attitude toward your offspring. Your emotions come strongly into the picture and if your Moon has challenging aspects, you must be careful not to smother your children with attention.

When **Mercury** is here, it suggests that communication is important and you often maintain a rather detached, intellectual attitude. This, of course, depends upon the sign Mercury is in. If Gemini is on the cusp of this house, it is important to you that your children are well educated. If Virgo is here, then you may have to beware of being too critical of your children's actions and values. You may also work with children — your own or other people's.

Venus rules the affectional nature and when it is in or ruling the 5th house, it can stress a loving and strong relationship. If you have this placement, it is necessary to be careful not to overindulge your children, as you tend to be quite lenient and sometimes permissive. Again, much depends upon the aspects and signs involved.

Mars in the 5th may describe annoyance through children and a certain amount of impatience with them. Often this position indicates a person who relates better to children as they get older, then enjoys their company and doing things with them. Mars in the 5th often symbolizes an active child. The parent feels a need for freedom and independence, so prefers older children; they tie one down less. If Martian assertion needs are projected, we may find willful children who annoy and irritate us because they are expressing the freedom, assertion, "me first" attitude we won't allow ourselves to manifest.

Jupiter connotes an expansive attitude which can be most beneficial or can lead to detrimental overindulgence. The best use of Jupiter in or ruling the 5th house is the ability to provide your children with a good moral outlook, strong philosophical beliefs and a broad-minded approach to life.

Saturn in the 5th house has a rather bad reputation. Some of the old books say it denies a family, makes you a cold and unfeeling parent and your children leave as soon as they can. I do not find that this is necessarily so. Often, by choice, this is the person who does not want a large family; but just as many times, as a compensatory action, this can be the person who has nine or ten children. Either way, this is the parent who feels a great sense of responsibility for her or his children.

The parent may be overly zealous and deny the child the opportunity for self-expression, or the parent may be self-critical and fearful of making any mistakes with the child. Often this is the placement of the person who takes responsibility for another person's child, through marriage or adoption, but sometimes as a teacher.

Uranian action is unpredictable; **Uranus** in or ruling the 5th house symbolizes just that...an unpredictable relationship. This can indicate the parent who is very close to one child and feels quite detached from another. It can also indicate a warm and loving attitude that suddenly changes to a cold and harsh one. This is a position that needs a great deal of examination. Sometimes it portends giving up a child. I have found it several times in the charts of women who give their children to the husband in a divorce, or who leave their children with other people to raise. Uranus indicates a need for freedom, uniqueness and individuality. If children interfere, the parent may react by leaving (giving up the child) or simply withdrawing into intellectual detachment. The challenge is to be able to love and be loved while still maintaining a sense of originality and independence.

Neptune in the 5th house often denotes the very indulgent parent who rarely sees her or his children clearly. Neptune here can involve adoption, abortion and unusual, hazy, nebulous relationships. Used positively, it indicates the parent who inspires and leads their children to productive use of their imaginations. Just as it can indicate a person who gives up a child for adoption, so it can signify the person who adopts and raises another's child.

Pluto in the 5th house often depicts a very intense or possessive love of children, almost to the point of obsession. The parent with this placement often expects a great deal from his or her children. Whether it is forthcoming depends upon the aspects to Pluto **and** the children. This placement can also describe a deep, psychic connection, a sort of "tuning in" to each other.

Which House for Which Child?

The 5th house shows your attitude toward all your children and specifically describes the first child. The 7th house is indicative of your relationship with your second child, the 9th shows how you interact with your third child, and so on around, skipping a house each time: 11th...fourth child; 1st house...fifth child; 3rd house...sixth child, etc. By careful perusal of each of these houses, you can determine your attitude and everyday working relationship with each of your children. I do not mean to imply that the sign on the cusp is the child's Sun sign, although this can happen. But basically the houses show how you view the child represented.

A client has Gemini on her 5th house cusp; Mercury is in Aquarius in her 12th house. Her oldest child is a son who has his Ascendant ruler in Gemini conjunct Uranus. They have a good, tacitly understanding relationship with excellent lines of communication. Her second child is represented by the 7th house which has Leo on the cusp and the Sun in Aquarius. He has a Leo Sun, and the Moon that rules his Ascendant is in Aquarius, opposing his Sun. They have a very close and loving relationship; but his early childhood was stormy and there were a lot of lessons learned on each side.

Her third child, represented by the 9th house, was a Pisces with Aquarius rising. She has Saturn in the 9th squaring her Sun and Neptune. This child lived only nine days.

Aspects

Another method for examining parent/child relationships is to look at the aspects between the charts of the child and the parents. If a parent's Saturn is conjunct the child's Sun, Moon or Ascendant, there may well be a desire on the part of the parent to dominate the child. Even though the parent may call it guidance, the child is likely to feel restricted by the parental authority. Both parties need to be realistic and practical without overdoing the rules in life. Jupiter conjunctions suggest expansion, and usually the child who has these contacts with a parental chart will benefit from the parent's largesse, compassion and understanding of their motivation. Sometimes there will be excesses, extravagance or overconfidence. Venus shows similar themes by conjunction, usually indicating mutual pleasures. Both positions suggest great reciprocal affection and material benefits.

Mars, Uranus and Pluto conjunctions all seem to suggest various types of conflict and need much love and understanding to work out. With Mars and Uranus contacts, both people need freedom, space and expression of their individuality in healthy ways. With Pluto, learning to share power and cooperate is vital. Manipulation, power plays and competition can ensue if there is not enough room for both parties to feel strong and in control of their own lives.

The strongest relationship is a Sun/Moon link. The child and parent who have a Sun/Moon conjunction are most blessed. They usually share emotional warmth and giving with one another.

Cycles

Another interesting observation is the seven-year cycle. All astrologers are familiar with the Saturn/Moon 28-year cycle, one quarter of which is the seven-year growth pattern. A Czechoslovakian, Dr. Swoboda, after studying thousands of cases came to the conclusion that mental and physical likenesses existed between parents and children only when they were linked to the seven-year cycle. If one of the parents has reached a year divisible by 7, such as 28, 35, or 42, the child born to them then will have pronounced physical and mental characteristics of that parent. The same applies to the grandparents and great grandparents.

Dr. Swoboda found that those children born in such a "seven" year became a channel for the experience and achievement of their forebears and are likely to be more physically and mentally robust than those not born under the seven-year law. Often it goes hand in hand with achievement and fame, to wit, Goethe and Darwin, who were both born when their fathers had reached a "seven" year. He also observed that in families with a high mortality rate, the survivors were usually born in a seven year of a parent.

The research done by astrologer/medic Dr. Eugen Jonas in astrological birth control suggests that in the future we may indeed control our family hereditary factors, and miscarriage and infant mortality could decrease dramatically.

I feel that astrology's greatest gift is our ability to view ourselves and our children somewhat objectively and see how the planetary patterns can help us in guiding and helping them.

AN INVESTOR'S PROFILE
by Marion D. March

Before we establish an investor's profile, we need to establish certain parameters. We are not going to discuss investment of time or talent or resources, but investment of money — cold cash or a facsimile thereof.

Financial Resources

Ideally this should be money beyond one's daily needs, so you can spare it and put it somewhere where it will grow and be available at some later time. That is the basic assumption of the word investment. According to the dictionary, to invest means: "To commit money in order to earn a financial return; to make use of for future benefits and advantages; to lay out money for income and profit." Nowhere does it say that some investments go wrong, that instead of profit or income, there may be a loss or reduction. Yet experience has taught all of us this sad but true lesson.

A good broker or financial advisor would therefore question all clients before deciding what kind of investment to recommend. "Do you have a safe roof over your head and own (partially at least) a house or apartment? Do you have some insurance for protection, such as health, life, accident, mortgage cancellation and so on? Is there adequate available cash in a checking or savings account, money fund, treasury bills or the like, to take care of unexpected emergencies?"

After ascertaining these common sense and logical facts, whatever money is invested has less urgency to produce immediate results, and therefore a better chance to succeed.

Investment Possibilities

The next parameter is to understand the myriad of available investment areas open to the public today.

There is **real estate** for business investment and opportunity. You can own land, houses, apartment houses, warehouses, shopping centers, gas stations etc. You can be a land developer; you can build for speculation or for a buyer; you can own a house and fix it up for resale while you live in it or you can develop a city block; you can be an active or passive partner in a real estate venture....it all depends on your personal needs, money availability and general disposition.

Aside from real estate many other investment areas are available. There are various types of **savings accounts**. There is **insurance** — annuities or single premium life insurance. There are **bullions** — gold, silver, copper and other precious metals. There are many **commodities** — mostly agricultural products such as eggs, soya beans, oats, pork bellies, but also oil and gasoline. All of these can be traded in futures or in cash markets, where you take delivery of the actual product (such as a trainload of eggs). Part of the futures market also includes all **foreign currencies**.

The word investment can get stretched pretty thin in some recently developed **financial indexes,** such as the Dow Jones Index, Oil and Gas Index, Computer Technology Index and others. With these indexes you actually guess at a possible closing price for a specific date. It's about as scientific and as safe as horse racing — yet to call a bookie is illegal, to call your stockbroker is legal.

Options offer another relatively new investment field, developed in the seventies. You can purchase options on many commodities, on most stocks and on some indexes. **Stocks**, of course, have been around forever. They simply represent an equity in a corporation, which means you own a share of it. Most stocks pay dividends. When you invest your money in stocks, you not only look for the return your money brings through dividends (compared to how much interest your money earns in a savings account), but you also look for the growth potential of the corporation. You may settle for a small dividend in exchange for a higher stock value in the future. This is the "Buy Low — Sell High" motto of all investors.

As a stockholder you have certain choices, depending on how safely you want to play it. You can own preferred shares and get your dividends before other nonpreferred shareholders, or you can own convertible preferred shares which entitle you to convert to regular shares whenever you wish. If you believe a stock will go down, you can sell "short" instead of buying.

Then there are **bonds**, where you lend money to a corporation or municipality in exchange for a fixed interest rate on your money. Bonds may not have growth potential, but they have other advantages, such as no federal tax on Municipal Bonds and a fairly safe investment. In the municipal field, for example, General Obligation Bonds are backed by tax revenue, whereas Revenue Bonds are backed by the income of the facility the bonds are financing.

United States Government Bonds are the safest. They are issued by the Federal Government; they also save you from paying state but not federal taxes. The safety of some bonds is not fail proof, as WHOOPS (Washington Water Power Nuclear Projects) proved when the five nuclear facilities cost $24 billion instead of $1½ billion and they had to declare bankruptcy on facilities 3, 4 and 5.

Some rather innovative investment possibilities have evolved since World War II for the person who wants to put away a few thousand dollars each year. **Mutual Funds** are one example, where an organization pools monies in order to buy a diversified portfolio in which you can participate by buying a share. **Unit Trust** is a similar setup, only the organization buys bonds, not stocks. The management can trade or change investments in Mutual Funds, whereas they cannot do that in Unit Trusts; what they start with is what you end up with.

Most people are familiar with **money funds**, where an organization invests your money in Treasury Bills, Jumbo Certificates of Deposit and other money market (cash) instruments.

Share Builders is a very interesting program sponsored by Merrill Lynch, where you can buy stocks by dollar amount rather than by shares, allowing you investments of as little as $50 after an initial $300 purchase.

Certificates of Deposit allow you to loan money to a bank which in return pays you interest; these have become available for the small investors for as little as $1000 since stockbrokers pool them on behalf of their clients. When dealing directly with the banks, the minimum is usually $10,000.

With **Treasury Bills**, you lend money to the U.S. Government for no longer than one year, in return for a set amount of interest; these bills cannot be bought for less $10,000. They are, of course, considered as safe as the government is safe.

Tax shelters are also considered investments in today's language, though actually many of them just save you money by giving you income tax deductions, and do not build up future advantages or give you a cash return.

What are Your Reasons for Investing?

How to choose amongst all these possibilities? This is where astrology can be of help. First and foremost, what kind of a client are you or are you dealing with? Can you face facts, such as the daily financial pages that give you the ups and downs to a fraction? Or would you prefer the approximate knowledge of real estate where no exact price is available until the day it is sold?

Secondly, do you wish money to buy you peace of mind or excitement? Within many of the fields just cited, both prospects exist and some shades in between. In the bullion area, for example, to be very safe, you can buy gold in form of coins which can be stashed in your safe for a rainy day. The butcher or landlord or ticket agent will always take a Canadian Maple Leaf, South African Krugerrand or Austrian Corona, while your greenback may be worthless in case of rampant inflation or other disaster. Gold bars, which are easy to trade in the stock market, but cumbersome for personal usage, would be considered an in-between hedge. You can trade in bullion futures, speculating on the ups and downs of the world value of gold or you can decide that any investment should bring you daily pleasure and buy gold jewelry. You wear your investment and hope that the actual gold weight will rise enough in value to cover or better the labor cost of manufacturing the jewelry. The CIA for example gives some of their personnel pure gold link bracelets; they can detach a link in exchange for cash when needed.

The same rationale applies to stocks and bonds. You can buy "widows and orphans" quality for safe investments. In the olden days in the United States it was railroad stocks, then American Telephone and now probably government bonds. For the hardy soul ready to take a risk and looking for growth as well as fun, there are many glamour stocks, there are commodities and indexes. In between are certain growth stocks, certain options and certain bonds.

With the help of astrology, you, for yourself or your client, can decide the fields of interest, the amount of risk and the attitude towards money and save everybody a lot of growing pains.

Astrological Basis of Information Presented

In forming conclusions for this article, I have used many timed and untimed charts of famous, rich and successful people — but none of them are my clients, nor do I know them personally; therefore I can hardly vouch for their investing practices. I can only go by written or oral biographical data. Instead, to help substantiate some of my assumptions, I will use charts of actual clients with whose investment habits I am really familiar.

Chart 1 — Rick

This young man has Leo rising, suggesting he may want to talk to others about all he does, including his investments. The chart ruler (planet ruling the Ascendant) is the Sun in Scorpio, indicating that despite his fun in showing off, or in bragging a little, he would never want to reveal all he does or thinks.

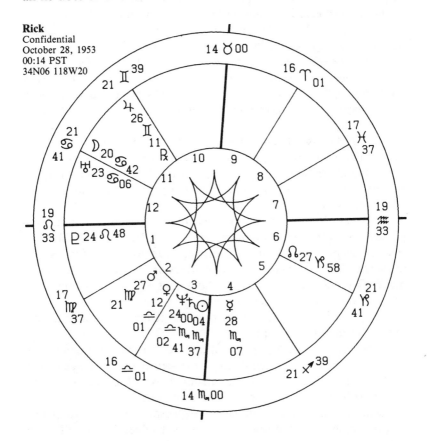

Rick
Confidential
October 28, 1953
00:14 PST
34N06 118W20

The only aspect the Sun makes is a conjunction to Saturn, describing that the need to prove himself, especially to his father, may overshadow many other needs and tone down some of the exuberance and go-getting attitude of the Leo Ascendant and Sagittarius on his 5th house of investments.

The Sun in Scorpio often has big ideas and enjoys doing things on a large scale, especially in business matters. Jupiter, ruler of his 5th house, squares Mars in the 2nd house of income, values and self-worth; we can assume that he will be a risk taker in investment matters and that he would optimistically expect large profits on all his undertakings.

Jupiter also inconjuncts (quincunxes) Mercury, ruler of the 2nd house and we would hope that he takes time to think clearly and plan carefully, lest he get carried away by his large vision and great ambition. Jupiter trine Saturn could be beneficial, if he uses the integration of the two planets to become patient and persevering, and to maintain better balance. Jupiter's trine to Neptune may signify a certain humanitarian approach, idealism and optimism.

Since the entire chart is contained within the Jupiter/Mercury quincunx, his need to expand and communicate may be evident from early on. Emotionally he could thrive on excitement (Moon conjunct Uranus), but he may be more sensitive than he wishes to admit (Moon in Cancer, Sun in Scorpio).

His 2nd house of values and money earned implies a practical approach (Virgo on the cusp), a deeply rooted wish to do everything in a big way (ruler Mercury in Scorpio in the 4th house) and a need to be actively involved in the money making process (Mars in Virgo in the 2nd house).

He may also get much enjoyment from his beautiful and tangible possessions (Venus in Libra in the 2nd house). He will probably earn most of his money through his profession (Venus, ruler of the MC is in the 2nd house), whereas his investments or speculations can fulfill his group needs (Jupiter in the 11th house), as well as his romantic and creative urges (Jupiter trine Neptune).

This brief look already enables you to see the type of investments the young man might enjoy.

There is some earth or practical evidence which could point to real estate, but upon closer examination it describes his basic need for a roof over his head and pleasant surroundings to live in, rather than a wish to be tied to land or building ownership.

The bullion field does not have enough expansion or growth potential, though he would probably enjoy a few baubles for himself or his wife under the heading of "investment." Insurance is too tame; commodities might be interesting in later years, after he's built up a large enough reserve, but it's too speculative for now (Sun conjunct Saturn). That leaves stocks and options.

Rick started buying various growth stocks with the first money he was able to put aside. He owns a small town house where his payments are reasonable, his car is nearly paid off and most of his insurance is paid by the firm he works for. He has a money fund for "rainy days" and everything else gets invested in the stock market.

He bears his losses stoically and reveals them to his broker, the U.S. government for income tax purposes and a chosen few (his astrologer). He enjoys his gains thoroughly and loves to talk about them, especially to his father. He loves the thrill and expectation of stocks and is sure that he will be a millionaire by combining hard work in his career with daring, yet relatively safe investments. In typical Scorpio fashion, he likes to dig up new businesses and research their potential for future growth.

Importance of 5th House

Why the emphasis on the 5th house? Isn't that the house of romance, creativity, children, fun and speculation?

Even in the old days investments were considered a 5th house matter — investment bankers, according to Rex Bills "Rulership" book are Sun and Leo ruled. I guess only the dictionary and very naive people assume that investments and bankers mean their money is safe for eternity. Astrology and astrologers realized long ago that investments also imply risk and speculation, a creative approach to making money or planning for the future, as well as fun while doing it. All are very 5th house activities.

The category called investors by Rex Bills is ruled by Venus, Jupiter, the 2nd and 8th houses. In most of my research in this matter, based on approximately 250 timed and maybe 50 untimed charts, people dealing with other people's monies, such as brokers and bankers, seem to have strong 8th house emphasis. But their own way of investing and understanding their basic needs, is best seen by checking the 5th house, the ruler and its aspects, as well as the 2nd house, Sun, Ascendant, chart ruler, Moon and Saturn.

Of course you always have to look at the entire chart in order to really understand a person's full potential — but to get an idea of what I mean, let's check some pertinent factors in a few more charts of clients of mine whose investment policies I am familiar with.

Chart 2 — Francis

Our second male has Libra on the cusp of his 5th house and the ruler

Venus is in Sagittarius in the 6th. His investments should somehow be connected with his line of work; in Sagittarius he wants freedom of movement. Venus makes only three aspects, opposition Uranus, trine Pluto and sextile Neptune, indicating the potential of good imagination, depth of thought and the ability to try new things as they come along.

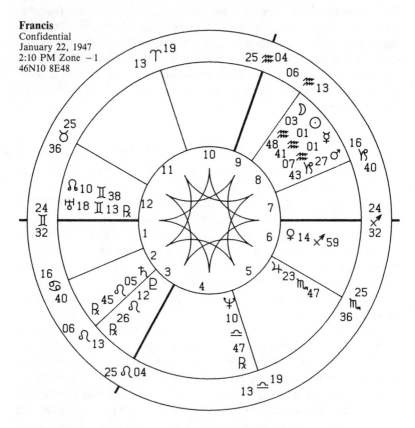

Francis
Confidential
January 22, 1947
2:10 PM Zone − 1
46N10 8E48

Jupiter is situated in the 5th house, implying a certain generosity and enjoyment in executing his affairs with largesse of spirit and action. His Sun is in Aquarius in the 8th house; so is his Moon, and Mercury which rules his Ascendant. Even Mars, planet of action, is in the 8th house. Other people's monies and resources become paramount in his scheme of things, and he could get — or will depend on — support from others.

Politicians often have heavy 8th house involvements, but this strong

Aquarian shows little indication of wishing to be involved with or serving the public at large. His real need for security through money and possessions (Cancer on the cusp of the 2nd house, Saturn in the 2nd, widely conjunct Pluto) points to a more practical career. He is a banker, earns very good money and lets his wife help in handling their daily finances as well as their savings structure.

His investments are made through a brokerage office, not his own bank. He scorns the money funds, treasury bills, mutual funds and/or bonds his wife favors. Instead he buys and sells options, mostly on stocks. He prefers to buy one large option (Jupiter in the 5th) rather than diversifying, as his wife would prefer.

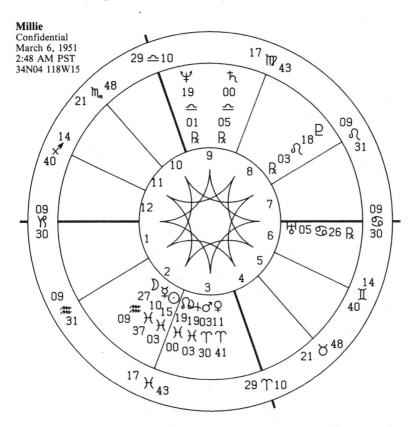

Millie
Confidential
March 6, 1951
2:48 AM PST
34N04 118W15

Chart 3 — Millie (Wife of Francis)

Her choice of the safer, but less exciting way of investing can be understood when you realize that she has a Capricorn Ascendant, involved in a T-square with Venus, which rules her 5th house, and Uranus, ruler of her 2nd house. If you use large orbs, you may even call it a grand cross and include Saturn, ruler of the Ascendant. Or you may view it as two T-squares: Ascendant in opposition to Uranus, and both square Venus and Mars; Saturn in opposition to Mars and both square Uranus.

The rulers of her Ascendant (outer personality), 2nd house (security), 4th house (roots), 5th house (investments) and Midheaven (status and ego) are all involved in challenging squares and oppositions, and she may feel the need of extra safety. She is probably happiest when she can control the 5th house actions; after all, the ruler Venus is in Aries, conjunct Mars.

The sensitive Pisces Sun and the Moon in Aquarius are both in her 2nd house, suggesting that she could gain better insights into her own values and find a more realistic kind of security by earning money through her own efforts, and not just through investments, however safe those investments might be. Work would also be important to her general state of health and her nervous system, since Uranus, involved in both T-squares, occupies her 6th house of health and service. By the way, so far his type of investments are doing much better than hers, since his have kept up with inflation.

Chart 4 — Frank

This gentleman, now deceased, was a very successful trader, respected for his investment and business savvy. Aquarius is on the cusp of his 5th house, the ruler Uranus is conjunct his Ascendant. Aquarius thrives on excitement, and the ruler's conjunction to the Ascendant would suggest that Frank liked excitement in his personal life as well as in his investments.

Actually, he was a banker by profession, (Pluto and Neptune, rulers of the 2nd house of money earned and 6th house of work in the 8th) a writer and philosopher by avocation (Mercury in the 5th house trine Uranus).

His real success was in taking advantage of the stock market crash in 1929. He had the guts to buy stocks at their low when everybody else was running scared. He risked his personal fortune and took this daring gamble. Aquarians are known to enjoy being different, to stick out from the pack and go against the trend. With his Sun and the 5th house cusp in Aquarius, and Uranus conjunct the Ascendant, he took the personal involvement by using his own money. Uranus trine Mercury and the Sun may have pointed to his ability to think in detached as well as avant garde ways.

Saturn in Leo in the 10th and involved in a yod with chart ruler Venus, denotes his potential need to prove himself to the world professionally and personally. Saturn's trine to Jupiter in the 2nd house may have represented the necessary impetus and confidence. Jupiter in the 2nd house seems to indicate people with a feeling of "riches are within my reach," "the sky is the limit in my earning capacity." The belief is often precursor to the fact.

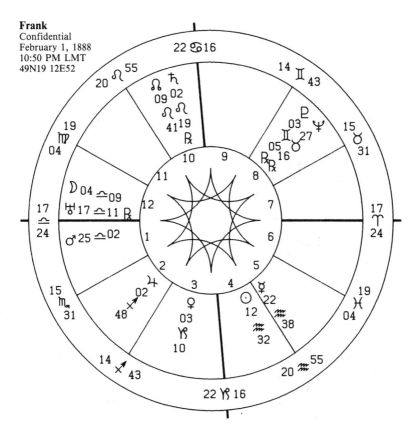

Frank
Confidential
February 1, 1888
10:50 PM LMT
49N19 12E52

After the stock market rebounded from the crash, he was a millionaire and retired in his late forties. He still continued advising friends and of course handled his own fortune, which he wisely had invested in many countries, giving him much freedom of movement during World War II.

Chart 5 — Ellen

In this horoscope we find Mercury, ruler of the 5th and 2nd houses, placed in her 6th house of work. She may want to earn and invest her money through her own work. Her chart ruler Venus is also in the 6th; so is her Sun (though the latter is definitely conjunct the Descendant). Mars, planet of action, Jupiter, planet of expansion and Saturn, planet of overcompensation, are all in the 5th house, placing a lot of emphasis there too.

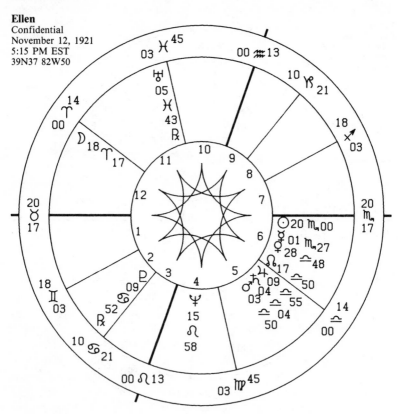

Ellen
Confidential
November 12, 1921
5:15 PM EST
39N37 82W50

With four planets in Libra she would want to seek out something that reflects beauty and harmony. The Scorpio Sun and Mercury could point to big ideas as well as deep involvement in whatever she undertakes. The Taurus (earth) Ascendant and an earth sign (Virgo) on her 5th house, could indicate her wish to invest in some tangible, touchable or concrete fields.

The Sun opposes her Ascendant and both square Neptune, forming a T-square and she also has a second (wide) T-square between her Moon, Jupiter and Pluto. With so much challenge and possible tension, she may prefer to do something she can control. Also, people with 12th house Moons like to be as much in control as possible, since they often feel emotionally vulnerable.

Ellen fulfills her chart potential very well. Her parents owned a very successful restaurant and bar, which she helped run. Upon her parents' death, she sold it, bought a large piece of land and developed it into a flower farm. She kept a few acres out to build her own house. Never one to shy away from hard work, she also went back to school to get a degree in horticulture. Part of her farm specializes in orchids and growers from all over come to her. Every penny she can set aside goes for improvements. Her flowers are her only investment.

She runs the place by herself with just a hired foreman and some helpers. She never got married, saying "You can't trust men as partners, so forget it and just enjoy them in bed."

Chart 6 — Werner

Here's the chart of a big time investor and risk taker. Leo is on the cusp of the 5th house, the Sun is in Leo in the 5th and trines his Aries Ascendant and Saturn, which in turn rules the Midheaven. Mercury, ruler of the 2nd and 6th houses is also placed in the 5th house at 29 degrees of Leo, potentially symbolizing a feeling of urgency, to still accomplish before the planet reaches 0 degrees of the next sign.

Mercury also trines the Ascendant and Saturn. The ambitious Capricorn MC is ruled by Saturn involved in a T-square with Neptune conjunct the Moon and opposed to Uranus in the 10th house. His need to achieve, do, go and be was only topped by his need to do it in some unconventional (Uranus in the 10th) and flamboyant way (Leo).

Werner, who passed away recently, was an ardent commodity trader, dealing in futures, including foreign currency ones. Though of the old school, he quickly caught on to Financial Indexes and loved it. He was a very successful writer by profession, but his investments gave him as many, sometimes more thrills than his books. To his family's chagrin, he had no hesitation to put their last penny into some wild gamble and sometimes they literally did not know where the next meal would come from. But all's well that ends well and he died a very rich man.

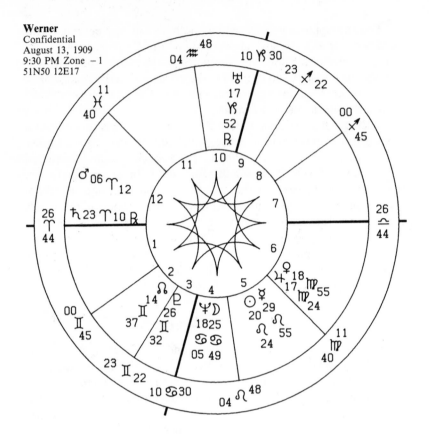

Werner
Confidential
August 13, 1909
9:30 PM Zone −1
51N50 12E17

Chart 7 — Laura

Laura is another big-time risk taker, in her work, her career and her investments. She has Cancer on her 5th house cusp and the ruler, the Moon is in Aquarius in the 12th house. Though sensitive and emotional, (Cancer) she can detach whenever necessary (Aquarius). With Mars and Pluto in the 5th house, she would want plenty of action and she feels intensely about all 5th house matters.

Mars is conjunct Saturn, and both are the focal point of a T-square involving Jupiter and Venus, illustrating that she could feel rather relentlessly driven to make money and appear successful — especially since Venus rules the 2nd (income) and Jupiter the 10th (worldly success) houses. These four planets interconnected through challenging aspects, may also symbolize feelings of inadequacy, of great vulnerability, of not being loved enough as a child; therefore they could express in the opposite way of "Look world, here I am, in charge, dependent on nobody, ready to prove and defend myself."

The Sun in Aries in the 1st house rules her 6th house, indicating how important work can be to her well-being. The Sun opposes Neptune, the chart ruler, in the 7th house, denoting possible over-idealization or misconception regarding her partner, as well as the potential of them not seeing her too clearly. She has gone through two marriages so far, and the third one is rather shaky.

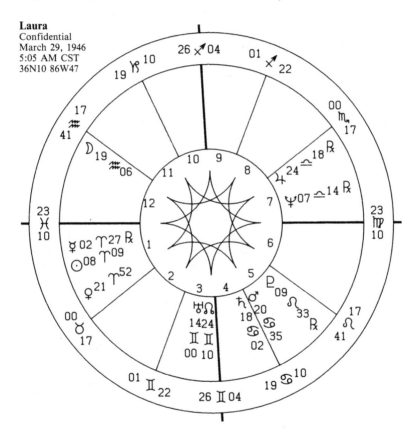

Laura
Confidential
March 29, 1946
5:05 AM CST
36N10 86W47

She ran a very successful "escort" service (an elegant way of saying call girls for hire), and earned as much as half a million per year. Some of these earnings were invested in such safe ventures as a big home for herself and her husband, a good size savings account, treasury bills and certificates of deposit. That was probably the Saturn part of the Saturn/Mars conjunction. The Mars part opted for high risk stocks and silver and gold futures.

The law caught up with her and all her investments had to be converted into cash to keep her out of jail and pay her lawyers. True to a 1st house Sun, she picked herself up off the floor and started all over. This time she is in a very legitimate business, which is paying off after only 18 months. She's started investing again with the little bit she manages to put aside. With Pluto and Mars in the 5th, she can't seem to leave a good thing alone and speculates more than she should at this stage of the game. Now that the business is tame and provides much work but little excitement, she uses the 5th house (speculation) more than the 10th (career) for her thrills.

Chart 8 — Charles

I am presenting this last chart mainly to show that attitude plays a tremendous role in the success or failure of any undertaking in life, including investments. You, the astrologer, cannot possibly know how much of the potential your clients or friends have used or how they feel about themselves at a given time, until you sit face to face with them and discuss the problems at hand. So be very careful with any glib analysis by mail.

Charles has used much of his potential in a negative way. The chart ruler, Mercury is involved in a T-square with Mars conjunct Saturn and opposed to the Moon. Neither Mercury nor Saturn have any easy outlets, but the Moon trines Jupiter and Mars sextiles it and trines the Sun, aspects which could indicate stamina, strength, optimism and the opportunity to use the tensions manifested through the square in many positive ways. Instead he feels sorry for himself, feels that fate is always against him, and that nobody really likes him.

Instead of enjoying the flow that his Sun in Libra trine Uranus and the MC, and sextile Pluto denotes, he indulges in being lazy, not delivering all he should in his work, and losing job after job. His marriages and affairs all end disastrously, with him literally being put out on the street.

His investments end nearly as badly as his love affairs. He likes to play it safe (Capricorn on the 5th house cusp, ruler Saturn involved in the previously mentioned T-square). His Sun is in Libra in the 2nd house and the ruler Venus is behind the Ascendant, in Virgo, where it does not feel very secure. To give you a typical example — in the late seventies, when "everybody" said silver would continue to rise, he bought bullions at $20 — and of course that was the all time high, before the Hunt brothers sold out and silver plummeted.

He also invested in an antique car venture with two "friends" as partners. They skipped to South America when tax time came around, and he was left holding the bag. He has lost his house and is barely holding on to his car. Though a computer expert, data processing consultant and programmer, he insists that he cannot find work. He goes through psychologists and psychiatrists like other people go through toothbrushes. As soon as one of them hits a nerve, he backs out of therapy. Until he learns to use the energies available to him in a positive fashion, neither his investments nor his love life nor much else will have a chance of succeeding.

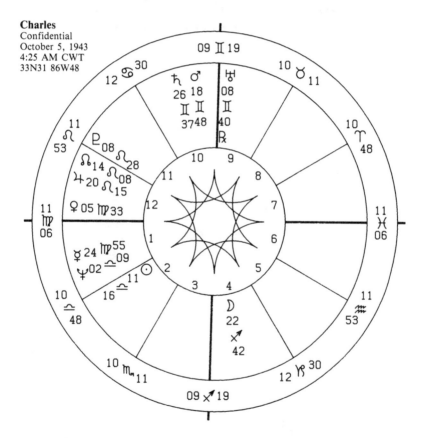

Charles
Confidential
October 5, 1943
4:25 AM CWT
33N31 86W48

Examine the Context of the Whole Chart

These eight charts only give you a beginning hint of what to look for. Your astrological knowledge can give you the rest.

Can chart No. 1 face the facts of daily losses? You bet. Scorpio is strong and fixed and will wait til the stock goes up again. He may make up a story as to how and why he bought the stock in the first place, in order to protect his Leo Ascendant pride, that's all. Does chart No. 6 want peace of mind or excitement when investing? Excitement, obviously.

Does Jupiter in the 5th indicate a wish for more of all 5th house matters and therefore you are ready to gamble for it? Yes in chart No. 2 with its sextile to Mars, quincunx to Uranus and the Ascendant and square to the Midheaven. With caution in chart No. 5, where Saturn can symbolize caution which can hold both Jupiter and Mars in tow. Look at your own chart and see what kind of an investor you could be!

THE BOOMERANG: A NEW CONFIGURATION

by Joan McEvers

Most astrologers are familiar with the **yod** configuration. Both Thyrza Escobar and Dane Rudyhar have written about it extensively. It is a configuration consisting of two planets sextile to each other and both inconjunct (or quincunx) a third planet. It is often referred to as the "Hand of God" or the "Finger of Fate."

In this particular configuration the life tends to fall into a pattern, one that goes along for a while, then veers into a new direction. At the proper time and place, attitudes are discarded and circumstances change. This cannot be rushed; things happen when they are supposed to — not before, not after.

Adjustment

The inconjunct is often associated with an upsetting feeling. The basic delineation of the inconjunct (quincunx) is adjustment. *Webster's New Ideal Dictionary* defines adjustment as: a correction or modification to reflect actual conditions. This seems to suggest that there is some event in the native's life which necessitates taking action in order to resolve whatever is bothering him or her. Some people make adjustments readily; others find it difficult to change habits or habit patterns and the adjustment becomes a challenge. This is why some find it easy to deal with inconjuncts in the chart and others find them challenging.

Generally speaking, those who are predominantly mutable or have many planets in cadent houses have the least problem with inconjuncts and yods. Making adjustments is second nature to them. On the other

hand those who are mostly fixed or who have many planets in succedent houses are the ones who may have trouble changing their attitudes
and outlook. Cardinal, angular people usually deal with inconjuncts
directly and are often willing to make changes if those changes involve
some kind of physical action.

Many astrologers feel the inconjunct has a Virgo/Scorpio quality. (In the flat chart the 150° angle is from Aries to Virgo or from Aries
to Scorpio.) This implies the characteristics of analysis and discrimina-
tion, especially in knowing what to keep and what to throw away
(Virgo); intuiting what is no longer worth hanging on to (Scorpio); dealing with deep and sometimes unconscious emotions.

Closet Cleaning

Zip Dobyns refers to the inconjunct as the "closet cleaning" aspect.
In using this aspect positively, we examine everything carefully, deciding
what is useful and worth keeping and discarding the garbage that piles
up. While doing this, we discriminate spiritually, emotionally, physically
and mentally and in so doing we may discover some buried treasures —
including unrealized talents.

When we use this aspect negatively, we hang on to the old negative
guilts and negative emotions, jockeying for position to avoid taking
the responsibility for our actions. This is the so-called "fated" quality
of the yod...refusing to deal with the necessary changes. People who
feel they were suddenly "forced" into action by a quincunx need to
examine their feelings, attitudes, actions and habits which they refus-
ed to alter long before the inconjunct was triggered by aspect.

People who operate with the symbolism of the inconjunct make
changes in their life direction and may indeed uncover a "buried
treasure" of such importance that they feel it essential to put it to use
in the world. When they realize they have been carrying around emotional baggage in the guise of resentment, anger, hurt and guilt, and
get rid of it, they will find it easier to develop happier relationships.
The important message is that we are in charge of our own lives.

A Very Challenging Aspect

I feel that the inconjunct is the most challenging of all aspects. The
square is made up of two straight lines at angles to each other and involves signs of the same quality. The essence of the square is direct
action, which when taken results in a sense of accomplishment. The
opposition is a straight line linking two opposing signs indicating the

opportunity to work out the challenge through interaction with another person. The inconjunct is neither a straight line nor a straight angle. The signs involved have no correlation with each other. If one is interpersonal, the other is personal or transpersonal. It is very difficult to find a way to express both ends of this aspect in a harmonious way. It takes work and discipline (Virgo), perseverance and patience (Scorpio) as well as willingness to look deeper into our psyche. But the rewards are great: a sense of control and self-mastery, knowing we are responsible for running our own lives.

The Sextile in the Yod

In the yod, the two planets that inconjunct the third are sextile to each other, therefore things have a way of working out to the benefit of the person with the yod — but only after the adjustments indicated by the inconjuncts have been made. After watching this configuration in birth charts for several years, I find the action is taken at the "Finger" of the yod: the planet receiving the two inconjuncts. It is as though the person is walking down life's pathway and comes to a fork in the road. It may appear foreordained at this point, but we are the ones who set it up. It's like getting on a plane for New York and then deciding you want to stop in Chicago after you leave Los Angeles. You can bewail your fate that "life won't let me go to Chicago." But you are responsible because you purchased the ticket.

We are dealing with two inconjuncts and these require compromise and reorganization on the part of the native. At the time it may seem unduly challenging, but actually people find themselves working out the challenge by using the opportunity afforded through the sextile.

Charles Dickens

For example, in Charles Dickens' chart, Uranus, ruler of his 4th house, is inconjunct Jupiter in the 8th. Mercury, ruler of the 8th, is also inconjunct Jupiter but Mercury and Uranus sextile each other. Let's consider the circumstances of this challenging yod. When Dickens was about 9 years old, his father (here represented by the 4th house and its ruler Uranus) was arrested and sent to jail for nonpayment of debts. Mercury, ruler of his father's 8th house (the 11th of the chart), is in the father's 12th (the 3rd house of the chart).

The system utilized here is derivative houses. This allows us to use the same chart not only for the person born with that chart, but also for anyone having a significant relationship to that person. The general principle is to establish the house symbolic of the other person (the one having a significant relationship to the person whose chart it actually is). Then count the number of houses away to symbolize the relationship to that other party. The house in which you begin is number one. For example, children are a 5th house relationship. Therefore, children of children would be the fifth house from the 5th house (counting the 5th as the first house tallied) or the 9th house.

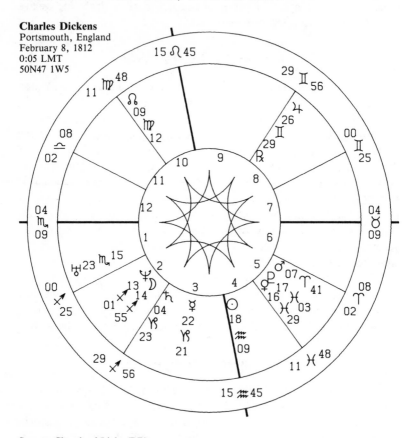

Charles Dickens
Portsmouth, England
February 8, 1812
0:05 LMT
50N47 1W5

Source: Church of Light (DD)

Thus, if Dickens' father is in the 4th house of Dickens' chart, in order to look at the father's 8th house (debts), we would count eight houses from the 4th house (to Dickens' 11th house) which would be his father's 8th house.

While visiting his father in jail, Dickens noted the conditions that he saw and later wrote (Mercury in the 3rd) about prison scenes with a tinge of horror and extreme sympathy. Thus did a difficult situation in childhood afford him an opportunity in his later years. The yod was triggered off at age 9 when solar arc directed Pluto squared Jupiter in the 8th house.

Psychologically speaking, Uranus in the 4th house indicates Dickens' inner conflict about roots, home and family. Part of him wanted a nest, security, comfort, and part of him wanted to be free, independent, doing his own thing. He was born with ambivalence about attachment versus independence, so, *karmic*ally speaking, he came to a family with the same conflicts, from whom he could learn.

Since the yod involves a ruler of the 8th house to a planet in the 8th house, conflict centers in that area: around the giving, receiving and sharing of physical possessions, money and pleasures. Parents teach us both what **to** do and what **not** to do. Obviously, Dickens got an early lesson about the handling of joint resources and debts (8th house) from his father. The question of "haves" versus "have nots" probably emerged early in his consciousness. Certainly it was a very positive integration for Dickens to later incorporate his experience into his writing and turn it into social commentary and criticism. But he may never have really resolved the conflict between independence and action as an individual versus dependency and emotional attachments. This is a theme that also appears in his work, e.g., *Great Expectations.* Pip loses his parents. The girl he loves has no parents. Miss Havisham loses a fiance. As each person reaches towards love and commitment, they lose it and end up with independence and loneliness.

Most configurations are activated when a progressed or directed planet contacts one of the planets in the configuration and thus energizes the whole pattern. This is why people who have configurations in their chart seem to live through many crises because the planets act in concert with each other.

Ferde Grofe

Another example is the chart of Ferde Grofe, composer of the *Grand Canyon Suite* and many other beautiful pieces of music. In his chart, Uranus inconjuncts Jupiter and the Sun in the 2nd house, and Uranus inconjuncts both Neptune and Pluto in the 3rd. He left home at age 14, when the Ascendant squared Neptune by solar arc direction. He held a series of jobs and lived in many different environments. Not only did he gain experience and insight, he was also exposed to diverse kinds of music in his wanderings. This nomadic existence and the need to adjust to many unusual people (Neptune and Pluto in the 3rd) enabled him to diversify his musical genius in his later career as a composer and conductor. (Sun conjunct Jupiter, ruler of the Midheaven.)

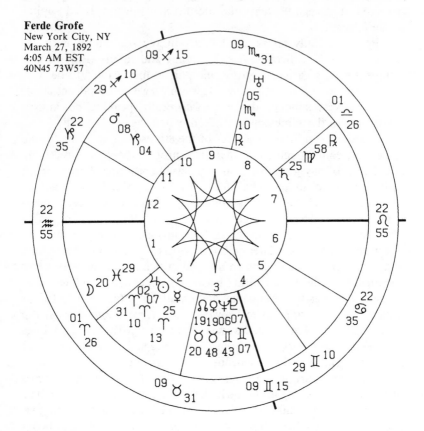

Ferde Grofe
New York City, NY
March 27, 1892
4:05 AM EST
40N45 73W57

Source: *Sabian Symbols* #412 (C)

This is a fascinating chart since it has so many inconjuncts. Saturn quincunxes Mercury and Mars inconjuncts the Pluto/Neptune conjunction. Thus there is another yod with the Mars/Uranus sextile inconjunct the Pluto/Neptune. People with many inconjuncts often experience life as a series of turning points. Where lots of fire and air are involved, the individuals feel **they** are making the changes and tend to like being drawn to new experiences. Those with lots of earth and water often feel threatened by new directions; they fear loss of security. They see changes as fated or beyond their control, unaware of how they have set themselves up through choices, attitudes and actions.

Ferde Grofe has lots of fire (Aries and a Sun/Jupiter conjunction closely square to Mars) and lots of air (Gemini, plus all the air houses occupied), so he appears to have consciously chosen the gypsy life in his youth — particularly with Uranus (independence) being a ruler of the 1st house and Mars, the natural ruler of the 1st house involved in the yod.

Walt Disney

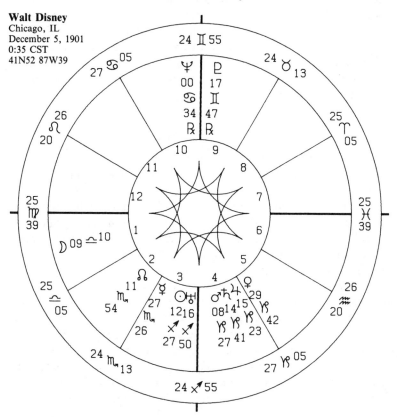

Walt Disney
Chicago, IL
December 5, 1901
0:35 CST
41N52 87W39

Source: Lyndoe, *American Astrology Magazine* (C)

The chart of Walt Disney is a classic illustration of the yod and how it works. Neptune in the 10th house inconjuncts Mercury in the 3rd and Venus in the 5th indicating his ability to create (Venus in the 5th house) fantasy (Neptune) through writing and drawing (Mercury in the 3rd). In 1923 at the age of 22 when transiting Mars trined his Mercury and opposed Venus, he moved from Kansas City to Los Angeles. Solar arc Mars inconjuncted Neptune and solar arc Moon had just passed the trine to Neptune. This was not a move that he had anticipated and looked forward to with joy; his job in Kansas City had evaporated and his brother Roy had suggested that Walt Disney might be able to find work in Los Angeles. When he arrived in July 1923, he went to live with an uncle. Times were tough and it was not until 1928 that he created Mickey Mouse and was able to ride Mickey's coattails to success. He was not enchanted with Los Angeles when he arrived and jobs were not easy to come by. Many times he regretted the necessity for the move, but in the long run, it was one of the turning points of his life.

But the activation of the yod clearly offered him a way to go, which, while not of his conscious choice, was still the right direction for him as later events proved. If one accepts the premise of "inner wisdom," he subconsciously knew it was right.

Boomerang

I have noticed charts where the yod configuration has a planet opposed to the inconjuncted planet: the "Finger." When this happens, it seems that the action indicated by the yod, instead of taking place at the "Finger," reacts at the planet in opposition, or **boomerangs**!

At first I thought of this as a slingshot type of action; but after careful perusal of many charts, I feel that the action involved is more in keeping with the **boomerang** principle. One of the definitions of the word **boomerang** is: "An enterprise that recoils and has an opposite effect of what is expected." It is easier to work with an opposition than an inconjunct, therefore we tend to neglect the yod by ignoring the inconjuncts and acting out the action of the opposition when dealing with the **boomerang**. All areas in the chart that are ignored can lead to eventual frustration and guilt, so it is necessary when working through the **boomerang** pattern to be sure to make the adjustments symbolized by the inconjuncts. This is what I have observed in the charts of people who have this interesting configuration.

Cher Bono Allman

Entertainer Cher Bono Allman has a yod involving the Moon in the 7th house inconjunct Uranus in the 12th and Mars in the 2nd. This could indicate that through changing her public image (Moon in the 7th), she could earn a great deal of money (Mars in the 2nd), in an unusual way (Uranus in the 12th, the house of films and television). However, the Moon is opposed by Saturn in the 1st house and this becomes the **boomerang** point. By changing partners, her personal image (1st house) was limited (Saturn).

The Moon rules her 1st house of personality and because it is in the 7th, she often projects her *persona* through her partner. When the partnership broke up, the reaction of the **boomerang** through Saturn in the 1st house contributed to the lack of appeal to her public. As a solo performer, she was not as well received as she had been when she performed with Sonny.

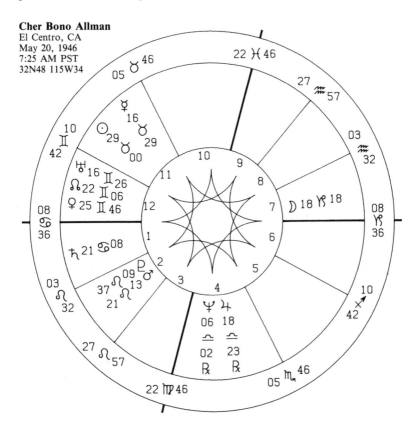

Cher Bono Allman
El Centro, CA
May 20, 1946
7:25 AM PST
32N48 115W34

Source: Quinn quotes "her mother" birth certificate (A)

With the 1st house ruler in the 7th, she is likely to feel her basic identity is in the hands of other people; she needs them to like her; she depends on them to validate her, especially partners. With Saturn in the 1st, there is the danger of being self-critical and judging herself too harshly. When we are hard on ourselves, others tend to sense it and contribute their criticism as well. Saturn in the 1st house identifies with work and can put much energy into a career, but Saturn ruling the 7th again ties her sense of self back to partnership. Yet with Mars in the 2nd house, she wants personal control of her money and resources.

So she is torn between pursuing a career and finding "herself" through a partner and she is inclined to be hard on herself for any mistakes or errors she feels she makes. Inconjuncts between planets in a house and planets ruling the house suggest conflict in that area. So here, both self-expression and partnership present challenges. Mars, natural ruler of the 1st, inconjuncts the Moon, the actual ruler. The Moon, ruler of the 1st, opposes Saturn in the 1st and Uranus, ruler of the 8th — representing partner's resources — inconjuncts the Moon in the 7th. Since she was not comfortable with herself or with her ability to be a partner, she handled her relationships with less than optimum skill. She is probably very hard on herself, and the public (7th house) reacted to her conflicts by withdrawing some approval.

Once she is truly secure and realizes she **can** have both love and work, she should be able to pursue a career successfully without castigating herself for her shortcomings and maintain a relationship without feeling that her sense of self depends on other people in her life.

Ralph Waldo Emerson

Ralph Waldo Emerson, the American essayist, poet, philosopher and lecturer, also has a **boomerang** configuration. Pluto in the 6th house inconjuncts Mars and the Moon in the 11th and Uranus in the 1st house. Pluto also opposes Saturn in the 12th house. After Emerson graduated from Harvard in 1821, he taught school and studied for the ministry. At age 26 when by solar arc direction Uranus squared the Moon, Pluto trined the Moon and Mars squared the Sun, he became minister of the Old North Church in Boston. His **boomerang** had been activated; but instead of finding pleasure and happiness in a job well done (Pluto in the 6th house), he found himself in an untenable position.

His temperament made him unsuited for the ministry in any conventional sense. Uranus in the 1st house often indicates a rebel. Jupiter there, plus his ministerial family background, indicated his original interest. Uranus rules his 6th house of work and inconjuncts Pluto there, so when the configuration was activated, it seemed logical that he would, by circumstances and the need to live up to his parents' expectations for him, move into a job that would prove to be unsuitable. If he had chosen an Aquarian kind of profession, one that allowed him the sense of independence and nonconformity he needed, that satisfied his idealism (12th house) as well as the need to earn a living, he probably could have maintained that situation — despite the boomerang configuration. Maybe he "needed" the experience of the ministry to further develop his own independent thinking and to clarify his vision of perfection and idealism. So, he unconsciously chose a career which he would later leave (satisfying the restlessness of the Uranian themes and the boomerang) that would please his family and that would stimulate his own mental, spiritual and idealistic development.

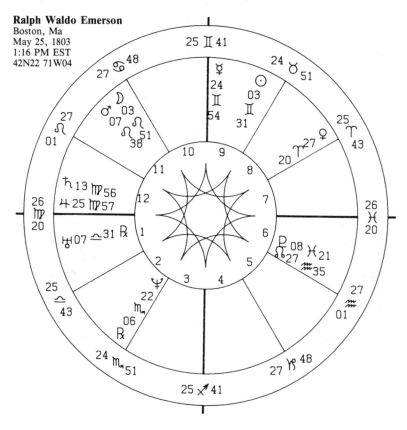

Ralph Waldo Emerson
Boston, Ma
May 25, 1803
1:16 PM EST
42N22 71W04

Source: Father's diary "while at Sunday dinner" (B)

He despised dogmatism and in 1832, after proposing to his church to discontinue the celebration of the communion and challenging all Christian orthodoxy, he left the church. The **boomerang** configuration was again being activated. This time Pluto opposed Uranus and trined

Mars. The unexpected event reacted through the opposition of Pluto to Saturn in his 12th house and it was while he was soul-searching that he realized the ministry was not for him. Instead he developed his transcendental philosophy and outlook and began to do some creative writing. Saturn rules his 5th house. So we can see that what, at the time, appeared to be an inevitable turning in the road (the yod) instead developed into an opportunity for unlimited soul growth (the **boomerang**).

There is much conflict involving the work area in Emerson's chart. Saturn, a natural key to career, opposes Pluto in the 6th house of work. Uranus, ruler of the 6th, inconjuncts Pluto in the 6th. The inconjunct from Pluto to Mars and the Moon in the 11th reinforces the freedom theme, both by the nature of Mars and the 11th house. The 6th/12th opposition is the struggle to integrate one's ideals, one's utopian vision of how the world ought to be, one's version of the beautiful dream with the nitty-gritty reality of the world and what is truly possible in terms of work and efficiency. This was complicated in Emerson's case because he had such strong needs for personal freedom and independence (Jupiter and Uranus, two of the three freedom planets in the 1st; Mars, the third freedom planet in the house of Uranus).

Summary

The **boomerang** seems to denote a reverse-type action. Things do not work out as expected. Instead, there is action at the inconjuncted planet and then a reaction working out at the planet opposed to that point. Oppositions can be a pulling apart and, used negatively, can be extremely disruptive, as in the case of Cher. Used positively, oppositions indicate that ability to balance two opposing factors and therefore enable you to become aware of different viewpoints and modes of operation. Your free will, of course, determines which path you choose.

A TRIBUTE: H.S.H. PRINCESS GRACE OF MONACO

by Marion D. March

(Since my daughter and son-in-law lived in Monte Carlo, I was privileged to have Princess Grace's secretary as my client who confirmed all the birth data used in this article, except Prince Rainier's time.)

Background

Once upon a time there was a quiet, rather plain duckling who developed into a beautiful swan, married a handsome prince in a faraway kingdom and lived happily ever after...but no, that's merely a fairy tale while ours is a true story with a tragic ending.

A brief biographical synopsis tells us that **Grace Patricia Kelly** was born November 12, 1929, at 5:31 AM in Philadelphia, Pennsylvania. She was one of four children: three girls and a boy. Her father, John Brendan Kelly, was a former bricklayer who became a millionaire contractor. Though shy and sickly as a child, Grace blossomed into a cool beauty who made 11 successful films, won an Academy Award and gave it all up to marry His Serene Highness Prince Rainier of Monaco and become the mother of three children.

An official Monte Carlo paper states: "Her Serene Highness Princess Grace, is an extremely conscientious sovereign, wife and mother. She personally initiates and contributes to numerous projects, charitable, scientific and cultural to bring about the betterment of mankind." And that's how it was until September 13, 1982, when her car missed a hairpin curve on the Moyenne Corniche and came to rest

120 feet below. She died on September 14, 1982, at 10:00 PM, when the family agreed to disconnect the life-support system that had sustained her body, though according to the attending physician, Dr. Jean Duplay, the brain had died hours earlier.

Delineation

Grace Kelly
Philadelphia, PA
November 12, 1929
5:31 AM EST
39N57 75W10

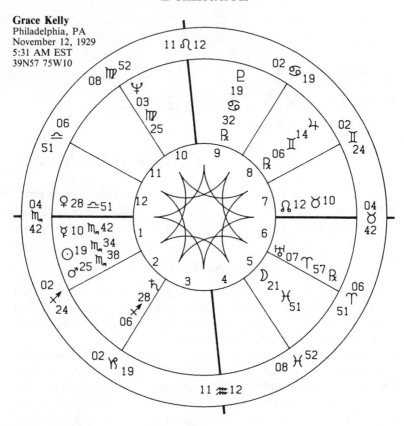

Source: Secretary quotes birth records (A)

The astrological profile reveals an interesting person. We find a strong Scorpio stellium, involving the Sun or inner individuality; the Ascendant or outer personality; Mars, the planet of action; and Mercury, the reasoning ability, in the 1st house of self-expression. The ruler Pluto is in the 9th house in Cancer, exactly trine the Sun; the Moon, her emotional essence, is in the 5th house in Pisces, giving her a grand trine in water.

She dreamed big dreams, had high aspirations and ideals (chart ruler Pluto in the 9th house); the harmonious aspects to the luminaries showed the ability to realize those dreams. Of course, we must also remember the classical 9th house interpretation of living in a faraway or foreign country, something which certainly applied to her.

The grand water trine not only indicates the possibility of great sensitivity, but Grace's Moon in the 5th house in Pisces added the potential of artistic inclinations, creativity and imagination. Her mother told Grace's biographer, Gwen Robyns:

> She was a shy child but with some sort of inner tranquillity and quiet resourcefulness [Scorpio stellium]. Though often sick with colds and asthma [sickness is often found when restless Uranus is in the 6th house of health inconjunct the Ascendant — body — and Neptune, forming a yod; when adjustments — positive use of inconjuncts — are made through work or service — 6th — the illnesses usually cease], Grace never minded being kept in bed and would sit there with her dolls for hours on end, making up little plays. She would change her voice for each doll, giving it a different character.

The Sun, Mercury and Mars in the 1st can be a means of self-expression, and of course privacy-loving Scorpio enjoys playing a role instead of revealing its true nature. States her brother Jack (lovingly known as Kell): "My sister blossomed as soon as she got in show business. She was more introverted than my sisters Peggy and Liz, and I think when she got on the stage, she sort of came out of her shell."

Early education and the way people communicate is described by the 3rd house. With Capricorn on the cusp and the ruler Saturn in Sagittarius in the 2nd house of values and income, Grace used her speaking ability to contribute to her earning power. She took advantage of Saturn's trine to Neptune to give form to her artistic talents. According to the *Los Angeles Times* of September 15, 1982:

> Grace's interest in drama surfaced early, she studied ballet seriously and already at age 12 appeared in a play staged by the Old Academy Players in East Falls, Pa. At that time she was attending the Raven Hill Academy, a strict Catholic convent. Grace also studied at the Stevens School in Philadelphia and then went to New York City to enter the American Academy of Dramatic Arts.
>
> She worked as a model, did some TV commercials and in July 1949, shortly after her graduation from the Academy, she made her professional acting debut at the Bucks County Playhouse in New Hope, Pa. and in November 1949 she opened in Strindberg's play *The Father* on Broadway.

The previously mentioned trine to Saturn is only one facet of Neptune. It is (together with Pluto) the most elevated planet in the horoscope and it rules both the creative 5th house and the Moon. Neptune, planet of mystery, glamour, magnetism and charisma in the 10th house of career and status is often the signature of royalty and film stars.

As told to biographer Gwen Robyns by producer John Foreman, who was then an agent, he vividly remembers a luncheon with Grace at the Plaza Hotel in New York.

> This aspiring actress shows up with gloves and a hat with a little veil. What a strange dead-assed girl, I thought. But by the end of the luncheon I realized that Grace had her act together — the act she put together for survival. Only Grace could have created Grace Kelly.... No one else did, no manager, no agent, no producer, not even her family. Grace's act, which has stood her in good stead for all these years, is one of the most efficient I have ever seen.

When she took this act, this self-creation, to Hollywood, the impact was tremendous. "Grace was a gentlewoman, something totally new to Hollywood," quotes her friend Rita Gam. While filming *Mogambo* in Africa, Grace was speaking Swahili, which she had carefully studied beforehand, with the natives. "She'll always have the class you find in a great racehorse," says her former costar James Stewart.

Besides the Neptune and 5th house integration, class and beauty are often seen when Venus is conjunct the Ascendant, particularly when placed in Libra, sextile Saturn and Neptune. The well aspected Venus in the 12th also helps to explain why her romantic involvements, supposedly with Clark Gable, Oleg Cassini, Jean-Pierre Aumont, Bing Crosby and Ray Milland, never created a scandal.

Parents and the parental background always play a major role in character development. Grace's Sun (father), ruling the 10th house (father), is placed in the 1st house (self), indicating that her father could play a very important role in her life. In Scorpio, conjunct Mars and quincunx Jupiter, he may have loomed as a larger-than-life, intense and ever-active figure. The trine from the Sun to the Moon could indicate that Grace experienced her parents as a loving couple and as a result the male and female principles within her were in harmony.

With the Moon in Pisces she probably viewed her mother as warm and sensitive, but also as unique, energetic and active, since Aquarius (unique) is on the cusp of the 4th house (mother) and the ruler Uranus is in Aries (active) in the 6th house.

According to *Newsweek* magazine of September 27, 1982:

> To suit the media's image of a family background befitting a fairy tale princess, the Kellys were bleached out to plastic pap.... while they actually were an Irish-American tribe right out of a John O'Hara novel.
>
> Grace's father, John B. Kelly, son of an Irish immigrant, was a great athlete: An Olympic rower who was refused permission by the British to race in their Diamond Sculls championship, because he had worked with his hands and was therefore not a gentleman sportsman. Nearly 30 years later Grace's brother, Jack, won the Diamond Sculls on the way to becoming as great an athlete as his father.

Grace's mother, the former Margaret Major, was also a known athlete, the first woman to coach a woman's team at the University of Pennsylvania. She was of German descent and her three daughters inherited her blond beauty. Pulitzer Prize-winning playwright (*Craig's Wife*) George Kelly was Grace's uncle and another uncle, Walter, was well known in vaudeville.

Despite riches and fame, the Kellys never could get into the Philadelphia Social Register, but father John was a power in the Democratic party and once was nearly elected mayor of Philadelphia.

The Moon in any chart describes not only the way we see our mother, but also our emotional nature and needs; it therefore assumes major importance. In Grace's case it is in her 5th house, explaining first her need to be creative; next, her need to love and be loved; and, most of all, her need to have children. By the time she met Prince Rainier at the Cannes Film Festival in 1955, she had starred in eight successful motion pictures, including Hitchcock's *To Catch a Thief* and *Rear Window*; *Dial M for Murder*; *The Swan*; *The Bridges at Toko-Ri*; and *The Country Girl*, for which she won an Oscar as best actress. As one palace insider remarked, "By then she may have been ready for a permanent, her last and best role." The marriage on April 18, 1956, made headlines and was a social, historical and media event.

According to palace sources, Monegasques were slow to warm up to Grace who at first spoke French with an accent. Roderick Mann (*Los Angeles Times* Calendar, September 19, 1982) quotes Princess Grace: "At first I thought I wouldn't be able to cope. Monte Carlo is a small town with a small town's attitudes. It took a lot of adjustments."

The positive use of the previously discussed yod involving Uranus, Neptune and the Ascendant, as well as the Uranus/Mercury and Sun/Jupiter inconjuncts, was to make many adjustments, which Grace did. As the Monegasques tell it, '*La Princesse*' threw herself into her new role with such dedication that the principality rewarded her with true love and admiration. "She can talk with royalty or movie stars, with presidents or me with the same ease, and make all of us feel good!"

a local taxi driver once told me.

My daughter, who at the time was active in a group called *Les Voisins* which helped newcomers get acquainted with Monte Carlo's ways, was surprised at how much personal interest the princess took, how naturally she acted and how totally charming she was.

It was Grace who made Monte Carlo the glamorous international center for which it is well known. "Before she came along," said Somerset Maugham, "it was becoming a resort for doddering dowagers" and a "sunny place for shady characters." By 1982 it was an ocean of skyscrapers whose footage had been increased from 375 to 464 acres by reclaiming land from the Mediterranean.

Rainier successfully regained control of the gambling casinos, and with Americans flocking to the principality, Loew's built a tremendous hotel and apartment complex, including an American-type casino, where craps, slot machines and Las Vegas techniques never cease to amaze the Europeans.

Typical of a 1st house stellium, which can find self-expression by throwing itself into action, Grace spared no efforts and, as head of the Red Cross, made it one of the most active international chapters. She founded a group for infants of working parents; the Garden Club of Monaco; an organization to protect artisan works of the principality; the Ballet School of Monte Carlo; the International Festival of Arts; and numerous other projects. She also enlarged and modernized the Centre Hospitalizier Princesse Grace (the hospital where she died). Some people feel the hospital is still not up to American standards and lacks many conveniences we take for granted.

Grace also did some exquisite flower collages which she exhibited in many places. She published *My Book of Flowers*, written in collaboration with Gwen Robyns, which covers the entire concept of flowers in art form. The proceeds from the book, as well as those from her needlework and poetry reading, went to one of the many charitable causes she espoused. (Venus, indicating what you might like to do, is in the 12th house of charitable institutions, sextile Neptune, which often depicts creative expression, and sextile Saturn, which can denote adding form to the creative ideas.)

But most of all, as befits a 5th house Moon in Pisces in a grand trine to the Sun and Pluto, Grace thrived on motherhood. In fact, everybody who has ever known Princess Grace emphasizes the importance of her family. "A real mother hen," state some of her friends. (The square from the Moon to Jupiter may have helped to show her tendency to overdo in this area.)

The Children

Princess Caroline Louise Marguerite was born January 23, 1957, at 9:27 AM; Prince Albert Louis Alexandre Pierre, Marquis des Baux, followed on March 14, 1958, at 10:50 AM, while Princess Stephanie Maria Elizabeth was born February 1, 1965, at 6:25 PM. All three were born in Monaco.

Newsweek quotes, "A close American friend states that the up-bringing of the 2 older children was straight out of the Victorian age, which may well have accounted in part for Caroline's rebelliousness and her marriage to French playboy Philippe Junot." I heard that up to the end all three children, including 25-year-old divorced Caroline, had to report to Maman, who would wait up for them at night.

Grace's Moon (mother/emotional nature) is square to Saturn (father/feeling of denial), which could account for her having felt a certain lack of parental affection or tenderness as a child, therefore she wanted to make sure her children would not feel the same way. She also defended them like a lioness against outside attacks.

Prince Albert fared best by graduating from Amherst College in Massachusetts. He supposedly is a good student and an excellent athlete who at this point is ready to carry on the Grimaldi stewardship of Monaco, which dates back to the thirteenth century.

Despite bodyguards assigned to the two girls in vain attempts to keep them out of the public's eye, their romantic flings made daily headlines. Even during and after the tragedy of Princess Grace's accident, the *Star* filled pages with "Jean-Paul Belmondo Jr. is keeping a loving vigil at the hospital bedside of his grief-stricken and injured girlfriend, Princess Stephanie." On the next page, "Princess Caroline and Robertino Rossellini split up earlier, but have been reunited by a common bond of tragedy — the deaths of Princess Grace and Robertino's mom, Ingrid Bergman."

Quotes Gwen Robyns in the *Star* (October 5, 1982):

> Grace was the most loving and caring mother I've ever known. She told me that she never minded what people said about her, but did mind terribly when they attacked her children. She felt that Caroline was a very responsible young woman, totally misunderstood by the public. Even this summer's interlude with tennis star Guillermo Vilas, as well as Stephanie's school antics and 'puppy love' with Harry Belafonte's son, were brushed aside as grossly exaggerated.

"Instead," states Robyns, "she was very happy that Stephanie had graduated and praised her decision to study under dress designer Marc

Bohan in Paris in the fall.'' (Accentuate the positive can be the motto of a grand trine.)

As configurations often do, this grand water trine assumed an all-important role in Grace's chart. The way she utilized the easy flow between the Sun, Moon and Pluto explains the basics of her character, her wish to bring love, life, the family and art all together. Her own words in *My Book of Flowers* best describe it:

> Through working with flowers we began to discover things about ourselves that had been dormant. We found agility not only with our fingers but with our inner eyes in searching for line, scale and harmony. In bringing out these talents within ourselves, we gained a dimension that enabled us not only to search for harmony in an arrangement, but also to discover the importance of carrying it into our lives and our homes. To create harmony in the home is the woman's right and duty. Home must be the oasis for the family — husband, children and others close to us. It should be a place where they can find a sense of well-being and strength, replenishment and renewal.

What a shame this vibrant woman had to leave us so early!

Aspects at Death

Can we see death in a horoscope? **No!** Thank God. The chart continues after death and the year, by progression, merely shows lots of activity, some challenges, responsibilities and hurdles to overcome — all aspects which could and often do mean many other things.

Of note are: solar arc Mars, ruler of the 6th house of health, opposing (possible feeling of separation) Pluto, ruler of her Ascendant (body) and Sun (inner individuality). Solar arc Ascendant conjuncts Saturn (new responsibilities), and all magnified by transiting Mars exactly conjunct natal Mars (superman syndrome) and transiting Saturn (ruler of 3rd house of communication and transportation) square to Pluto. Mundanely, this square is often called 'violent', but in a personal chart we would indicate possible power struggles, best solved by spending time alone in contemplation (transiting Saturn in the 12th house), or fighting for causes we believe in (charities, etc.).

Also solar arc Pluto squared Jupiter, ruler of the progressed Ascendant and natally situated in the 8th house of surgery and death, which is a handy after-the-fact interpretation, but usually indicates people motivated to reach for new achievements. Some astrologers may place great importance to the solar arc nodes in exact square to the natal Part of Fortune. Personally I don't work with Arabic parts, but

I find it very important that transiting Pluto and Saturn were both preparing to enter the sign of Scorpio and activate the stellium there.

Children's Aspects

A tragedy such as death is usually more noticeable in the survivors' charts, where the possible loss of a parent or partner can be detected, than in the person's chart.

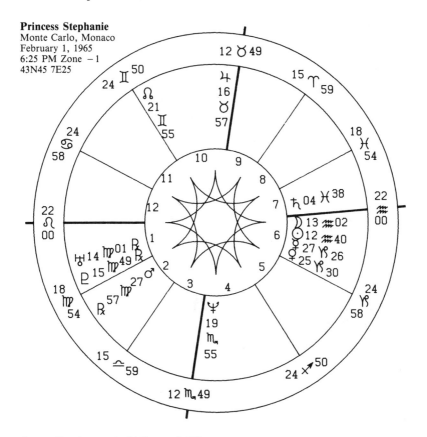

Princess Stephanie
Monte Carlo, Monaco
February 1, 1965
6:25 PM Zone − 1
43N45 7E25

Source: Secretary quotes birth records (A)

Stephanie's solar arc Venus was conjunct her natal Sun and, together with solar arc Mercury, touched off her natal T-square. That can readily signify that she may experience some major changes. The solar arc Sun and Moon had just entered 0° of Pisces, and the Midheaven was at 0° Gemini, all three pointing to the possibility of important new beginnings and also endings. There were many Saturn aspects: solar arc Saturn inconjunct the Ascendant, solar arc Jupiter square Saturn, secondary Ascendant opposition Saturn, connoting her readiness to accept new responsibilities and sometimes depicting a possible loss.

Worth noting is how interwoven Stephanie's natal chart is with her mother's: especially her Neptune exactly conjunct Grace's Sun as well as her MC/IC axis conjunct to Grace's nodal axis.

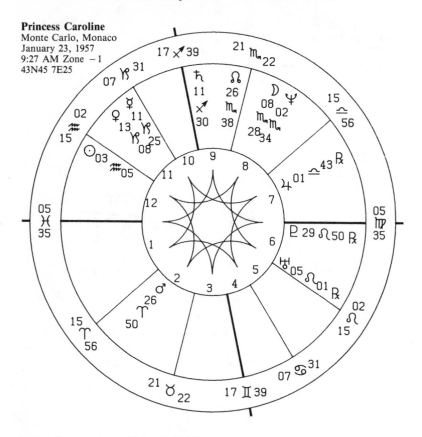

Princess Caroline
Monte Carlo, Monaco
January 23, 1957
9:27 AM Zone −1
43N45 7E25

Source: Secretary quotes birth records (A)

Caroline's natal chart also has a T-square which had been activated, first by secondary Mercury, then by transiting Jupiter. It would again be affected when Saturn entered Scorpio in December 1982 and later when Pluto got there. Her progressed Sun opposed Pluto, and just like Stephanie's, it was switching from Aquarius into Pisces. Most of

Caroline's Saturn aspects are separating (secondary Mars inconjunct Saturn, solar arc Saturn inconjunct Uranus, transiting Saturn opposition Mars). Transiting Saturn was moving through her natal 8th house.

There are many more aspects by progressed and transiting planets, too many to cite here, but it also looks like a serious romance could be in the making since there are many pleasant Venus and Moon involvements.

Caroline's chart also shows a strong bond with her mother. To mention just a few links: her Moon is conjunct Grace's Mercury, her Neptune sits on Grace's Ascendant and her north node conjuncts her mother's Mars.

Prince Albert
Monte Carlo, Monaco
March 14, 1958
10:50 AM Zone −1
43N45 7E25

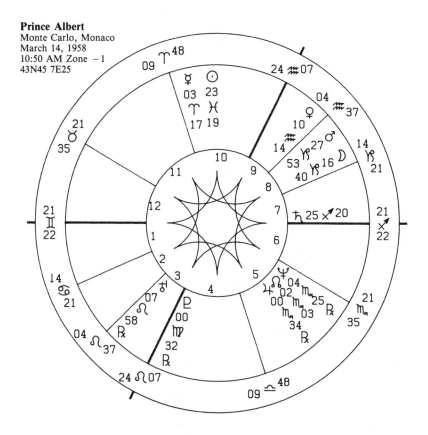

Source: Secretary quotes birth records (A)

Of all the children, **Albert**'s horoscope was the most activated, showing the potential of tremendous changes in the making. His mutable T-square, which involves the Ascendant, Sun and Saturn, was being filled by solar arc Pluto. When the empty point of a T-square is occupied by progression or direction, it nearly always indicates a key development in the life of the native. Also, transiting Neptune was activating the T-square by its conjunction to Saturn.

Just like his sisters, Albert also has a fixed T-square natally which related to Grace's stellium in Scorpio. It too had been affected by solar arc Moon conjunct Venus, transiting Jupiter conjunct Neptune and transiting Saturn ready to touch off the Scorpio planets. Additionally, solar arc Mercury (chart ruler) squared Mars, the solar arc Ascendant opposed the Moon, solar arc Jupiter squared the Midheaven and the progressed Sun was just separating from a square to the Moon. All these progressed and transiting aspects symbolize activity and upheavals which can force Albert to take stock and go through a tremendous growth period.

Grace and Albert must have had an innate understanding. His Sun is conjunct her Moon, his Jupiter conjuncts her Venus and Ascendant, his Neptune is on her Ascendant, his Saturn on her Saturn, his Venus on her IC (4th house cusp) and his Uranus on her MC. Of course all 3 children have many aspects to their mother's horoscope (sextiles, squares, trines, quincunxes and oppositions); I am just citing the conjunctions for strongest impact and feeling of belonging together.

The Husband

The most interesting astrological aspects are the links between **Prince Rainier** and his wife because they are not necessarily those generally encountered in a marriage comparison. His Neptune conjuncts her MC (he brings her his princely status); his Sun and Mercury sextile her Uranus (unusual attraction and unique communication), inconjunct her Ascendant (reorganize his thinking and life style) and square her Neptune (learn to accept her glamour image and importance). His Moon is widely conjunct her Saturn (she can bring him discipline), squares her Moon (mutual emotional challenges) and inconjuncts her Pluto (power struggles); his Ascendant inconjuncts her Mars, opposes her Saturn and squares her Moon (all personal adjustments and tensions to be worked out).

His Mars trines her Venus. This classic aspect for physical attraction and falling in love is magnified by her Scorpio stellium falling in his 5th house of love and by his Sun, Mercury and Ascendant falling in her 8th house of sex. To complete the picture, his Venus opposes her Mercury (tenderness and love verbally expressed). His Saturn trines her Jupiter and sextiles her Midheaven (they can help each other in many ways). His Jupiter conjuncts her Mercury (he can help her to expand her mind) and his Uranus conjuncts her Moon, explaining the quick attraction they felt for each other. Grace has a Pisces Moon and Rainier a 12th house Sun (also considered a strong bond).

Prince Rainier
Monte Carlo, Monaco
May 31, 1923
6:00 AM Zone − 1
43N45 7E25

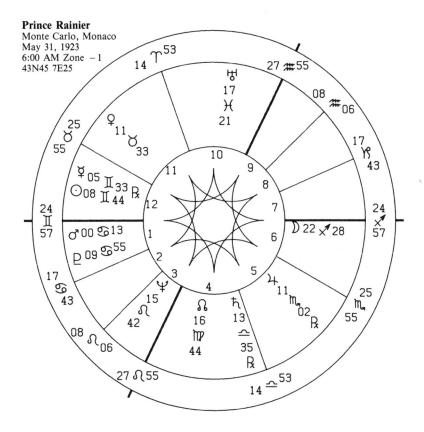

Source: Church of Light old file (C)

Rainier, just as his children, has a fixed T-square aspecting Grace's Scorpio stellium; and her Moon, together with his Moon opposition Ascendant, forms a T-square which often seems to be present in marriages that last.

His progressed horoscope reveals that his natal T-square was activated by secondary Mercury at 13 Leo. (I have found that the activation of the T-square starts when a progressed planet first aspects any of the planets involved and ends when the last planet of the configuration is touched off — the square to Jupiter took place August 1981, the conjunction to Neptune December 1982. The entire time span should be considered important, dynamic, challenging and action-filled.)

Transiting Jupiter conjuncted its own position, a Jupiter return, indicative of new beginnings in partnerships, since Jupiter rules the 7th house and Moon. Rainier has many inconjuncts (I count eight), all active within a two-year period and indicative of a need to make massive adjustments and of the necessity to reshape much of his life-style. Solar arc Mars is opposition his Midheaven (status) while transiting Mars squares it.

By May 1984 solar arc Venus will conjunct his natal Pluto which may indicate other changes and transformations in his life direction.

Bibliography

Grace, Princess. *My Book of Flowers*. New York: Doubleday, 1980.
Les Voisins (Monte Carlo), October 1979.
Los Angeles Times, September 15, 1982.
Los Angeles Times, Charles Chaplin, September 16, 1982.
Los Angeles Times, Roderick Mann Calendar, September 19, 1982.
Newsweek, September 27, 1982, 36-47.
Robyns, Gwen. *Princess Grace*. New York: McGraw-Hill, 1976.
The Star, October 5, 1982.

THE IMPORTANCE OF CORRECT BIRTH DATA

by Marion D. March

Most modern astrologers pride themselves on exact chart delineations, and even more exact chart computation, by calculating all cusps to the minute and the Sun and Moon down to the second. Yet few of them worry about inexact or sloppy birth data. But without the proper time of birth we cannot possibly have an accurate delineation!

My respected friend and colleague Lois Rodden has been the foremost crusader in this field and has made all of us aware of our gullibility. Time and again she has presented us with 2, 3 or even 4 different birthtimes for the same person. Her *The American Book of Charts* (published by ACS Publications, Inc.) brims with DD (dirty data) horoscopes. A perfect example is architect Frank Lloyd Wright, supposedly born June 8, 1867, at 8:00 PM LMT.

States Rodden: "The *Penfield Collection* quotes documents at Columbia University for June 8, 1867; these include his mother's diary. He himself also stated that he was born in the evening, in the middle of a storm. Yet the Church of Light (for many years a good source of data) quotes Ziegler who states that Frank Lloyd Wright was born June 8, 1869 at 6:05 AM; *World Book* and other encyclopedias also quote 1869."

Not as far back in history but every bit as confusing is the data on the "king" of the movies, Clark Gable, born February 1, 1901, at a minimum of five different times. Quotes Rodden:

Penfield Collection quotes *Dear Mr. Gable* by Jean Garceau [1961] which quotes on p. 18 "...made his entry into the world at 5:30 that morning." *Gable* by Chester Williams [1968] gives the date but no time. Dewey quotes "doctor's data" given in *The King* by Samuels as 9:15 PM CST but LMR has been unable to locate that biography. McEvers quotes Jan Moore "from doctor's records 3:30 AM CST." Church of Light gives 8:50 PM LMT, Sabian Symbols #361 gives 9:00 PM and Kraum's personal notebook has 4:40 AM.

Rodden has divided her data into four categories:

A   **Accurate Data**: birth certificate, in person, hospital records
B   **Biographies:**
C   **Caution**: nondocumented or no source of origin
DD   **Dirty Data**: with two or more conflicting statements

In our books Joan McEvers and I have gratefully adopted this system. But I would also urge great caution in accepting the personal testimony of birthtime without some certificate to back it up.

Elisabeth Kubler-Ross

A case in point is the chart of psychologist and care-for-the-dying expert Elisabeth Kubler-Ross. In a biography titled *Quest - the Life of Elisabeth Kubler-Ross* by Derek Gill, with an epilogue by Kubler-Ross, it states:

> In the late afternoon of July 8, 1926 all appeared normal in the delivery room of a maternity hospital in Zurich, Switzerland. . . . The fair-haired woman on the table seemed in the final stages of labor. . . . as the delivery room drama moved to a climax, the obstetrician cupped her hands to receive the infant now struggling to escape the birth canal. One minute later a child was born. . . . It weighed exactly two pounds. But shortly after Emma Kubler was delivered of a second child, a two pound replica of the first; a moment later a third child, weighing a healthy six pounds, was born. . . . The firstborn triplet was named Elisabeth.

A brief synopsis of Gill's biography will help in our delineation. This book reveals a life marked throughout by a sense of destiny, courage, resolution and service to others. Elisabeth became almost an alter ego to her identical triplet Erika, who was very sick as a teenager. At 18 she left home alone to see what she could do for the war-ravaged people of France and Poland. Against the wishes of her formidable father, she struggled to become a physician. After her marriage to an American medical student and her emigration to New York, she became a psychiatrist working among mental patients labeled hopeless. With her determination and dedication, she brought many of them back to health. Eventually she was drawn to those most truly abandoned by our society, namely, the dying. Her accomplishments in this field are legion, as was her best-selling book *On Death and Dying*.

According to Gill, Kubler-Ross is an ardent hiker, mountain

climber and skier. She admits to a short fuse, great highs and lows, and an overly idealistic nature. She has an excellent memory, nearly total recall, and she is a workaholic. She has a son Ken born in in 1960 and a daughter Barbara born 1964.

Since the biography has an epilogue by Kubler-Ross, it should signify an endorsement of the facts stated in the book. Therefore "late afternoon," the time quoted for the birth of the triplets, should be between 5:00 and 6:00 PM.

Elisabeth Kubler-Ross (#1)
Zurich, Switzerland
July 8, 1926
5:30 PM Zone −1
47N23 8E32

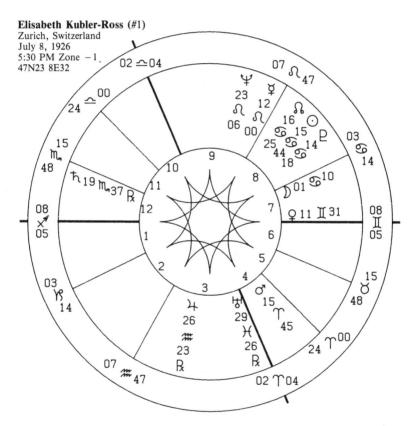

Source: Biography by Derek Gill (B)

A chart erected for 5:30 PM and labeled "B" according to the Rodden system has Sagittarius rising (see Chart # 1); the ruler Jupiter is in Aquarius in the 3rd house of communications and siblings. It is involved in a challenging T-square with Saturn falling in the 12th house of psychology and hospitals, and Neptune in the 9th house of philosophy and expansion. The Sun in caring and nurturing Cancer is conjunct Pluto in the 8th house of death and dying. Pretty convincing case, wouldn't you say?

But read on! After a lecture by Kubler-Ross in California, one of my students questioned her on the time of her birth. The rather firm reply was: "I was born on July 8, 1926 in Zurich at 10:15 PM." That chart has a 27° Aquarius Ascendant. The ruler Uranus in the 1st house would indicate her need for self-expression and probably a unique (Uranus) approach to life. The Sun, Pluto and the Moon are in the creative 5th house, all in the caring sign of Cancer. The T-square, always an indication of how the planets integrate and where the individual will feel much energy and emphasis, falls in the 12th house of hospitals, in the 9th of foreigners, visions and life philosophies, and in the 6th house of health and service (see Chart #2).

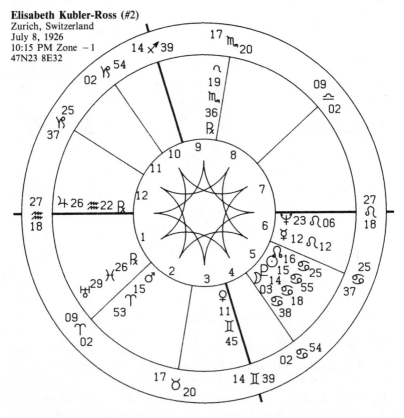

Elisabeth Kubler-Ross (#2)
Zurich, Switzerland
July 8, 1926
10:15 PM Zone −1
47N23 8E32

Source: Elisabeth Kubler-Ross (A)

Again, a very convincing chart, and one rated "A" since the data was received from the lady herself. But read on!

In September 1980 Lois Rodden received the copy of a letter from Mrs. Kubler-Ross, written in response to seeing a published chart based on her own quote of 10:15 PM. Part of that letter reads: "I **am** aware that until recently I presumed my birthtime was 10:15 PM, but I have since found out that it was 10:45 PM on July 8, 1926 in Zurich, Switzerland." She then goes on asking for some information regarding this new horoscope (see Chart #3).

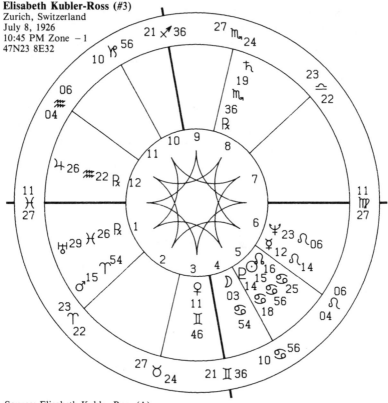

Elisabeth Kubler-Ross (#3)
Zurich, Switzerland
July 8, 1926
10:45 PM Zone − 1
47N23 8E32

Source: Elisabeth Kubler-Ross (A)

Well — now we finally have the real "A" data (we hope!). What does this chart tell us? We see a caring and sensitive Pisces Ascendant. Ruler Neptune is in the 6th house of health and service, involved in the previously discussed and ever important T-square with Jupiter in the 12th house of doctors and Saturn in the 8th house of death in the transmuting and transforming sign Scorpio.

The Sun and Pluto are still in the 5th house of love, creativity and children. Uranus still occupies the 1st house to explain her need for uniqueness, but now we also find Mars there to help us understand her need for independence of action and her self-determination (rather than Mars in the 2nd house of possessions and financial emphasis, as the 10:15 PM chart indicates). Venus, planet of affection, is located in the 3rd house of siblings.

What is the moral of all this? First of all, we should be very careful with our acceptance of data, especially when someone gives us a time of birth without first checking the birth records. Very few people have as good a memory as they think, and even those who do, often reverse figures. I have learned the hard way that "Mother said I was born at 9:07" is frequently 7:09 when the birth certificate or hospital records are consulted. "I remember exactly" can mean as much as twelve hours off, since morning and afternoon can become muddled in the mind as time goes by.

Secondly, please realize that we can find substantiation for many character traits if we look hard enough. In hindsight, or by knowing what to look for, we can easily fit a chart to a person; in fact, as we just demonstrated, we can make two or even three charts fit. Therefore, approach each Midheaven and Ascendant with a grain of caution and distrust, and rely on a more in-depth interpretation than just zooming in on some house positions.

Bibliography

Gill, Derek. *Quest - The Life of Elisabeth Kubler-Ross*. New York: Harper & Row Pub., 1980.

RECTIFYING THE BIRTH CHART
by Joan McEvers

All astrologers run into situations where there is no birthtime available. What to do? There are several answers. One of these is to rectify the chart. This is a long, involved process and requires a lot of dedication on the part of the astrologer. I like to do rectification, but most people are not able to pay an astrologer enough for the time necessary to do it properly. However, over the years, I have learned a lot about rectification.

In speaking of rectification, I am referring to the instance when you do not have a birthtime or when you only have a very general one, like around six in the morning. The method I will outline here is not for rectifying the birthtime on the birth certificate. That is a whole other story. You will find that it is much easier to rectify a chart for someone who has lived a whole lifetime than for a young person who has had relatively few life experiences. When I rectify a chart for a client, they have to fill out a 99-question list, provide a picture or two and give me samples of their handwriting which I send off to a grapho-analyst. Rectification is not an easy thing to do.

How to Begin

Numerology, grapho-analysis and use of the pendulum are all helpful in rectification. The best way to start when there is absolutely no time reference available is with a **solar equilibrium chart**. This is the chart where you put the degree and sign of the Sun on the Ascendant; the degree and sign of the ensuing zodiac sign on the 2nd cusp; and so on, setting up an **equal house chart**. After you have done this, take the planets right out of the ephemeris and place them into the wheel.

I feel that everyone should have two charts beside the **natal chart** in their file. One is the aforementioned **solar equilibrium chart**; the other is the **flat chart** which has Aries on the Ascendant, Taurus on the 2nd and so on around the wheel and using the planets right out of the ephemeris on the day of birth. From this chart you get a picture of yourself in relationship to everyone else born on the same day. The house position of the planets is not significant as it repeats the themes of the sign placement. For instance, if your Sun is in Leo, in this type of chart it is also in the 5th house, intensifying the Leo behavior pattern.

The solar equilibrium chart gives you a frame of reference for the day. Of course, both charts show the interrelationship of the planets. The Moon, naturally, can move as much as $6°$ to $10°$ backward or forward and remembering this motion can be of help in bringing the chart into line. The solar equilibrium chart is more particularized than a solar chart (when you put $0°$ of the Sun sign on the Ascendant).

Thyrza Escobar says you are more consciously aware of the content of this chart than of any of the other charts for your birth. If you have a planet within a degree or two of a cusp, the themes it represents are given outstanding emphasis, consciously, in your life. Activation of that planet points to major issues. The events depicted by the house that planet is in likewise have a strong effect. This is a subjective chart and as such does not indicate other people in your life, only your own attitudes.

There is another method for setting up a chart when there is no birthtime available: a **Johndro chart**, which localizes the horoscope and is quite accurate in delineation. Barbara Watters' book *An Astrologer Looks at Murder* is an excellent example of the use of this type of chart. However, I have not found these to be particularly good for rectification purposes.

Solar Equilibrium Chart

In looking at Chart 1, which is the solar equilibrium chart for **Ira Gershwin** (born December 6, 1896 in Brooklyn, N.Y.), we can see that he could be freedom loving (Sun in Sagittarius). We cannot state that he is self-motivated (most of the planets east) because with this type of chart, the hemispheric factor has no significance. Communication will be important to him; Mercury conjuncts the Sun. Both oppose Neptune suggesting imagination; they oppose Mars denoting drive and energy applied to creativity because in this chart Mars rules the 5th house. They also oppose Pluto indicating a certain stick-to-itiveness.

Saturn conjuncts Uranus, the ruler of the 3rd house. This conjunction is in the solar equilibrium 12th house describing possible sorrow through a sibling and/or an artistically gifted relative. It also characterizes Gershwin as having a creative imagination. There is a T-square involving Sun, Mercury, Jupiter, Pluto, Neptune suggesting drive, energy and possible inner conflicts and stress. Pluto is conjunct the cusp of the 7th house, illustrating that partnerships will be an important part of his life.

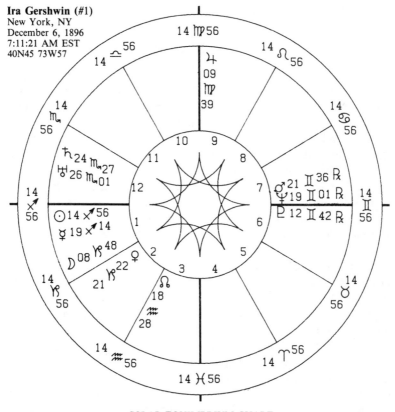

Ira Gershwin (#1)
New York, NY
December 6, 1896
7:11:21 AM EST
40N45 73W57

SOLAR EQUILIBRIUM CHART

The Moon is in Capricorn and is not close enough to the beginning of the sign to move back into Sagittarius. Because the Moon represents the mother, we can say that his mother was probably quite ambitious for him — perhaps a bit cold, traditional and conservative (all Capricorn characteristics). There may have been a grandparent who played an important role in his life. (The 7th house symbolizes grandparents as well as partners. The Moon in Capricorn often shows a strong grandparental tie.) Since the Moon has a trine to Jupiter (even if the

Moon moves forward 6° to 10°, this trine is still in orb), we expect that he is interested in journalism, sports and travel.

The Moon also signifies the wife, and she could be quite social, ambitious and purposeful. The Moon rules the 8th house in this chart, implying that he would get backing and support from the women in his life. The Moon in Capricorn indicates someone who would try to be protective of his emotions, control his feelings and try to live up to society's rules and expectations.

Life History

Let's look at the biographical material we have on Ira Gershwin. He was the oldest of four children of Russian immigrant parents and was somewhat overshadowed by his younger brother George. His mother was a nervous, ambitious, purposeful woman who wanted the best for all her children, especially education. She opposed George's interest in music but did not stop him or Ira from following that as a profession.

His father was easygoing, philosophical and took things as they came. He earned a living as a small businessman: owned a Turkish bath, cigar store, etc. While Ira was a child, the family made 25 moves between Manhattan and Brooklyn. When he was 10 years old, they purchased a piano, but he was not interested, so George got the music lessons.

Shy and modest, Ira was short, somewhat heavy and totally devoted to his brother and the rest of his family. In fact, when George died in 1937, Ira withdrew for three years, and friends who knew him well said he never really recovered from the loss. His literate rhymes and his brother's jazz-influenced tunes and rhythms put the brothers at the forefront of American musical theater in the 1920s and 1930s.

At age 20, he was writing lyrics under a pseudonym, so as not to trade on the Gershwin name, which George was in the process of making famous. He collaborated with George on *Lady Be Good* (1924) and a number of other successful Broadway shows including *Of Thee I Sing*, which was the first musical drama to win a Pulitzer Prize. They went on to write for the movies and in 1935 collaborated on the folk opera *Porgy and Bess*, which, though slow to catch on, has been recognized as one of the truly great works of the American musical theater.

After George died, Ira went on to collaborate with Kurt Weill (*Lady in the Dark*), Richard Rodgers, Jerome Kern (*Cover Girl*), Harold Arlen (*A Star is Born*) and others. Besides his lyric writing, he was a fine painter, an avid poker player and quite a social bon vivant. He was a racing fan and liked to travel. He was a collector of books and paintings and had a fabulous art collection.

He married the former Leonore Strunsky on September 14, 1926. They never had children. In 1928 the whole family went to Paris. His first trip to California was in April 1930. In August 1936 he, his wife and George all moved to a rented house on Roxbury Drive in Beverly Hills, California. George was living there when he passed away. In 1940 Ira and Lee bought the house next door where they lived until Ira's death. The last 20 years of his life were spent in almost total seclusion. He died August 17, 1983, at 8:00 AM PDT in Beverly Hills at the age of 86.

Knowing these facts about Ira, we will try to turn the solar equilibrium chart, so that what we know about him fits. Since he was a collector, was quite short and roly-poly, perhaps a Cancer Ascendant will work. (See Chart 2.)

Cancer Ascendant?

This chart does not support the strong partnership drive although it does indicate his creative streak (Sun, Mercury and Uranus in the 5th). Since the degree on the Ascendant was selected arbitrarily, perhaps Uranus would be in the 4th house indicating the many boyhood home changes. This chart supposes a birthtime of around 7:20 PM and the Moon would have moved forward about 7° and would be at 15° Capricorn conjunct Venus. This may be an indication of the working collaboration that he was noted for because the conjunction is in the 6th house. Mars ruling the 10th house and placed in Gemini in the 11th could connote his peripatetic father; and Saturn in the 4th and Venus in Capricorn ruling it present a fairly accurate picture of his mother. Eureka, we have it!

Certainly Jupiter in the 2nd fits, but why is there such an emphasis in the 11th house? There is nothing in this chart that indicates his withdrawal periods. Let's see how this chart works for events in his life. He married at age 30, and the 7th and 10th houses should be aspected by progressions or directions. Solar arc Mars, ruler of the MC, opposed Venus, and Venus trined Mars. By secondary progression Mars trined Venus. There are no aspects to the 7th house. In 1937 his brother George died and we would expect to find aspects to his 3rd house (brother) and to his 6th (brother's 4th) and his 10th (brother's 8th). Secondary Mercury (ruler of the 3rd) inconjuncts Jupiter (ruler of the brother's 4th).

This is a way of looking at his relationship to his brother by the derivative house system. This system carries interrelationships in the horoscope to their logical conclusion. The basic idea is to begin in the house of the basic or primary relationship. Then count the number of houses around the wheel as signifies the desired relationship. When counting, the house in which you begin is always counted as number one. For example, grandparents are parents (4th and 10th houses) of one's parents (4th and 10th houses). Thus, we can count 4 houses from the 10th (reaching the 1st house) and 4 houses from the 4th (reaching the 7th house). Or, we can count 10 houses from the 10th (reaching the 7th house) and 10 houses from the 4th (reaching the 1st house). Either way, we end up with the 1st and 7th houses signifying grandparents.

Ira Gershwin (#2)
New York, NY
December 6, 1896
7:20 PM EST
40N45 73W57

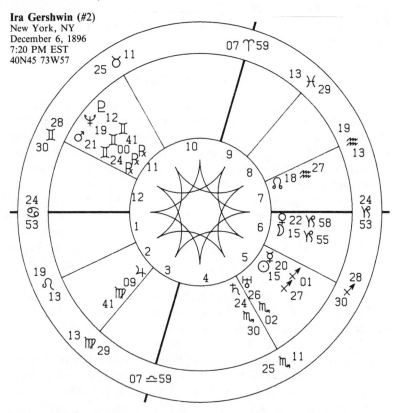

In this case, Ira's brother is signified by the 3rd house. Ira's 6th house would be his brother's 4th house (signifying endings). The 6th is the 4th house from the 3rd house. This chart seems to work, but some things we know about his life are unexplained.

Pisces Ascendant?

Let's try another water sign: Pisces (see Chart 3). In this chart the Ascendant ruler Neptune is in the 3rd house, which fits very well because it is in Gemini, the sign of brothers and writers. Mercury, ruler of the 4th house (mother), is conjunct the MC which could indicate that she is quite dominant. But again, nothing indicates his periods of withdrawal, nor is there much illustration of his gambling or collecting interests. At the time of the marriage, Mercury inconjuncted Neptune. Since Mercury rules the 7th, this is valid.

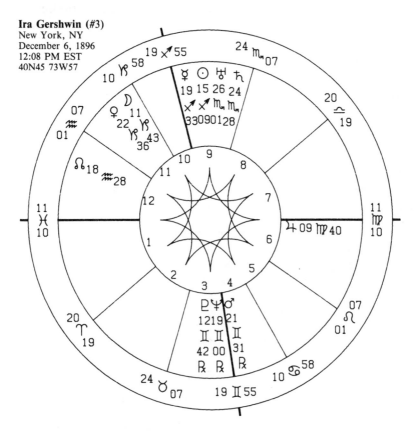

Ira Gershwin (#3)
New York, NY
December 6, 1896
12:08 PM EST
40N45 73W57

Scorpio Ascendant?

Let's try a Scorpio Ascendant (see Chart 4). In this case, we have to decide if we want the Saturn/Uranus conjunction in the 1st or the 12th.

If we put Saturn/Uranus in the 12th, the Sun will be in the 1st. He was not outgoing enough for a 1st house Sun, particularly in Sagittarius. So perhaps, Saturn/Uranus should go in the 1st house. Since Saturn rules the 3rd, we can see the potential of a strong attachment to a brother. Also the ruler of the 7th is in the 3rd signaling a partnership with a brother which was ended by death (Venus in the 3rd inconjunct Mars in the 8th). Venus ruling the 7th also depicts the marriage partner. Venus is in Capricorn and Lee was described as slender, very chic, a rather grande dame...somewhat resembling Helen Gurley Brown. The description fits Venus in Capricorn in Gemini's house. Uranus, the ruler of the 4th being in the 1st house clearly establishes the importance of home and family.

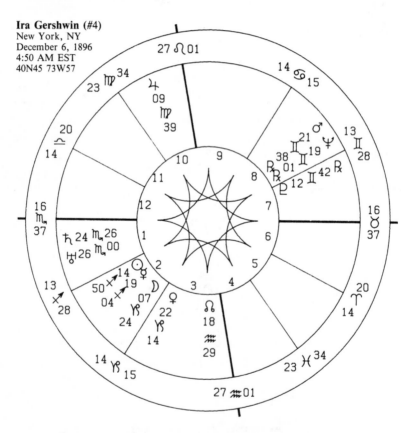

Ira Gershwin (#4)
New York, NY
December 6, 1896
4:50 AM EST
40N45 73W57

Scorpio rising can be withdrawn at times and Mars, the co-ruler, is in the retiring 8th house. Pluto is conjunct the 8th. Since Venus rules the 12th and is in the house of siblings, the loss of the brother could very well have activated his need to withdraw from the world (12th). This placement also indicated his brother's artistic talent. Before George died, Ira was known to be quite social and it was only after the loss of George that he showed his reclusive side.

Scorpio rising also fits his appearance. Scorpio is a short sign and with a Sagittarius Sun, we would expect a short Ascendant sign. Pluto and Mars (both in Gemini) depict his writing ability, and the opposition to Mercury and the Sun could characterize his intermittent reticence.

Uranus ruling the 4th house could denote the many moves when he was young and then the reluctance to move in his older years. In whichever area of the chart Uranus is placed, there are many changes. You can act one way one day and another on another day. Jupiter in the 10th illustrates the potential for awards. Jupiter ruling the 2nd house and square to Pluto in the 7th shows the capacity for earning with a partner. The ruler of the Ascendant in the 8th house supports this. So does the ruler of the 6th in the 8th. Saturn in the 1st conjunct Uranus indicates wit and a way with words since Saturn rules the 3rd house. The Sun ruling the 10th opposing Neptune is a good characterization of his father. Jupiter in the 10th shows that his father may have been quite a philosopher.

Charles Carter says that musical ability (to put his lyrics to music) is indicated by 16 Taurus/Scorpio and Saturn on an angle. He also likes Neptune on an angle and Saturn connected with the Moon. In this case, we have the Moon in Capricorn. The reason I chose the second decanate of Scorpio rising is because it is the Pisces decanate and I like to get as much Neptune into a creative chart as possible.

Progressions

Let's see how the progressions work with this Ascendant. When his brother died, Uranus conjuncted the Moon, Jupiter trined Mars in his 8th house and the MC had just passed the square to the Moon. When he married Lee, the MC sextiled Uranus; Mars opposed Venus (ruler of the 7th); Uranus trined the MC. These were all solar arc directions and could be quite indicative of what was going on. By secondary progression, the Moon inconjuncted Jupiter in his 10th house showing a change of status when he got married and Venus (ruler of the 7th) opposed the MC. When George died, the progressed Moon conjuncted Mars in the 8th house and inconjuncted Venus in the 3rd; the Sun inconjuncted the MC and sextiled Uranus; Mercury inconjuncted Jupiter in the 10th (George's 8th).

Transits

Now it is necessary to check transits on the specific days we are considering. He married on September 14, 1926. On that day the Sun squared natal Mars; the Moon of the day conjuncted the Sun and Mercury during the day; Mars squared his mean nodes and Jupiter conjuncted the north node; Saturn inconjuncted Mars. Uranus inconjuncted the MC; Neptune conjuncted it; Pluto inconjuncted the Sun. In comparing those aspects to the 3 charts, the Scorpio rising chart seems to be the most accurate. In men's charts particularly we find aspects to the 10th house for marriage because it suggests a change of status. Ira had plenty of these and he also had aspects to the 7th.

On the day George died, July 11, 1937, Mars inconjuncted Mars, and Jupiter conjuncted Venus in his 3rd house.

Numerology

Numerology is an excellent additional tool for rectification. He was born Israel Gershvin but was always called Ira, which he assumed stood for Isadore. He did not find out his real name until he was about 30, probably when he wanted to marry. George had changed Gershvin to Gershwin and Ira had adopted this change also. Numerology relates well to astrology, but you cannot say that each number relates to a specific planet or sign. However, Israel Gershvin is a #4. Four can refer to Saturn and the Moon, which is verified in Ira's Scorpio rising chart with Saturn in the 1st house. The Moon in Capricorn supports this. The confusion about his name is suggested by Saturn inconjunct Neptune. Neptune rules confusion, and the 3rd house (which Saturn rules) has to do with names. Ira Gershwin is a #5. This number seems to relate to the planet Mars, which in this case co-rules his Ascendant. The pseudonym he used in his early days (Arthur Frances, the names of his brother and sister) added up to a #8, which coincides with the Uranus in the 1st house and Leo on the MC. Eight is a power number and relates to Uranus, Leo and Saturn.

Death

Ira Gershwin died August 17, 1983, at 8:00 AM in Beverly Hills (see Chart 5). The death chart should link to the natal chart. I have found that in the death charts of prominent people, the Ascendant or MC usually falls on a natal angle. In this case, the Ascendant is in the natal 10th house and the MC falls on the 8th house cusp of the Scorpio rising chart. Of course, it also conjuncts the natal Pluto. The Sun of the day squares Saturn in the 1st house. The Moon conjuncts Mercury and opposes Neptune. It has been my experience that transits do not have to be exact to the minute to work. A degree or two approaching is often valid, and occasionally even a degree or two separating works. The slow transits seem to set up the action and then when a fast-moving planet reaches an aspect everything is set off.

Gershwin's Death (#5)
Los Angeles, CA
August 17, 1983
8:00 AM PDT
34N03 118W15

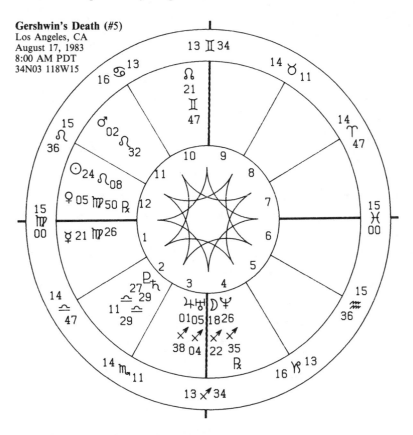

Neptune by transit trined the MC, indicating an easy release. He had been sick for quite some time and was probably relieved to go on. By secondary progression the Sun squared Pluto; the Moon opposed Jupiter; Mercury, ruler of the 8th, trined the Mars/Neptune midpoint; Mars was conjunct its own position in the natal chart and the progressed

MC was conjunct Uranus and square its own position. By solar arc direction Venus sextiled the Mars/Neptune midpoint; Mars squared the Mercury/Neptune opposition making a T-square; Uranus squared Saturn; the north node was conjunct the 7th house cusp; the Ascendant sextiled the Sun, and the MC conjuncted the Saturn/Uranus midpoints. In my experience, aspects to midpoints are quite prominent in death charts.

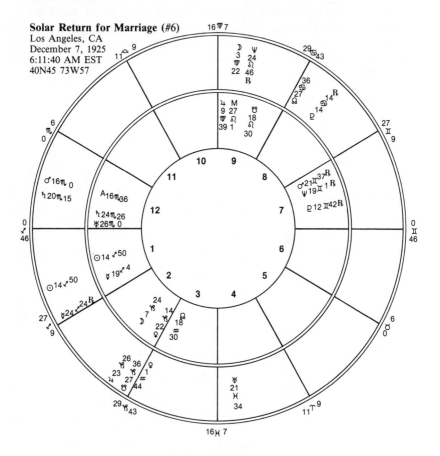

Solar Return for Marriage (#6)
Los Angeles, CA
December 7, 1925
6:11:40 AM EST
40N45 73W57

Solar Returns

As a checkpoint in rectification, it is always wise to set up some solar return charts. Chart 6 is the solar return for December 7, 1925, the birthday prior to his marriage to Lee. The 1st house of the Scorpio rising chart comes to the Ascendant and the Sun is in the 1st. This is always an important year in the life and since natal Jupiter that rules the Sagittarius Ascendant is in the legal 9th, we can see that it is possible he may legalize a relationship. With SR Jupiter in the 2nd, his values may change; he will probably gain some sensual gratification and indulgence through marriage and it is likely he would spend money on a partner since it conjuncts natal Venus, ruler of his natal 7th house.

By progressing the SR chart 1° every 4 days across the MC, we find that by September 14, when he married Lee, the MC was at 28° Scorpio conjunct his natal Uranus suggesting he might be ready for a change in his home life. (Uranus rules the 4th.) The Ascendant had progressed to 6° Aquarius just past SR Venus, a nice aspect for marriage. The 11th house cusp conjuncted his Sun, signifying a social event, and the 5th house cusp was conjunct natal Neptune/Pluto midpoint, implying sexual feelings and magnetic attraction.

Solar Return - George's Death (#7)
Los Angeles, CA
December 6, 1936
6:52:11 PM PST
34N03 118W15

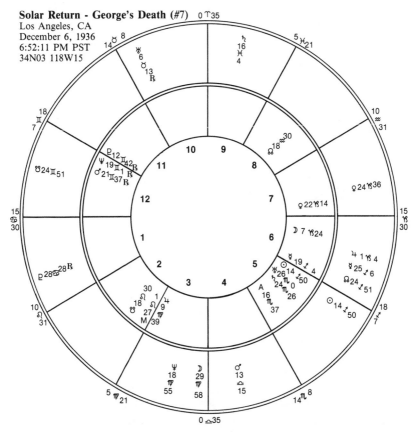

In the SR chart for the death of his brother (Chart 7), there is a Pluto/Venus opposition across the angles linked to his natal chart by the SR Venus conjunct natal Venus. The Moon is conjunct the 4th house cusp and Mercury, ruler of the SR 3rd, is in the 6th (the brother's 4th). Progressing the SR chart to the date of George's death, July 11, 1937, we find the MC opposing the Saturn/Uranus midpoint at 25° Taurus; the Ascendant at 28° Leo has just squared natal Uranus; the 12th house cusp conjuncts transiting Pluto at 28° Cancer, and the 3rd house cusp at 26° Libra squares SR Pluto/Venus opposition.

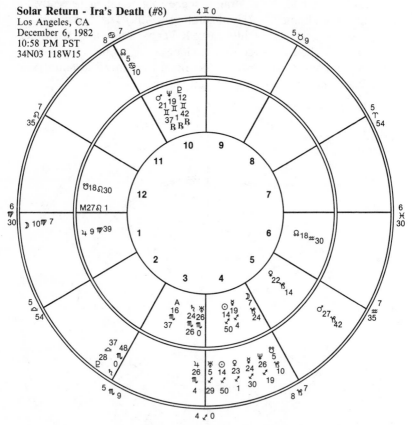

Solar Return - Ira's Death (#8)
Los Angeles, CA
December 6, 1982
10:58 PM PST
34N03 118W15

The solar return chart (Chart 8) for Ira's last year, 1982, brings his 10th house to the Ascendant. His Sun, natal Moon and Mercury — as well as SR Uranus, Venus, Mercury, Neptune and south node are all in the 4th house of endings. SR Jupiter, ruler of the 4th, is conjunct natal Uranus, ruler of the house of health (the 6th); SR Moon is conjunct natal Jupiter near the Ascendant; SR Uranus and natal Uranus are straddling the meridian. I have found that in SR charts for the year of death, the meridian is often conjuncted by two or more planets.

When the SR chart is progressed to August 17, the Ascendant at
4° Scorpio trines the SR north node; the 12th house cusp at 5° Libra
squares SR nodes.

George Gershwin

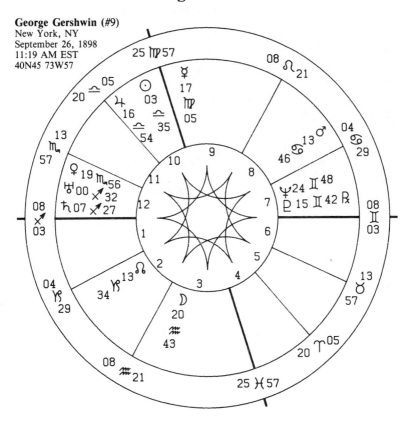

George Gershwin (#9)
New York, NY
September 26, 1898
11:19 AM EST
40N45 73W57

Source: *Sabian Symbols* #384 (C)

Whenever possible when rectifying a chart, it is wise to look at as many
family charts as are available. The only chart we have to compare with
Ira's is the chart of his brother George (see Chart 9). Venus rules
George's 6th house and is in his 12th house, illustrating that much of
his work was done behind the scenes. George's Venus conjuncts Ira's
Ascendant if the Scorpio rising chart is correct. It also conjuncts Saturn,
the ruler of Ira's 3rd house of siblings. George's Ascendant has a wide
conjunction to Ira's Sun, but that is active regardless of which

Ascendant we use for Ira. George's Moon in the 3rd house trines Ira's Mars which rules his 6th house of work, indicating the collaboration between the brothers. These links are not present in the Cancer or Pisces rising charts.

Summary

I feel that these illustrations support the validity of the Scorpio rising chart. Since there is no record of a birthtime for Ira Gershwin, we will be unable to prove whether this assumption is correct. My coauthor Marion D. March knew Ira personally and had often asked him for his time of birth. He always replied that he didn't know. One day when she was visiting with him, he told her that a famous astrologer from New York had written, asking for his birth information because he wanted to put his chart in a book.

He told Marion he had sent it. She was surprised and asked again for his time of birth, figuring he might have found a record of it. He airily replied, ''Oh I just made one up.'' Needless to say, Marion was appalled. But how like a Scorpio Ascendant with Pluto and Mars in Gemini.

POTENTIALS AND LEVELS OF SEXUALITY IN THE HOROSCOPE
by Marion D. March

Since sexual activities and mores have crawled out of the Victorian closet, we have realized that whether enjoyed, repressed or overdone, sex is a motivating factor in most people's lives. The word sex has become all encompassing and includes desires, love and affection; just as the words sex appeal comprise charisma, glamour and popularity as well as that real aura of sensuality which is indescribable and can be sensed more than seen.

What about astrologers? Can we find sexuality in a horoscope? The answer is a resounding yes, but with this yes comes a warning: Do not only look at the obvious. We must consider the entire chart, because sex is not something that can be isolated — it is an integral part of the whole personality.

In this article we will discuss some of the traditional factors that should be considered when delineating sexual potential, psychological variables and archetypes of the signs, and so as not to get lost in details or single factors, we will use some actual horoscopes.

Sexual Overview

Here are some of the important areas to explore:

The **5th house** for love, romance, sexual enjoyment and attitude.
The **8th house** for the actual sexual performance.
Mars for the sexual drive and energy.
Venus for feelings of love and affection.
Pluto for passion, intensity and even obsession.

Neptune for romance and excessive idealization of love.
Uranus for excitement and experimentation.
Mercury for the sexual fantasies and mental approach.
Saturn for overcompensation due to feelings of inadequacy or inferiority, or a desire to be in control, as well as the principle of loyalty.
Jupiter for optimism and ease, as well as indulgences of all kinds.
The **Sun** for all ego expression.
And, most important, the **Moon**, indicating our emotional personality which will influence everything mentioned before.

Naturally we read house and sign placement as well as its aspects. (Please note that all planets should be observed.)

Sexual Mythology

To delve a bit deeper into the sexual implications we must realize that the Anglo-Saxon version of **Venus** as pure and virginal is quite mistaken. According to mythology, Venus is the Roman name for Aphrodite. When Cronus (Saturn) overthrew his father, Uranus, he castrated him and threw his genitals into the sea. Around these gathered white foam, *aphros*, and from this the goddess Aphrodite/Venus arose. Venus had many lovers; among the better known were the Olympian gods Ares (Mars), Hermes (Mercury) and Poseidon (Neptune). Being very fruitful, she bore them all sons. She also loved the mortal Adonis, whose name has become synonymous with masculine beauty. The French have a more realistic approach to what Venusian love is all about. It's sensuous (Taurus) and beautiful (Libra); it involves pleasures of the senses in every possible way and most important — it has to be shared and equally enjoyed by a partner to be really meaningful.

    Mars is also maligned by many cultures. He's no sexual deviate or coveting male ready to rape an innocent female. He is frank and up front — what you see is what you get. In Roman myths he was the most important god next to Jupiter, best known as the god of war. Originally the patron of vegetation, he was important to an agricultural people who were often at war. In the Greek version he is known as Ares, son of Zeus and Hera. Aside from his lusty encounters with Aphrodite, he is also known as the first god who stood trial for murder. He killed Halirrhothius who had raped his daughter Alcippe. After he was heard by his fellow gods, he was acquitted. The Martian energies are straightforward and open. The glyph of Mars with its barb is meant to represent (among other symbolic meanings) the male penis, erect and ready to penetrate. No behind-the-scenes shenanigans for Mars, just overt enjoyment of the sexual act.

The covert, passionate and multifaceted sexuality of **Pluto** is what people seem to have in mind when they talk of wanton behavior, overly permissive attitudes or promiscuity. Pluto, also known as Hades, is the archetype of the god of darkness, since he rules the regions of the nether world. What better way to describe certain sexual urges that seem to burst forth from some unknown depth within us.

There are many Plutonian myths; the most famous one is about Demeter, goddess of fertility and her daughter Persephone. Pluto/Hades, with the permission of his brother Zeus, snatched Persephone while she was picking flowers and bore her off in his black chariot to his kingdom. Demeter's grief while searching for her daughter caused all nature to wither and a famine threatened Earth. Zeus, seeing the blackened soil, sent Hermes to fetch Persephone back, but she had eaten part of a pomegranate and was already beholden to Hades. A compromise was reached and she spent part of her time with Hades and the other part with her mother as the carefree girl tending the fields. Allegorically, this was supposed to show that sex cannot and should not be denied, but also that it was not meant to become the end-all of existence. The forbidden fruit inherent in darkness can be temptation and sexual fulfillment as well as transformation into other ways of living. Pluto/Hades should never be confused with our idea of the devil, a concept alien to the Greeks who saw actions as good or bad rather than sinful. Even the occasional description of Pluto/Hades with a pitchfork prodding the dead is only reminiscent of Satan to those raised with Christian morals and ethics. The "pitchfork" is really a trident, symbol of power — the power to rule over the dead.

Marilyn Monroe

Let's discuss a known sex symbol as our first example: Marilyn Monroe. She has Sagittarius on the cusp of her 5th house and the ruler, Jupiter, is in Aquarius in her 7th. She loved to be free and easy, unhampered and detached in her romantic pursuits; yet Jupiter in the 7th shows that she wanted her romantic involvements to marry her or at least be serious one-to-one commitments. Jupiter also reveals other inconsistencies in Marilyn's life. The opposition to Neptune suggests her romantic expectations were unrealistic and overblown. (If the idealism denoted by that combination is not handled properly, people tend to expect more than is humanly possible in a relationship.) The conjunction to the Moon suggests she was very emotional, wanting nurturing experiences.

If not integrated, her emotional vulnerability could easily throw her off balance, particularly since Jupiter squares Saturn in the 4th house revealing that she probably lacked self-esteem and constantly had to prove that she could get and keep lovers, as a form of reassurance and security.

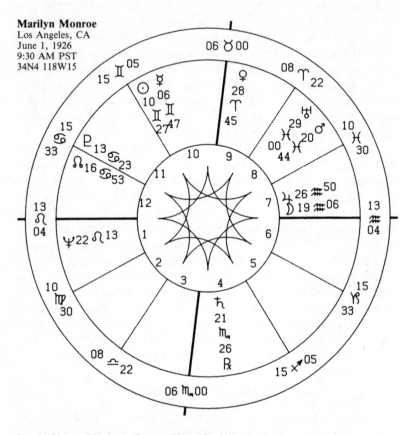

Marilyn Monroe
Los Angeles, CA
June 1, 1926
9:30 AM PST
34N4 118W15

Source: Photo of birth certificate in biography (A)

Marilyn's 8th house tells the same story in a different way. Pisces on the cusp and ruler Neptune in Leo in the 1st house show a romantic dreamer who wanted to be wooed and loved and idolized. But Jupiter, ruler of her 5th, is in opposition to the ruler of the 8th and both are involved in a square to Saturn, forming a powerful T-square which indicated inner tensions between the ideal she sought and the reality that was possible in this world. With the Moon also involved, she probably experienced a denial of parental love or lack of parental role models and doubted her own sexual ability and capacity to find emotional security (no father and an unstable mother who had to be institutionalized). Her role as a movie star encouraged her to rely on her glamorous and sexy image as projected by Neptune in Leo in the 1st house rather than finding a more secure foundation for feeling like a worthwhile person.

Mars in the 8th house frequently indicates a sensual person to whom sex is very important, but in Pisces it mirrored her emotional unpredictability, her sensitivity, vulnerability and idealism. Mars is inconjunct its own ruler Neptune, which called for adjustments in personal relationships, especially her habit of expecting too much from others and promising others more than she could deliver.

With Uranus in the 8th house, she was not adverse to all kinds of sexual experimentations and probably enjoyed them as long as her emotions were not involved. She found it easier to be successful on the casting couch, where she pursued her career ambitions in an emotionally detached fashion, than in her marriages where love and feelings took over. (The Moon is in her 7th house of partners.)

Her Moon, though in supposedly cool and collected Aquarius, squares Saturn, an aspect which shows the potential of feeling blocked or inhibited emotionally, of feeling a lack of nurturance. Her Saturn is in the 4th house (home) and Marilyn felt unwanted, lonely and unloved much of her youth. (This aspect used positively could indicate people who are comfortable with pragmatism and will work doubly hard to stand on their own feet.) The Moon/Neptune opposition showed how she veiled her pain by moderating reality but added to the distorted picture she had of herself. Because she found it easy to seduce men with her body, sex became her security blanket and her undoing, because it validated her fears that she had nothing else to offer but her body.

Marilyn's Venus in ardent and restless Aries rules her 10th and 3rd houses and it has only flowing aspects. Her Sun is in Gemini in the 10th and its one aspect is a conjunction to Mercury. Marilyn actually had the good mind implied by that placement, but felt trapped by the sex symbol role believing it to be the only road to success for her. She wanted to shine (Sun) in her career (10th), and her Venusian sensuality (Taurus on the MC) and charm in expressing herself (Libra on the 3rd) helped her succeed.

The Happy Hooker

Chart 2 is another Gemini female — Libra on the 5th house and ruler Venus in Leo in the 2nd. Here's a woman who really enjoys love and sex (Venus conjunct Pluto), wants plenty of it (trine Mars and sextile Uranus) and wants to be applauded for it (Leo). With Venus in her 2nd house, she may want to make money through it (and, of course, all other 5th house matters). Her intensity in sexual matters is confirmed by the Moon in Scorpio in the 5th house. It reveals a strong desire nature; she would not shy away from many affairs in pursuit of her pleasure. But it also shows a moody nature which can be jealous and possessive (Moon square Venus and Pluto) and has a great need for real love and affection as well as physical possessions and security. Her drive for security was probably exacerbated by childhood difficulties with one of the parents, most likely the mother.

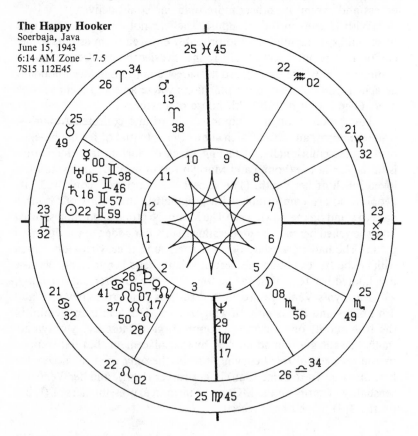

The Happy Hooker
Soerbaja, Java
June 15, 1943
6:14 AM Zone −7.5
7S15 112E45

Source: *Profiles of Women* (C)

The 8th house with Capricorn on the cusp is ruled by Saturn in Gemini in the 12th. Saturn — teacher, taskmaster, restrictor or denier — can symbolize feelings of inadequacy or insecurity; as a result, wherever Saturn rules or is placed, we tend to overcompensate. Saturn conjunct her Sun could confirm certain childhood problems, resulting in feelings of frustration of never living up to parental expectations, which in turn made her feel the need to prove herself — this time in some behind-the-scenes (12th house) matters involving the 8th house. Mars is in fiery and lusty Aries in the 10th where it indicates much physical energy and, possibly, an ardent love nature (it trines Venus). It can also denote a competitive woman seeking status and a successful career.

This is the horoscope of **Xaviera Hollander**, New York's notorious "madam." In her book *The Happy Hooker* she openly discusses her enjoyment of sex since her early teens. Born in Indonesia, she spent three years in a concentration camp and was raised in Holland after World War II. Her cultured family gave her a good education and she speaks seven languages. After global travels she decided to make her hobby her career and opened her own high-class brothel in New York.

Her good business sense (Jupiter in the 2nd trine the MC and sextile Mercury) and way with words (the strong Gemini emphasis in her chart) helped to make her autobiography a bestseller which was also sold to the movies. The challenge to live up to something or somebody, shown by the Saturn/Sun conjunction as well as the squares in her horoscope, propelled her into decisive action. Marilyn Monroe succumbed to the overexpectations symbolized by her Moon conjunct Jupiter opposition Neptune as well as the potential put-down of her Moon/Saturn square. Xaviera rose to the challenge of her chart.

One More Gemini

Our third female example is another Gemini, this time a client of mine. She is a beautiful woman who looks cool and distant, but believe me, every man can sense her aura of sexuality. Gemini is on the cusp of her 5th house with the ruler, Mercury, in Cancer in the 6th. Mercury makes only one aspect, a conjunction to Pluto. She pretends to take love and romance lightly and she enjoys variety and fun (Gemini); but deep down inside, this lady has feelings (Mercury in Cancer) and her involvements become intense (conjunct Pluto). Her Sun is in the 5th and she loves to shine in all 5th house matters. This is where she best expresses (Gemini) her true individuality, which she does not only through sex, but also as a very talented artist.

Her 8th house is Virgo, often a sexually unsure or even disinterested sign (since they sometimes view sex as a task or chore rather than something to enjoy); it too is ruled by Mercury in Cancer. Neither her 5th nor 8th houses show tremendous sexual needs, nor does her Gemini Sun or Capricorn Moon; but, lo and behold, she has Venus conjunct Mars in Leo, both involved in a grand fire trine with Jupiter, Uranus and Saturn. This Venus/Mars conjunction implies a magnetic effect, and particularly in Leo where the attraction to and for the opposite sex is tremendous. This combination shows her zest, charm, great sexual potential and endurance. As she herself says, she likes some sexual activity at least once a day, even now at 56 years of age. Her husband likes the challenge of conquest better than sex with only one woman, so they have a truly open marriage with him chasing new nymphs every month while she has steady lovers.

Female Client
Confidential
June 16, 1927
0:02 EDT
41N57 85W0

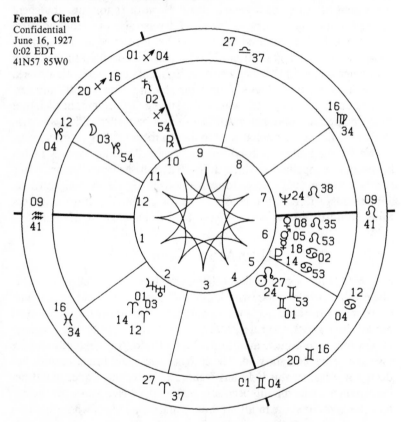

It was not always this way. Her Capricorn Moon inconjunct Venus/Mars and square Jupiter/Uranus illuminates her demand for lots of security, and watching her husband's antics was not exactly the medicine she needed. It took lots of urging from her husband and others to convince her to try having an affair instead of a divorce. By now she has an excellent marriage and has learned to relish her Venus/Mars conjunction. When her latest lover had to end the affair because his wife found out, she told me, "I lost my lover and my hairdresser in the same week and I'm not sure which one is harder to replace!"

No Absolutes

As our examples so far have shown, astrology is astrology is astrology, whether you talk about character potential, vocational potential, marriage potential or sexual potential. Though looking for specifics, the entire chart must be taken into account. There are no astrological absolutes, because every existing rule changes as it is blended with all else in the horoscope. Scorpio is a very sexual sign, but how much, how little and how enjoyable will depend on Pluto's placement as well as which planets are in the house with Scorpio on the cusp. We should also be careful not to judge what is sexually right or wrong, normal or abnormal. These are terms that depend on your background and upbringing as well as the mores of your environment. In Roman times homosexuality was totally accepted; so were orgies. In Victorian times we would have been jailed for either. In some cultures incest was the only way of assuring procreation while in others it was a great sin. With these different thoughts in mind, let us look at the archetypal sexuality inherent in the signs of the zodiac.

Sexual Archetypes

Aries can be brash, ardent, aggressive or assertive. They usually enjoy early sexuality, love to be the seducers, relish the conquest as much as the actual sexual act and rarely think before they leap. They like a quick and responsive partner who understands their need to experience rather than dream.

Taurus is the most sensual sign of the zodiac. Taureans like to touch and their tactile sense is highly developed. The old-fashioned game of "footsies" must have been invented by a Taurus Sun, Venus or Mars. Petting is also right up their alley. Sexually loyal, they are much easier to satisfy than their neighbors Aries or Gemini.

Gemini is an air sign, and as such works more through the mind than the body. They can detach from their emotions when necessary. Their need is to verbalize their feelings, and talking or reading about sex can greatly arouse them. Variety is their spice of life, be it in numbers of lovers or the lover's ability to offer a number of ways of making love. They can easily handle more than one affair at a time and without guilt, since social morality is of little interest to them.

For **Cancer**, feeling is the name of the game. To them even casual flirtations need to be meaningful. They love to nurture or be nurtured, to alternate between playing the strong parent or the little child who needs tenderness and protection. As sexual partners they can be quite demanding, expecting total devotion even while they may be off on some promiscuous errand. Their innate need to cling can become passion. Moody by nature, they are easily distracted by outside noises and happenings.

Leo is the sign of romance, flowers, self-assertion (the "Look at me, world" syndrome) and applause. Leo lovers need applause like most people need food. Not a grateful smile as Cancer would appreciate, or a gentle hand squeeze as would satisfy Taurus; Leo wants big words — "You are the greatest," "Nobody else ever," "Only you." Leo females should really be courted by Italian males — they have the greatest line; not a word of truth but, oh, how good it sounds! Leos are basically loyal; they may fall for the glitter of gold, but come back to their chosen mates. Their sexual approach is fiery and starts at a young age. They not only enjoy receiving pleasure, but love to give it. Since they greatly fear being laughed at, they will not stray too far from accepted mores.

Virgo more than any other sign (except Pisces) can go in two distinct directions: prim and proper like the puritans who founded the United States, or wantonly, making a job (Virgo/6th house) out of sex by becoming the perfect male or female prostitute. They often think that cleanliness equals godliness and shower before and after sex, or they can delight in messy sheets, strange odors and a pornographic atmosphere. They often are sexually highly skilled and also pride themselves on their ability to analyze their partners' sensual needs.

Libra's key phrase is "in love with love." This, after all, is the other side of Venus. Instead of Taurus' earthy and tactile approach, Libra loves the genteel touch. Soft music, candles and good manners are all prerequisites, but once the *mise-en-scène* is over, anything goes. The one-night stand is a bore to all true Librans who are basically lazy and prefer to know their lovers' likes and dislikes. Despite their reputation for needing one-to-one relationships, sexually Libras manage quite well with more than one, especially if everything is harmonious, beautiful and going their way. Inventive and romantic, they love to please and to indulge themselves as well as their loved ones. Loud noises or shrill voices can turn them off in a hurry.

Scorpios have a reputation of thinking of just one thing, but that's unfair because big money and power play an equally big role in their lives. Actually they are no sexier than Taurus or Libra or many other signs, they are just so intense about it that it seems sexier. As a fixed sign they pursue their course with total absorption. Their investigative nature leads them to many different approaches. Possessive and often jealous, their desire nature is deep-seated. Where the sexual act is an art form to Libra, it is a physical need to Scorpio; yet they are the ones with enough control to totally abstain when necessary.

Sagittarius likes the wide open spaces, but actually prefers large rooms and big, comfortable beds to meadows and mosquitoes. Most of all, they need personal space, the feeling of doing things on a voluntary basis without being fenced in. No Scorpionic power trips for them, just missionary zeal. They really enjoy many loves as easily as one or none, whatever their mood calls for. To them sex is fun and recreation or some idealized vision — the Rajneesh version of religion (Bhagwan Shree Rajneesh, Indian-born guru now living in Oregon, who advocates that free love is one of the roads to God). Sagittarians excel in sexual fantasies and love to indulge in such games as champagne baths.

Capricorn is nearly as maligned a sign as Virgo, yet the glyph depicts the goat — goats are horny and lusty. Capricorn's prerequisite is to be sure. Their fear of rejection or put-down makes them seem cold, whereas they are only self-protective. Once secure, they are down-to-earth lovers who work hard to please a partner. Because of their feelings of inadequacy, they are rarely the aggressors, but once involved, they can compete with the best of them. Capricorns prefer lasting relationships and are quite loyal. Though willing to try everything with a trusted mate, they usually nix threesomes or orgies.

Aquarius is the true experimenter of the zodiac. If it exists, at some point it should be tried. Now please remember that we are speaking of sexual archetypes of a sign, not necessarily the Sun in the sign. Aquarians are notorious for preferring groups to one-to-one relationships, yet they get bored with noninvolvement and as they settle down to one partner, they become interested, inventive and fun lovers. They, nearly as much as Geminis, like to communicate their sexual feelings and thoughts — not necessarily in an intellectual or abstract way, but on a rather earthy and salty level. Aquarius' biggest turnoff is too much routine or being told what to do when. Freedom is their true motto.

Pisces is a sexual surprise. As a water sign they are sensitive, but like water they know no barriers and embrace all. Romantic and idealistic, they will tell you that they are not promiscuous, but are good samaritans who fulfill mankind's needs. Though very touchy and quite insecure, their sexual urges are strong enough to make them seek lovers at the cost of possible rejection. Rejection to a Pisces is not as bad as it sounds; the martyrdom syndrome can work sexually too. They, more than any other sign, will submit to sexual behavior forced upon them by others. They prefer to react rather than act. They love to please their partners and enjoy making love in the dark.

Since most of us have a mixture of many signs indicating our sexual nature, we must do a lot of blending. For a few more examples, let's switch to some male charts.

David Bowie

David Bowie
Brixton, England
January 8, 1947
11:50 PM Zone 0.0
51N28 0W6

Source: *The American Book of Charts* (B)

David Bowie is a star of many faces and an artist of many styles, from rock to Broadway to serious movies; from hippie to punk to Ziggy to the Elephant Man. Typical of Aquarius on the 5th, he not only enjoys unique sexual experiences, but loved the shock waves he created when publicly discussing his bisexuality. Uranus which rules his 5th is involved in quincunxes (inconjuncts) to Jupiter, Mars and the Sun, forming a yod. David needs to make some adjustments in sexual as well as other matters, especially since he has no planetary oppositions which suggests potential problems in understanding his partners' needs, as well as a need to develop empathy.

Venus in Sagittarius in the 2nd rules his 8th house, indicating that David likes a free and light-handed approach to sex. The Taurean part of his sexual nature enjoys true sensuality, especially since Venus has only one aspect, namely a trine to Saturn (which in turn rules his Sun). The Sun/Mars conjunction shows David as ardent and forceful; and though impulsive, in Capricorn he is on top of the situation and fully aware of what effect he is producing. This ardor and intensity are confirmed by the Moon in Leo exactly conjunct Pluto. With the Moon (his emotional needs) and Saturn in the 10th house, his career will probably always take precedence over his sexual needs. With Libra rising and Neptune right on the Ascendant, he can charm and entice everybody. His lovers couldn't care less how much or how little they received, as long as they got a piece of him.

Richard Pryor

A different kind of sexuality is presented by Richard Pryor who has Scorpio on the 8th house cusp, Venus and Mars in Scorpio in the 8th and ruler Pluto in Leo in the 5th house. Need we say more? Venus and Mars are involved in a strong T-square opposing Jupiter/Saturn and squaring Pluto (which is their ruler). We don't have time to really delve into this fascinating chart; suffice it to say that this complex and insecure man probably feels surest in his sexuality. All that fixed emphasis (by planets, houses and signs) suggests absorption (even obsession) with sexuality, sensuality, money and all the physical indulgences. He grew up in Peoria where his family ran a string of whorehouses, managed by his grandmother. As a kid he saw his mother sleep with drunken white men and turn the money over to his father. Pryor has had 4 wives, so far, and one child by each of them. Notoriously crude and vulgar in his language, he also seems to attract violence into his personal life, including the terrible accident when, while high on drugs, he set himself afire and nearly burned alive.

Richard Pryor
Peoria, IL
December 1, 1940
1:02 PM CST
40N42 89W36

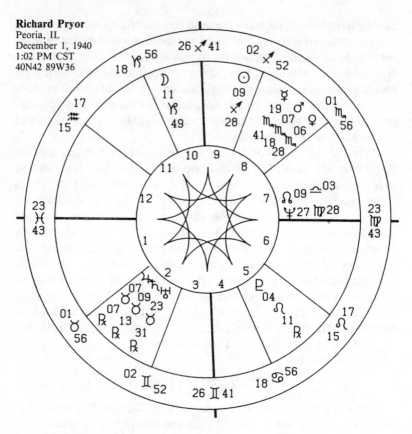

Source: *Gauquelin Book of American Charts* (A)

Old Blue Eyes

As our last male example we have a long-lasting sexual symbol: **Frank Sinatra**. Leo is on the 5th, the Sun is in Sagittarius in the 9th and Mars is in Leo in the 5th. Mars is the chart ruler (Aries Ascendant), revealing why Sinatra has so much sex appeal that his charisma has lasted from the bobby sox days of the '40s to date. It also indicates Sinatra's attraction to "broads," as he calls them, who are beautiful film stars or very glamorous women (Leo). Mars is in wide trine to the Sun which rules it, showing ease in 5th house matters. The Sun's near exact square to Jupiter suggests the excesses (sexual and others) he is known for.

The 8th house with Scorpio on the cusp is ruled by Pluto in Cancer in the 3rd. He communicates his sexuality even in his songs, caressing the mike and the air waves with his voice. Pluto's only major aspect is a sextile to Mars, indicating support from partners and many sexual opportunities. Sinatra's Venus is more troublesome. His love and affections are very bound up with his career, ego and the status he seeks. The T-square involving Venus (opposition Saturn, square Ascendant) doesn't look promising for marital matters either (Venus rules his 7th house), unless he learns to make peace between love and work, power and sharing. Maintaining control of his relationships may be the only way he feels safe, but it prevents equality.

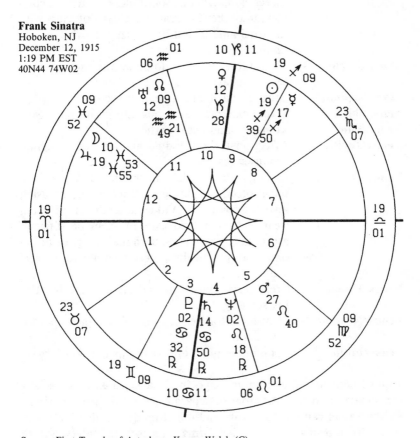

Frank Sinatra
Hoboken, NJ
December 12, 1915
1:19 PM EST
40N44 74W02

Source: First Temple of Astrology, Karma Welch (C)

Planets' Sexual Interrelationships

Here are some key words that may help you to integrate two planets as they relate to sexuality:

Mars/Moon	— A certain innate understanding of the other sex.
Mars/Venus	— Sex appeal; easy arousal; very sexual; often overemphasis on sexual matters.
Mars/Sun	— Much vitality and sexual energy.
Mars/Jupiter	— Sexual overindulgence and possible overdoing of a good thing.
Mars/Saturn	— Drive for security can lead to overcompensation; need for self-satisfaction. This can be a difficult aspect in male charts, sometimes even a penis complex, until they integrate the energy of Mars with the discipline of Saturn rather than the fear of failure.
Mars/Uranus	— Willful, they want to do things their way; erratic sexual behavior.
Mars/Neptune	— Great sexual fantasies and eroticism.
Mars/Pluto	— Sexual extremes, even obsessions and fetishes.
Venus/Sun	— Romantic and enthusiastic.
Venus/Jupiter	— Affectionate, self-indulgent; lots of hugging; promiscuous.
Venus/Saturn	— Feeling of lack of love in childhood may lead to self-protection. May experience others as using love to dominate. Vulnerable, therefore often wears mask of cold exterior. Can be difficult aspect in female charts, until they integrate affection and practicality, partnership and career, equality and power.
Venus/Uranus	— Great flirts. Quick, on-and-off love affairs. Enjoy sex as game.
Venus/Neptune	— They look for perfection in love, passion with compassion.
Venus/Pluto	— Compulsive in love; sexual appetites are large.

Moon aspects have important messages in sexual experiences, especially for females who find it harder to separate sex from their emotions. **Saturn/Moon** can connote fears and might result in individuals who cling to their own gender, or other forms of security and safety. **Saturn** aspects can be sexual downers if childhood traumas have not been worked out. But keep in mind that in synastry a woman's Saturn conjunct a man's Mars can point to impotence in one case, sexual endurance in another. The same principle applies in the natal horoscope; it all depends on how well we work with our potential.

How do we know that Richard Pryor will become a famous

comedian and not a male prostitute or a pimp? (Venus, ruler of his 2nd — how he earns his money — placed in the 8th house of sex in Scorpio conjunct Mars.) We don't know. All we can see is the potential.

Marlene Dietrich

Marlene Dietrich, another of the world's lasting sex symbols, has Capricorn on the cusp of the 5th and ruler Saturn in the house, as well as Jupiter and Mars which in turn rules her 8th house. The overcompensation shown by Saturn and the drive represented by Mars brought all 5th and 8th house matters to the fore. But where does it show that she was also bisexual?

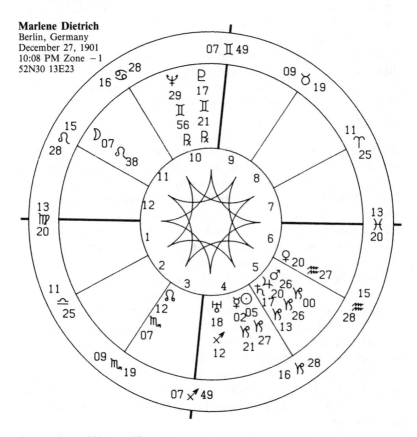

Marlene Dietrich
Berlin, Germany
December 27, 1901
10:08 PM Zone − 1
52N30 13E23

Source: Copy of birth certificate (A)

Other Sexual Styles

That brings us to another theme of sexuality, homo- and bisexuality. There are all kinds of "signatures" for homosexuality floating around and they should all be viewed with great skepticism. According to recent statistics, 1/6th of the population of Western civilized countries is homosexual. They can't all have the same signature, just as religion or race has no signature. In fact, unless told, we don't even know if a horoscope is male or female.

What can we tell? There are certain psychological problems that may or may not lead to the preference of one's own sex. Strange parental role models, an overly demanding or domineering parent, a weak parent, an uncaring or unloving parent, can all be contributing factors; but they can contribute to a number of other problems besides homo- or bisexuality. Sun square Moon can show tension between the male and female parts within. Saturn in challenging aspects, especially the square, to Venus, the Moon or Mars can be indicators for possible identity crises. (It can also simply show someone struggling to make room in life for love as well as work, home as well as career, self-assertion as well as following the rules.)

A Venus/Mars conjunction may illustrate sex appeal but it can also be a key to excesses. Venus and/or Mars square, opposition or inconjunct to Neptune can symbolize confusion, as well as spiritual or artistic talents. In a male chart a strong Moon (a domineering or dominant mother) might signal future confusion, or simply a strong emotional nature. The placement of the Moon or Venus in Virgo can denote the "Madonna" complex, or simply a love of work, artistic work or satisfaction in dealing realistically with the emotions. These are all possible warning signals to make us pay closer attention.

Certain maligned signs — Capricorn, Libra, Cancer and Gemini for males, Aquarius for females — don't hold up to large samplings. Capricorn's insecurity could lead to fear of failure with the opposite sex, but just as easily to a success-oriented individual who wants to fit into existing society and will avoid anything that stands out as being different, such as homosexuality. A male with lots of Cancer in his chart could have a mother complex which might lead to homosexuality, but he could also be a loving husband and father who enjoys home and family. Be wary of signatures! Astrology reflects the uniqueness of each individual human being.

For additional study I'm including the charts of Tennessee Williams and Gertrude Stein — neither of them could come to grips with their sexuality — and also a new sex symbol, cute and easygoing Tom Selleck.

Where does his appeal lie? Is it sexuality or just charm and charisma? I'll leave the interpretation to you. William Masters, who along with Virginia Johnson has helped a number of people enhance their sex lives, is also included for further investigation.

Tennessee Williams
Columbus, MS
March 26, 1911
2:30 AM CST
33N30 88W25

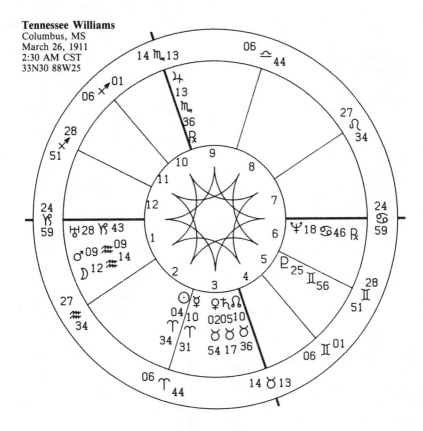

Source: Lockhart, Emma Cates from him (C)

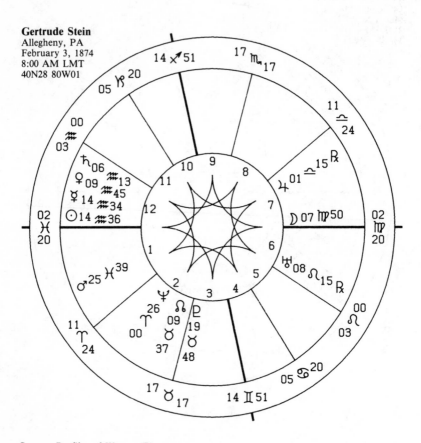

Gertrude Stein
Allegheny, PA
February 3, 1874
8:00 AM LMT
40N28 80W01

Source: *Profiles of Women* (B)

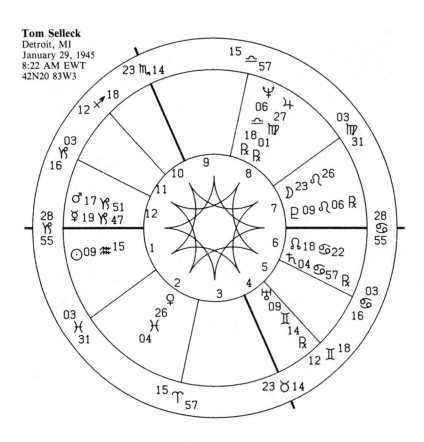

Tom Selleck
Detroit, MI
January 29, 1945
8:22 AM EWT
42N20 83W3

Source: Barbara Ludwig quotes birth certificate via Penfield (C)

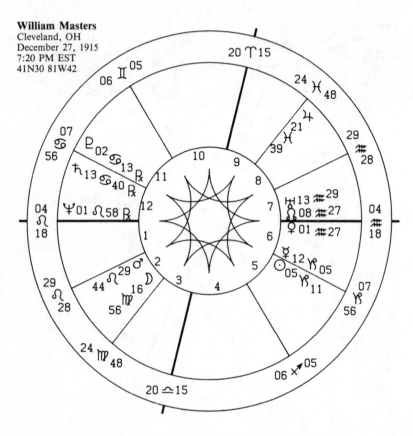

William Masters
Cleveland, OH
December 27, 1915
7:20 PM EST
41N30 81W42

Source: *Gauquelin Book of American Charts* (A)

IN-DEPTH DELINEATION: THE PROFILE OF A RAPIST

by Joan McEvers

Approach to Delineation

In any "in-depth" delineation, the astrologer should start with an analysis of the overall chart: the division of planets above and below the horizon; east and west of the meridian; by quality and element; distribution by houses; dignity; exaltation; detriment and fall; planetary pattern; final dispositor and mutual reception (if there is one); critical degrees; and any configurations. From this "once over lightly" much information can be gleaned. Then, especially for the beginning astrologer, it is wise to proceed in an orderly way through the chart, starting either with the Sun, Moon, Ascendant and following with the other planets — or the way I prefer, which is to start with the Ascendant and proceed through each house, delineating each planet as you get to it.

Frederick Harlan Coe

The latter will be the procedure used in this article. This is the natal chart (Chart 1) of convicted rapist **Frederick Harlan Coe,** who now goes by the name of **Kevin Coe.** Fred Coe is a highly verbal, handsome, six-foot, clean-cut, teetotaling young man. He is as conservative-looking as his native Spokane, with feathered brown hair and a predilection for button-up, three-piece suits. An athlete and student leader in high school, he dropped out of Washington State and Gonzaga universities and became a Las Vegas disco deejay, author of a lampoonish paperback called *Sex in the White House,* and founder of a one-man booster group which he grandly called Spokane Metro Growth. He has a history of minor offenses and an impassioned explanation for each.

His father **Gordon Coe** was managing editor of the then *Spokane Chronicle* (it is now defunct). His mother, **Ruth Coe** is a former fashion model who is very socially oriented. She was diagnosed in 1971 as a manic-depressive. His only sibling, a sister, is married and lives in the Seattle area.

In May 1971 Coe had his first formal brush with the law. He was arrested for second-degree burglary for entering the open door of a 20-year-old woman's apartment and "rubbing her body." The woman later left the state, and the charges were dropped. Shortly after this Coe moved to Las Vegas, where his mother would go to visit him frequently. Ruth Coe began to recover from her illness in 1976 after lithium carbonate treatments. This was also the year that Fred Coe returned to Spokane. After several brief visits to California, he settled in Spokane for good in 1978 and began working as a real estate salesman.

According to Ruth Coe's psychiatrist, who last saw her in 1979, she was very upset with her son. He hadn't lived up to her expectations and she claimed she was going to disown him. But, according to testimony at Fred's trial, mother and son were talking about going into business together. They also had another joint project: trying to find the South Hill rapist.

South Hill Rapist

For more than two years a rapist had prowled the thick bushes, vacant lots and terraced lawns of Spokane's South Hill, an old, tree-lined neighborhood peopled by the city's power elite. Operating only in darkness, the rapist chose his victims from joggers and walkers, his *modus operandi* easily identified. He dragged his quarry down, threatened death by knife, asked urbanely in a resonant voice about his victim's sexual experience, then rammed his heavily gloved hand deep into her mouth and committed rape.

The undermanned police department and the city's business establishment seemed unwilling to admit the rapist's existence; but sales of mace and tear gas pens zoomed as the women of Spokane attempted to protect themselves. In January 1981 the *Spokane Spokesman-Review* broke the story. Its sister paper, the *Daily Chronicle*, offered informants up to $1,000 in a "secret witness" program. Tipsters were impressed to find that their calls went straight through to the *Chronicle*'s managing editor himself: Gordon Coe, a respected second generation Spokanite. Everyone was after the rapist.

Six weeks after the newspaper revelations, an elite detective team, acting on a tip, attached a transmitting bug to the underside of a silver-gray Chevrolet Citation and began trailing it. The car's driver, usually dressed in warm-ups, would follow buses and check out jogging paths, sometimes spurting away on side streets as though he suspected a tail. On a Sunday in March 1981 a man in a blue sweater accosted an 18-year-old jogger; he exposed and fondled himself, and made lewd remarks. When the woman turned on him and yelled, he ran to a silver-gray Citation and sped away. Passersby noted the license number and called the police. It was the same car.

Two days later detectives arrested the driver, 34-year-old Frederick Harlan Coe, the managing editor's son. He hotly denied the charge, claiming that he was trying to find the rapist and collect the reward. His mother declared, "We were amateur sleuths. Son would jog and I would follow in the car. That's why police saw him in many of the areas where the rapes were being committed." That was the testimony from Fred and his mother at the trial. But the jury didn't buy it.

Five women identified Fred Coe as their assailant and the jury also heard corroborating evidence from Coe's live-in girlfriend, among others. Coe received one of the longest rape sentences in Washington history: life plus 75 years.

In a last-ditch effort to have Coe sent to a mental hospital rather than prison, a psychiatrist testified that Coe confessed to one of the rapes and needed treatment as a sexual psychopath. "Denial and rationalization are part of his personality," he said. He also claimed that Ruth used repression and denial to a very large extent in her relations with her son.

Delineation

AN OVERVIEW

Let's observe Frederick Coe's natal chart (see Chart 1). His planets are evenly distributed above/below and east/west so there is no outstanding characteristic indicated here. He has six planets and the Ascendant in fixed signs, five planets in air signs and no planets in earth; however he does have two planets in earth houses. His signature is Aquarius (predominant fixed air) which is the same as his Sun sign, emphasizing all Aquarian qualities. We can assume that he is determined, set in his ways, somewhat stubborn and has a good sense of self (fixity). People who have no planets in the earth mode often lack practicality and a sense of organization. He may have trouble keeping his feet on the ground, but if he is overcompensating for the lack, and sometimes people do this, he may pay more attention than necessary to minor details and feel that he is the epitome of steadfastness and reasonableness. We will discover how he reacts to this lack as we proceed through the chart.

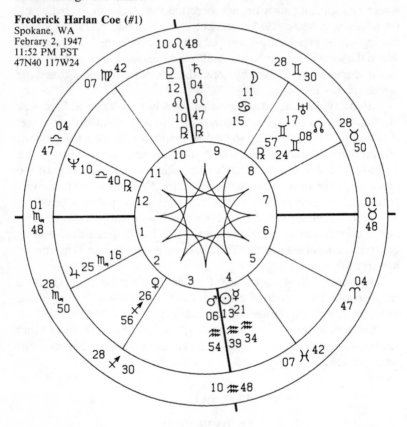

Frederick Harlan Coe (#1)
Spokane, WA
Febrary 2, 1947
11:52 PM PST
47N40 117W24

Source: Spokane Health Dept. birth certificate (A)

Saturn, an earth planet, is strong in his chart, but in double fire (Leo and the 9th house) he can be determined to express his own will. (Fire equals "I know what I want and I have the energy and confidence to get it.") Earth not being strongly represented can indicate unwillingness to be realistic in terms of necessary discipline and "non-fun" parts of work (Virgo and Capricorn). Pluto and Saturn often show organizational skills and thoroughness when prominent in the chart (his are widely conjunct and elevated). Concentration is evident, but there is potential disinclination to work, except on his own terms in exciting (fire) vocations.

SIGNATURE

There are four ways the chart signature can work. If it is the same as the Sun sign, as it is here, it emphasizes the qualities suggested by the Sun and the person will usually evince an even flow of his inner force. If it is the same sign as the Ascendant, the person often has an easy flow of personality. When the signature is the same as the Moon sign, the person is capable of integrating the emotional side of his nature into the rest of his chart. If the signature is a totally different sign, which occasionally happens, then it describes another dimension to the personality which is not always visible. But it is an underlying quality that must be judged in delineation because it will give you insight into how this person thinks and acts.

Here we have double emphasis on Aquarius. How might a typical Aquarian think and act? There could be a strong need to be noticed, to be an individualist in some way. The key phrase is **I know** and most Aquarians think they **know** everything. Some of the positive attributes are progressive, intellectual and independent. Some of the negative expressions are temperamental, bored by detail, eccentric, cold.

In Coe's case we know from his life story that he is intellectually oriented, and the Sun in the 4th house helps explain why he is not particularly independent even though he tried to be. He received love, admiration and attention mostly at home, probably from Mom. He chose to use the lack of planets in earth signs to overcompensate by being particularly interested in details, but the Sun's opposition to Pluto and conjunction to Mars suggests a lively temperament and eccentricity. Pluto, Mars and the Sun are all very into power and will, also. With the Sun and 3 other planets in ending (water) houses, he is quite receptive, sensitive and perceptive. The Sun rules his 10th house, so we see his ego need to attract attention to himself. With Pluto here opposed to the Sun, it is likely the kind of attention he attracts may not always be positive.

The Moon in Cancer is dignified and usually a dignified planet rates extra emphasis in the chart. His Sun is in detriment. A planet in detriment or fall does not need to represent a negative way of being, just something different than you expect. The Sun is considered ego-oriented through its association with the sign Leo; in Aquarius it would be more other-people-oriented. So it is somewhat harder for someone with this Sun to express his individuality when it is in Aquarius, hence he may act unpredictably.

Mercury and Uranus are on critical degrees and they are also in mutual reception and trine to each other, which symbolizes an original and inventive turn of mind. These planets assume a great deal of importance in his chart. Venus is unaspected (no major interplanetary aspects), so at times he may feel unloved, unwanted and alone. Also an unaspected Venus suggests a single-minded value system. Since Venus rules his 7th house, perhaps it being unaspected implies that he had trouble seeing things from another's point of view. This may also have suggested his lack of sensitivity to his victims' feelings.

CHART PATTERN

His chart pattern is a locomotive (all planets in ⅔ of the chart, leaving an empty trine), with Uranus as the engine planet. Uranus symbolizes the need for freedom and independence and Coe sought this through his bizarre sexual behavior. The engine planet in this position puts the focus of his chart in the 8th house depicting an interest in sex and other people's values. It is in Gemini, indicating a need to communicate in an unusual way. His victims told of his explicit sexual comments while engaged in the rape act. The chart rulers are Mars and Pluto (Scorpio rising). Mars is in the 3rd house reinforcing his need to verbalize. Pluto in the 10th house could substantiate his desire to attract attention and his almost obsessive need to be a leader and outshine those around him.

It is important to note how the Sun expresses through the Ascendant since the Sun represents the inner self, and the Ascendant, the outer personality. The Sun in Aquarius expressing through a Scorpio Ascendant could account for Coe's natural aspirations, loyalty to family, dogmatic opinions, and his gypsy behavior pattern. Outgoing, gregarious and popular, what counts most with him is his good opinion of himself, and this came over quite dramatically at the trial when he tried to dismiss his attorneys and represent himself in court. This combination often acts as his own judge and jury, convinced in his soul that because he deems his actions correct, they are.

CONFIGURATIONS

Coe has two significant configurations in his chart: a **T-square** between Mars, Saturn and the Ascendant; a grand air trine with Sun, Neptune and Uranus. The T-square can signify stress, energy and frustration. The empty leg is the 7th house cusp, implying that he needs to learn how to deal on a one-to-one basis with others. The action point of this T-square is the Ascendant; he may often feel the need to take physical action. Unfortunately he chose to use the energy of this configuration negatively. The action he took was to force himself at knife point on the women he assaulted. Mars and the Ascendant, both keys to personal action and self-will, in conflict with Saturn can show going against limits of the world. Saturn represents what we can do, can't do and have to do. The T-square repeats the issue of dealing with successful work, responsibility and realism in the world (like less emphasis in earth signs) and danger of him wanting to live life only on **his** terms. (Self will conflicts with societal standards and rules.) Eventually the *karmic* laws and consequences symbolized by Saturn win out!

The **grand air trine** could represent Coe's highly idealistic and individualistic personality. With Neptune (illusion) and the Moon (emotions) square, he is likely to drift and be subject to frustration. Disliking routine and menial work, Coe opted for jobs where this was not required. This configuration also highlighted his communicative ability. The grand air trine seems to have the need to impress others with their verbal talents and imagination with the Moon, Neptune and Sun aspects. If this trine had been integrated into the T-square, perhaps his energy could have been more positively dispersed.

DECANATES AND DWADS

Decanates and dwads add dimension to the analysis of the planets, especially the Sun, Moon and Ascendant (which is not a planet, but an important angle in the chart). His Sun is in the Gemini decanate, confirming his need to verbalize. Mercury ruler of the decanate is in the 4th house, reemphasizing the Cancer quality of the Sun in the 4th. This further highlights his attachment to his family, especially his mother. The Sun is in the Cancer dwad, again reinforcing the Cancer feeling. The Moon is in the Scorpio decanate and dwad; so is the Ascendant. This strong accent on the 8th house sign reaffirms a substantial interest in all 8th house matters.

INTERCEPTED AXIS

I feel that the intercepted axis is vital in chart interpretation. In Coe's chart, the 3rd and 9th houses contain the intercepted signs, Capricorn and Cancer. Seven planets are involved here. Jupiter, Saturn, Uranus by rulership of and Mars in the 3rd; Mercury, Moon, Sun ruling the 9th. I have also observed that by being intercepted a planet can gain strength. In this chart, the Moon is intercepted in the 9th house, so all things the Moon represents — emotions, home, mother, public — gain importance in his life.

THROUGH THE HOUSES

We have looked at the overall picture of Frederick Coe's chart. Let's start with the 1st house and work our way around the chart. Scorpio rises. Being in control is important; he is very possessive, investigative, secretive and at times distrustful. Incisive, he can go after what he wants with zeal, but it takes him a long time to commit. However, once committed, he is extremely tenacious. Positively used, this Ascendant is into self-analysis and self-mastery. The placement of the rulers has already been discussed.

His **1st and 2nd houses** are tied together (the same sign on both cusps) suggesting that he decides on his own value system; his self-worth is tied to his physical image and he probably equates that self-worth to his sexual prowess (Scorpio). Jupiter is in Scorpio in the 1st house; it rules the 3rd house, again stressing the importance of expressing his views. Jupiter in Scorpio is often intense and uncompromising in manifesting beliefs and standards. Jupiter in the 1st house can take the law into their own hands and when the energy is improperly handled, self-indulgence can be a problem. Jupiter is the natural ruler of the 9th house and when it is in Scorpio, it can be indicative of legal/sexual problems, as is definitely the case here. This placement (Jupiter in the 1st house) often describes a person who likes to be physically active. Coe was into sports, jogging, golf, etc. Jupiter square Mercury can be a good bluffer (or skilled communicator) and since Jupiter rules the 3rd house, Coe certainly has ability as a salesman. Mercury rules the 9th house; the square implies an interrupted education especially when the 3rd and 9th houses are involved, as they are here. This aspect often marks a person who talks more than is necessary. During and previous to his trial Fred gave many interviews to the media and later some of the things he said came back to haunt him.

With Scorpio on the 2nd house cusp, he feels intensely about his values and possessions. He felt a need to prove himself to others, particularly to authority figures (Pluto, Scorpio's ruler in the 10th house). The challenging aspects to Pluto could show his inflated idea of his own self-worth and obsession with power. Coe has the south node in Sagittarius in the 2nd house and the north node in Gemini in the 8th house. According to Van Toen this may indicate sexual difficulties, lack of regard for other's values or needs, and in extreme cases trouble with the law — all of which are evident in Coe's personality. He should have developed self-control and self-discipline instead of worrying about being noticed and appreciated. Trying to balance self-control versus indulgence around money and sex was necessary with the nodes across the 2nd and 8th house axis. Power struggles are a potential with this placement. Sharing is often learned through intimate relationships and there can be problems giving, receiving or sharing with the nodes here.

Venus in Sagittarius can express as sociable, friendly, outgoing, freedom loving. Coe tried to impose his values on others; he is flighty, fickle and self-indulgent. Venus rules his 8th house, which may explain why his sexual excesses cost him money; but his parents were very supportive of him and bankrupted themselves to help him.

Sagittarius on the **3rd house** cusp often indicates literary ability, and Fred had a fling at writing. It also depicts his fondness for travel. Saturn ruling the intercepted sign and placed in the 9th confirms the travel opportunities. It suggests that in his early years he may have felt misunderstood or had trouble expressing his true feelings. Mars in Aquarius may show someone who is sexually experimental, often speaks before he thinks and seldom works well unless he is in charge. This placement can describe someone who can be quite revolutionary. Mars' position in the 3rd house symbolizes an impulsive, argumentative, forthright person. Curious and aggressive, he could come on too strong and be tactless, impatient and critical of others. All these characteristics were very evident as the trial progressed and he would go on talking binges, declaring his innocence. He made contact with newspapers and TV stations and gave long, detailed interviews when the judge in the case was trying to keep the media from interfering with Coe's right to a fair trial.

Mars rules his 6th house, signaling that his work related to communication. Mars conjuncts his Sun, characterizing physical strength and an interest in sports, as well as strong leadership ability, but the opposition to Pluto suggests he had a hard time controlling his physical energy and properly channeling it. Mars opposes Saturn, which emphasizes his tendency to selfishness and egotism, or it could manifest as self-criticism and put downs if not expressed through productive work. It also indicates that timing is not his strong point. Mars squares or oppositions to Saturn are classic aspects for males with sexual problems. The negative form of this aspect indicates fear and anxiety (Saturn) regarding sexual prowess (Mars) which can lead to impotence. Sometimes, the desire for control (Saturn) is an issue as well. Controlling one's spontaneity tends to cut back on pleasure. (When integrated, such aspects show someone who knows when to charge full speed ahead and when to hold back — appropriately.)

The trine to Neptune implies imagination and creativity, since Neptune rules his 5th house. He was able to create verbal pictures for other people. This can also be an aspect of escapism, since Neptune is in the 12th house. When reality became more than he could handle, he would escape into a fantasy world where he was successful, a leader and looked up to. Positive use of the talents indicated by Neptune would be to utilize artistic ability or pursue one of the healing or helping professions.

Mars and the Sun oppose the MC showing a conflict with authority, possibly stemming from childhood, when he felt a parent tried to dominate him. From the information available, this may have been his father; but his mother sheltered and protected him, and eventually his father gave up disciplining him. He would not heed good and well-meant advice. His attorneys constantly admonished him for his outbursts in court and his overweening desire to see his name in print and his face on television.

Aquarius on the **4th house** cusp depicts a family that he perceived as not too warm or emotional and since Uranus, the ruler, is in the 8th, he is quite a private person regardless of how friendly and outspoken he appears to be. This is reaffirmed by Scorpio rising. It is important to him what others think of him and there is almost an obsessive need to be noticed. With both the Sun and Mercury in the 4th, his strong familial ties are evident. He is very close to his mother, but though his father and sister were supportive of him all through the trial, his relationship with them pales in comparison to the closeness with his mother. The Sun in the 4th often indicates a strong identification with a parent; also a need for nurturing and security. He played one parent against the other (Sun opposed Pluto in the 10th). The Sun is a part of the grand air trine and this typifies the good lines of communication between him and his mother.

Mercury in Aquarius is exalted and illustrates his ability to be charming, persuasive and convincing, as well as eccentric and unpredictable. It denotes that he came from a cultured and comfortable background; that his parents were interested in his education, philosophy and ethics (Mercury rules the 9th). The challenging aspect to Jupiter suggests that he can be irritable and high strung at times. Since Jupiter indicates ethics and moral principles, conflicts can be problems in that area. Coe's behavior could certainly be considered unprincipled as well as unethical.

Wherever Pisces is located, we often find some sense of frustration. The person is usually searching for some infinite ideal in that area, so risks chronic disillusionment and disappointment unless he finds some way to reach for something inspirational without demanding it like manna from heaven or playing God to other people. In Coe's chart, Pisces is on the **5th house** cusp implying that he never felt he had the time and money to develop his creative nature. Also, there were problems in his love life. He is a romantic and by his own admission, always had affairs with women whom he felt leaned on him and then disappointed him. His only marriage was of relatively short duration to an alcoholic who was older than he was.

Aries on the **6th house** cusp is another affirmation of his need to work for himself, of his dislike of authority or interference. He functions best when he feels needed and appreciated. A positive way for him to have used all the Pluto/Mars energy in his chart would have been law enforcement. Instead, he ran afoul of the law. It is often noted that criminals and law enforcers have similar charts. They just choose to use the energy differently.

With Taurus on the **7th house** cusp, he is looking for a partner who is sensual and charming, who enjoys beautiful surroundings, who is placid, domestic, easygoing and who will applaud his efforts. Venus, ruler of the 7th is in the 2nd house, so he treats a partner as a possession and will not allow her as much freedom as he demands for himself (Venus is in Sagittarius). The 7th and **8th houses** are tied together (Taurus on both cusps), so a sexual relationship is important to the partnership. With Uranus, the ruler of the 4th house in the 8th in Gemini, he was probably able to communicate these needs to his mother, if not verbally, at least tacitly. Often with Uranus here, there are difficulties in coming to terms with your sexual attitudes, and the act of rape could be a symptom of this difficulty. Since Uranus has such flowing aspects in his chart, these acts came easily to him. The detachment evident in his makeup suggests little or no conscience, and the psychiatrist's reports in court confirmed his arrogant and cavalier attitude in these matters.

Gemini is on the **9th house** cusp; the ruler Mercury is in the 4th. The Moon is in this house in Cancer, showing that his reigning need is mothering or being mothered and a sense of security. He needed to travel and learn about different cultures and ways of life; to get away from the home situation, to get some perspective. But the Moon inconjuncts the Sun in the 4th, and he was always pulled back to the nurturing and indulgence of the mothering situation. Neptune square the Moon may have alluded to his cloudy perception of women. He probably feels that his mother is perfect and no other woman can live up to her. He was his mother's darling little boy and when he was young, she took him everywhere with her. She was very socially active and always brought little Freddie along to teas and bridge parties. Friends remember him as a precocious child, always interrupting and distracting his mother with his needs and demands. His relationship with his mother dominated his whole life, except for the times when he was living away from home. Even then she came to visit him (Moon in the 9th house). According to Jack Olsen, the author of *Son*, the story of Frederick Harlan Coe, he and his mother had a "love/hate" relationship. At times they were cordial and loving. Two minutes later, they would be hurling invective and insults at each other.

After Fred's arrest, trial and conviction for 4 of the 37 rapes that had occurred, and when he was serving his sentence, Ruth Coe, his mother, hired a hit man to kill the judge and chief prosecutor in Fred's case. In affidavits, police claimed that Mrs. Coe wanted prosecutor Donald Brockett dead "for allowing the entire trial to be televised and photographed." Unfortunately for her, the hit man was a wired policeman. She was convicted of soliciting murder and sentenced to jail for one year. Testimony in her trial suggested the separate sicknesses of a mother and a son feeding off each other to disastrous ends.

A psychiatrist who treated the 61-year-old Ruth Coe said there were two things she couldn't come to grips with. One was her relationship with her son. He called it "an abnormal, atypical thriving off one another beyond what is normal or healthy or optimal." The other thing she didn't want to acknowledge was getting old.

Fred Coe didn't want to get old either. According to an ex-girlfriend, he watched his diet carefully and used skin creams and emollients to keep his face looking young. Geminis are often concerned with staying young and Fred's Sun ruler is in Gemini.

The Moon in the chart is one of the astrological indications that symbolizes the mother. In Coe's chart, the Moon is dignified, signifying a possibly nurturing relationship. It rules the 9th house, suggesting that his mother might travel to see him, that she may be instrumental in any legal dealings he would be involved with, and that she may influence his morals and ethics.

The Moon has very challenging aspects and no outlets (sextiles or trines): inconjuncts to Mars and the Sun and a square to Neptune. The square to Neptune suggests that both Fred and his mother might have trouble coming to terms with reality. Improperly used, this aspect may surface as a complete lack of touch with the world around you and the tendency to escape into a world of fantasy. The Moon inconjunct the Sun is quite difficult to deal with and often necessitates coming to grips with the way you handle your emotional needs (Moon) and the way you express your will (Sun). The Cancerian nature of this aspect in this chart (the Moon in Cancer and the Sun in Cancer's house) pictures the unhealthy relationship between mother and son. He remained his mother's baby boy into adulthood and never learned to handle his sexual and aggressive drives properly.

The inconjunct from the Moon to Mars signals the need to align the emotional nature with the desire nature. Inconjuncts are difficult aspects to integrate unless the person is willing to face the problem indicated and get help and, in severe cases, some counseling. Venus, ruler of the 7th house (which represents counselors), is unaspected; perhaps that avenue was not open to him before now. In prison, he is getting psychiatric counseling.

Saturn in Leo often depicts a tremendous drive for personal recognition and control, which other things in Coe's chart have verified. He is a member of the Saturn-conjunct-Pluto generation about whom Liz Greene says, "There is a lot of violence inherent in this conjunction...it seems to indicate a real hatred of any authority figure, a very strong anarchistic streak...which may be expressed on a physical or emotional level, but either way the responses are closer to jungle law than so-called civilised (sic) behavior." Naturally not all people who have this conjunction will live their lives in complete disregard for law and authority, but in Coe's chart, Pluto is his Ascendant ruler and both Saturn and Pluto oppose Mars and conjunct the MC which in this case indicates his arrogant attitude and the ability and desire to place himself above the law.

Saturn squares his Ascendant from the 9th house illustrating that at some time, due to legal matters and ethical, moral issues, he may be restricted or limited in his action. Saturn conjunct the MC indicates that one must learn to deal with authority figures. Fred never managed to do this, at least not up to this point in his life, so not being able to learn this lesson contributed to his downfall.

Saturn is a *karmic* point in the chart, not to be ignored in this lifetime. It marks the place where we **must** learn something and then give it to the world. Saturn in the 9th house points to a lesson of faith, moral principles, ethics, the law. Of course, one doesn't have to be a criminal with these placements. Some people teach the law and base the whole structure of their lives on moral principles and spiritual ideals. Other people have lessons of too much faith, too little, or putting their faith in the wrong place. But Jupiter in the 1st has been known to "play God" personally on occasion (faith in the wrong place). So, by using his potentials in the way he did, Fred Coe now faces well-deserved consequences.

The person with Pluto in the **10th house** cannot stand to be ignored and will attract attention one way on another. He has an obsessive need to be best and outshine those around him. But with the oppositions to the Sun and Mars, Coe did not develop the patience to learn, to achieve recognition because of his contributions to society. Instead, he used the potential violence of the Mars/Pluto/Saturn combination to draw attention to himself in a very dramatic but negative way.

With Virgo on the **11th house** cusp and Mercury in Aquarius in the 4th, Fred Coe sought out his family for friendship. As an adult, he has very few male friends and those few who came forward and supported him were family, rather than personal friends. His goals were linked to his nurturing family and his seeming lack of career success may be attributed to his psychological dependence upon his mother. He had two close friends during his school years, both of whom were convinced of his guilt and could not testify for him, because of their conviction that quite possibly he was guilty as accused. He berated these two men and his mother swore to "get them."

The **12th house** signifies your hidden strengths and weaknesses. It is the house behind the Ascendant (outer personality) and it represents what you brought with you from past experiences and is a very important house in the chart. However, it is also the house of your undoing if you persist in seeking impossible dreams. Venus rules Coe's 12th house and it is in the 2nd house, unaspected. He has his own unique value system, especially as regards legal affairs (Venus is in Sagittarius). Neptune is in the 12th house and rules his 5th. Perhaps his creative imagination (5th house) got him into trouble. Or it could have been his unrealistic relationship with his mother (Neptune square Moon). Neptune has a trine to the Sun and a sextile to Pluto. When he was in Las Vegas, away from the family influence, he was able to use his creative energy in a positive way by writing.

Progressions

I have progressed his natal chart to 1978 when two of the rapes he was convicted for took place. Coe was living with his girlfriend of the moment in an apartment but, according to his testimony in court, had breakfast and dinner every day with his parents. He was dabbling in real estate but not really holding down a full-time job. He had tried some writing and some political work, but nothing was going his way. The real estate market was in the process of falling apart. He was 31 on February 2, 1978, and by secondary progression Venus at 1° Aquarius was square his Ascendant; secondary Mars was trine it. His progressed Moon was moving through his 10th and 11th houses. In April when one of the rapes took place, the progressed Moon in Virgo inconjuncted Mars. (Natally the Moon inconjuncts Mars from Cancer to Aquarius.) In August when the second rape occurred, the progressed Moon inconjuncted the Sun. As discussed earlier, these are natal aspects that were being activated by progression. Natally these aspects indicated the need for him to pull both the male and female sides of his nature together, to deal with his feelings toward his parents in an acceptable way instead of playing one against the other.

Now the progressed Moon was setting up a yod configuration. He had never dealt with his psychological dependency on his mother, had been unable to stand on his own two feet. In other words, he had not cleaned his closet (the inconjuncts) and now he had to deal with the accumulated garbage pile-up. With the Venus and Mars aspects to his Ascendant, it was easy for him to choose sex, aggression (Mars) and sensuality (Venus) as modes of expression.

Solar Arc Directions

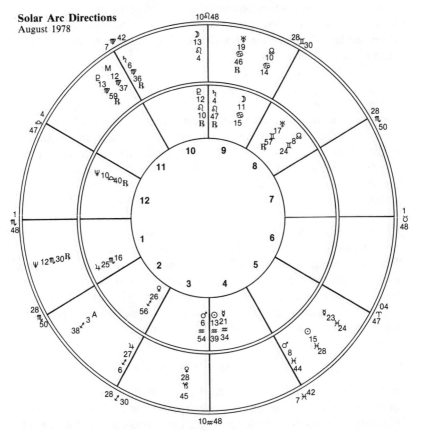

Solar Arc Directions
August 1978

Rape is a violent act. It is intercourse by force. If we look at the solar arc directions for 1978 (see Chart #2), we see that the SA Moon at 13° Leo conjuncted Pluto, a need to get recognition (Pluto is in the 10th house) by force or violence (Pluto opposed Mars and the Sun) through some kind of interaction with women (Moon). Jupiter at 26° Sagittarius conjuncted Venus, amplifying and expanding his tenuous value system; and since Venus rules both his 7th and 8th houses, it is easy to see why he decided to take out his excesses on others in a sexual way.

Solar arc Saturn at 6° Virgo inconjuncted Mars, again creating a yod with the natal Moon/Mars/Sun. He may have felt he had to act out the hostility and sexual frustration. He apparently has never dealt with his Oedipus complex. SA Mars, the sexual motivator at 8° Pisces, squares the nodes. According to Ivy Jacobson, a planet in the same degree as the nodes can indicate a crisis. SA Neptune at 12° Scorpio squares Pluto, his Ascendant ruler, and SA Pluto at 13° Virgo inconjuncts his Sun — both indicative of a need to come to terms with his sexuality and willfulness. Instead of seeking counseling or finding some other acceptable way to deal with these drives, he was motivated to commit assault and rape.

Transits

On April 26, 1978, the day of the first rape, transiting Saturn at 24° Leo was square natal Jupiter. Neptune and the Moon in Sagittarius opposed his 8th house Uranus. Venus was conjunct the Pleiades at 29° Taurus, Mercury had just turned direct and Mars in Leo was approaching the opposition to his natal Mars. All of the placements are challenging, activating his 8th house and his natal Ascendant ruler, Mars.

On August 30, 1978, another rape occurred and the police connected Coe with this rape also. On that day transiting Uranus at 13° Scorpio was square his Sun/Pluto opposition, setting up a T-square that dumped out in his 7th house. Transiting Sun at 6° Virgo was inconjunct his Mars, activating the natal inconjunct to the Moon; Mercury at 21° Leo, again was stationary direct and opposing his natal Mercury suggesting lawbreaking since Mercury rules his natal 9th house.

Solar Return

His solar return chart for that year (see Chart #3) brings his natal 8th house to the Ascendant and the Sun is in the 9th house. Both these placements could indicate sexual activity that is not within the law. SR Mercury, ruler of the SR Ascendant, is also in the 8th house, putting even more stress on 8th house activities.

SR Jupiter is in the 1st house of the SR chart and exactly opposes natal Venus and inconjuncts SR Mercury and natal Jupiter. This sets up a boomerang configuration. The action took place in the 7th house — his assaults on other individuals — but the reaction boomeranged to the Jupiter in the 1st house and later led to his arrest and conviction.

Frederick Harlan Coe Solar Return (#3)
February 2, 1978
12:29:58 PM PST
47N40 117W24

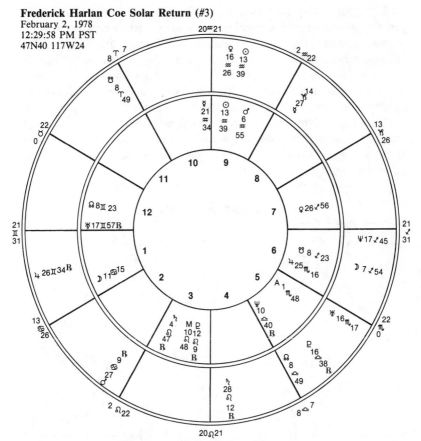

Progressed Solar Return

If we progress the SR chart (1° for every 4 days at the Midheaven and take the rest of the wheel from the Table of Houses), on April 26 the whole chart is activated by cusps aspecting both SR and natal planets. The progressed MC is 11° Pisces trine his natal Moon. The progressed SA Ascendant at 10° Cancer conjuncts natal Moon, activating the all-important inconjunct. The 11th house cusp at 6° Taurus squares natal Mars, motivating the desire for physical/sexual action. The 9th house cusp at 21° Aquarius conjuncts natal Mercury, setting off the natal square to Jupiter (the desire to do his own thing — his personal version of morality).

When we progress the SR chart to August 30, the date of the second rape, there are almost as many contacts. The MC is 13° Aries trine natal Pluto. Since Pluto is the natural ruler of the 8th house, this could suggest sexual activity of some kind. The 5th house cusp is conjunct natal south node, a possible indication of risk-taking and *karmic* lessons. The progressed SR Ascendant is 2° Leo square the natal Ascendant which usually marks a challenging day or two in the life. It is also conjunct Saturn, the planet of overcompensation. The 2nd house cusp is conjunct SR Saturn. All this Saturn activity highlights the challenging aspects to his natal 9th house Saturn bringing possible lawbreaking activity. The progressed 4th house cusp conjuncts natal Neptune bringing into play the square to natal Moon (the confusion about women). Two of the keys to *karmic* lessons, Saturn and the south node are highlighted at this time.

Lunar Returns

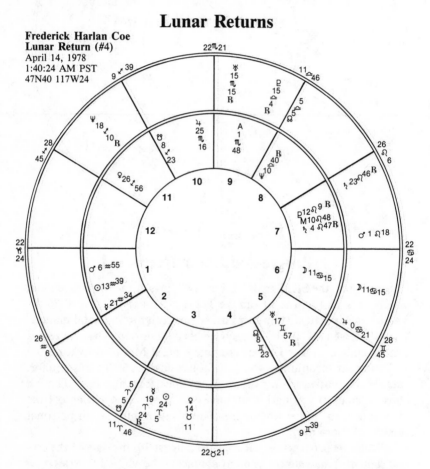

Frederick Harlan Coe
Lunar Return (#4)
April 14, 1978
1:40:24 AM PST
47N40 117W24

Coe's lunar return chart for April 1978 (see Chart #4) puts great emphasis on the 7th house with natal Saturn, MC and Pluto there plus LR Saturn and Mars. Since Saturn rules the LR Ascendant, its dual placement in this house is particularly significant. The Moon is in the 6th house, the 12th of the 7th, and rules the 7th house, indicating possible behind-the-scenes activity which involves another person. Natal Jupiter is conjunct the LR MC, emphasizing the legal aspects that have shown up all through the progressions and the Solar Return. There is a T-square formed by LR Saturn at 23° Leo opposing natal Mercury square Jupiter. The empty leg is in the 4th house, characterizing his need to act out his parental frustration.

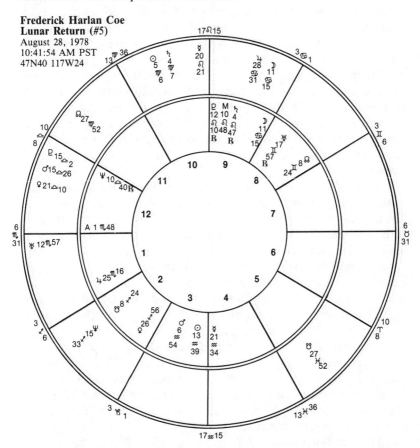

Frederick Harlan Coe
Lunar Return (#5)
August 28, 1978
10:41:54 AM PST
47N40 117W24

The lunar return chart for August 1978 when the other rape took place (Chart #5) is a return of his natal chart with the 12th house strongly highlighted. LR Mars and Pluto, the Ascendant rulers, are both in the 12th house along with the natal Ascendant. LR Uranus is rising, mirroring his desire to be unique, independent, even eccentric. Uranus rules the 4th house. Perhaps his acts of rape were a reflection of his sexual attitudes toward his mother. That theme is well represented throughout the chart. The Moon, always significant in the lunar chart, trines the 1st house Uranus from the 9th typifying his luck in avoiding being apprehended by the law.

Aspects for Arrest

Frederick Harlan Coe was arrested on March 10, 1981, and charged with six rapes on Spokane's South Hill. He was convicted on July 30 and sentenced August 17. When we look at the progressions for 1981, his secondary Sun at 18° Pisces squares Uranus activating his natal 4th and 8th houses — again the mother/sex theme. Venus at 4° Aquarius 45 opposes Saturn, the classic aspect of "nobody loves me." He had been getting away with his bizarre behavior and now he had been caught. His insecurities had caught up with him. This aspect also describes his loss of freedom. Progressed Venus, ruler of the 12th house (confinement) opposed natal Saturn in the 9th conjunct the MC (legal authority).

By solar arc direction Mercury, ruler of the legal 9th at 26° Pisces, squared the natally unaspected Venus. Often when a planet is unaspected natally and it receives an aspect by progression, the tendency is to overreact. These stressful aspects indicated events that he would have trouble dealing with and since natal Venus is in Sagittarius and natal Mercury rules the 9th house and is in the natal 4th, his home (4th) changed. He was taken into legal custody. Natal Venus rules the 7th and 8th houses and it had progressed to square the Ascendant. There were two other rapes early in the year. The 7th and 8th houses were activated in 1978 and now they are again.

Solar arc Mars at 11° Pisces trined the Moon, possibly signaling his overconfidence that he could beat the charges. This is the aspect that symbolized his desire to talk to the media. Mars comes from his 3rd house. His attitude when he was first arrested was confident and cocky, a reflection of the trine. This is also symbolic of the support he received from his parents.

His 1981 Solar Return chart (see Chart #6) highlights the 1st, 3rd, 7th and 9th houses representing the legal activity, his feeling of self-importance and the need to communicate his ideas. The natal 3rd house comes to the SR Ascendant; the Sun is in the 1st; and natal and SR Saturn, the Ascendant rulers, are in the 7th and 9th houses respectively.

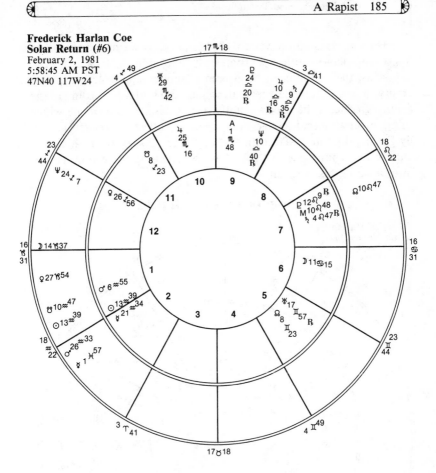

Frederick Harlan Coe
Solar Return (#6)
February 2, 1981
5:58:45 AM PST
47N40 117W24

Other Rapes

There was a rape on February 5, 1981, just three days after his birthday; another was on the 9th. On the 5th, transiting Mercury at 4° Pisces
inconjuncted natal Saturn activating the violent opposition to Mars/Sun
in his chart. Transiting Venus at 1° Aquarius 34 squared his Ascendant and conjuncted his SA Venus, mirroring the solar arc direction.
Transiting Jupiter/Saturn at 10° Libra conjuncted his natal Neptune,
representing his illusion that he could "beat the law."

On February 9, 1981, Mercury made a retrograde station, which
is significant only because on two other occasions he committed rape
when Mercury was stationary. Transiting Venus at 6° Aquarius was
conjunct his natal Mars, two planets that have been prominent in each
rape. Transiting Mars trined his Ascendant, and Jupiter and Saturn
were still within range of his Neptune.

He was arrested on March 10. Mercury, as we have seen, is an important planet both by progression and transit. It was at 23° Aquarius, the midpoint of his Mercury/Jupiter square activating his ability for conceit, tactlessness, arrogance and bluff. According to the arresting officers, he tried valiantly to talk his way out of the whole thing, protesting that he had been trying to collect the reward money by finding the rapist. Transiting Mars, at 25° Pisces, trined his natal Jupiter and conjuncted his SA Mercury, stressing the energy he put into debating his position.

Aspects at Conviction

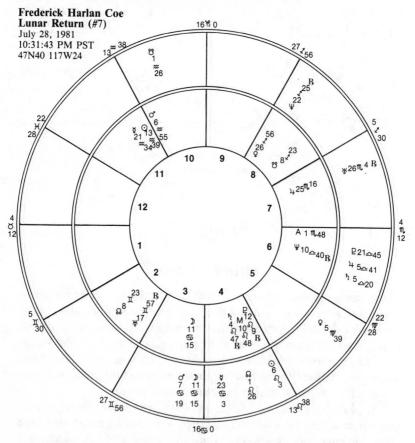

Frederick Harlan Coe
Lunar Return (#7)
July 28, 1981
10:31:43 PM PST
47N40 117W24

July of 1981 was a significant month. The new Moon of the month was conjunct his natal Moon in the 9th house, highlighting legal affairs. On the 30th, the day he was found guilty of four of the six rapes (the ones indicated in this article), the transiting Sun was opposing Mars; the Moon transited over his Saturn, MC and Pluto; Uranus conjuncted Jupiter and Pluto trined his Mercury.

His lunar return took place the day before on July 29, 1981 (see Chart #7). It is interesting to note that the 7th (the house of open enemies) comes to the Ascendant and that natal Venus, the ruler of that Ascendant, is conjunct the legal 9th house cusp. Natal Jupiter is in the 7th trined by LR Mercury. Could this indicate that justice was served?

His sentence was handed down on August 17, 1981, and the transits on that day are significant. The Sun squared natal Jupiter; Mars inconjuncted Mercury; Uranus was still conjunct Jupiter. There were trines from Saturn to Mars and from Pluto to Mercury plus sextiles from Mercury to the Ascendant and Neptune to Mercury. Saturn trined Mars, but one always returns to the nature of the natal aspects: progressed aspects show timing. He had **not** learned the lesson of his natal Mars opposition Saturn.

Prenatal Eclipse Chart

According to Victoria Shaw, who has done extensive research on murderers' charts, the prenatal eclipse chart is quite significant when dealing with the lives of criminals. She used it effectively in analyzing Son of Sam killer, David Berkowitz's chart. She feels it shows the pattern for life. The prenatal eclipse chart is one that is erected for the solar or lunar eclipse just prior to birth. It is set up for the location of birth, and the planets on the day of the eclipse are placed in the wheel.

Fred Coe's prenatal eclipse chart (Chart #8) has Capricorn rising with the ruler, Saturn, in the 7th house conjunct Pluto; Venus and Jupiter are in Scorpio conjunct the Midheaven. All of this signifies a need for recognition in a Scorpionic or Plutonic way. Venus/Jupiter contacts are classic aspects of possible excess and indulgence, in this chart through sex because the conjunction is in Scorpio. The lunar eclipse falls across the 5th/11th axis and the Moon is conjunct Uranus, precursor of the importance of Uranus in the natal chart. Mercury is angular in Scorpio portending his need to verbalize.

I have not done much research with prenatal eclipse charts, but judging from this one and a few others I have observed, there does seem to be some significance in them. Saturn and Pluto in Coe's 7th house square Venus and Jupiter in the 9th. These are both legal houses and the ramifications are interesting, to say the least. The strong Pluto/Scorpio indications are carried over into the natal chart. The progressions and transits to this chart for the key years and days are intriguing but much too involved to go into here.

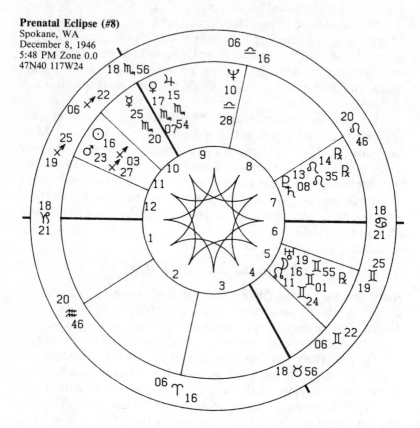

Prenatal Eclipse (#8)
Spokane, WA
December 8, 1946
5:48 PM Zone 0.0
47N40 117W24

The Mother

Mamie Ruth Enfield Coe, Fred's mother, was born on June 30, 1920, at 11:00 AM PST in Spokane, Washington (see Chart #9). According to Jack Olsen, her acquaintances recalled her as a beautiful child who got prettier with time and knew it (Venus conjunct the Sun in the 10th house). The words that best described her were "luscious" and "sensuous." But she was never cheap or promiscuous. She was flamboyant, given to overstatement, effusive (Mercury, her Ascendant ruler is conjunct Neptune in Leo).

Just before she met Gordon Coe in 1945, the twice-married Ruth had planned to leave Spokane for California; she'd never spoken highly of her native city and had felt rejected by its high society. (The Moon in the 4th house opposes the Sun/Pluto/Venus conjunction in the 10th. It also inconjuncts her Ascendant ruler Mercury, suggesting difficulties in the home arena. Pluto rules the local environment 3rd house.) Early in 1946 she married Gordon, just home from the war. (By solar arc, Neptune, ruler of her 7th house opposed Uranus; the Sun inconjuncted the Moon, ruler of 11th (3rd marriage); the Moon trined the Ascendant.)

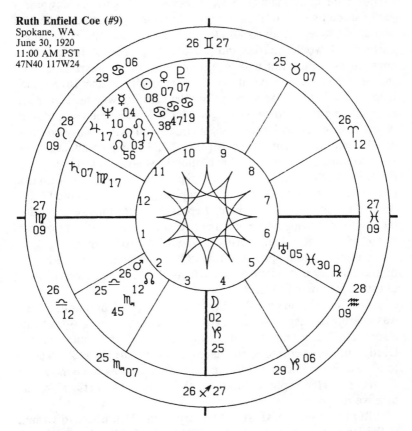

Ruth Enfield Coe (#9)
Spokane, WA
June 30, 1920
11:00 AM PST
47N40 117W24

Source: Spokane Health Dept. birth certificate (A)

The South Hill neighborhood where the Coes raised their children was very social, but the Coes received few invitations, and Ruth had quickly established a reputation for being different (Sun trine Uranus). A friend of her daughter remembers her as consistently eccentric — devoted to her children and dogs. (Uranus, ruler of her 6th house, is trine her Sun/Venus/Pluto conjunction and Saturn, ruler of the 5th, sextiles it — all evidence of her dedication.) She was always well groomed, given to wigs and five-inch heels. She spent a fortune on clothes and dry cleaning; she would wear an outfit a few times, then put it up for resale on consignment. This is consistent with a Virgo Ascendant ruled by Mercury in Leo. The need to be flamboyant (Leo) but, in the final analysis, the need for thrift (Virgo).

She and Fred both would berate Gordon Coe because he did not support them in the manner to which they would like to be accustomed, yet he stood by both of them until the bitter end. The ruler of her 7th house, Neptune, conjuncts Jupiter, the ruler of the 4th, describing a partner who would nourish and provide. Neptune and Jupiter, both connected to inspiration and aspirations, may indicate expecting more than is reasonable from partners (7th). Mercury inconjunct Uranus may help explain her manic-depressive problem as it shows a need to adjust her reasoning ability to great changes. Manic-depressive illness is basically seen as an emotional issue, with extreme mood swings. Fire and water are the emotional elements in astrology, and strong combinations of fire and water show the potential of mood swings. Fire symbolizes optimism and extroversion, while water represents introversion. Ruth Coe has fire and water signs strongly occupied, plus the Sun exactly conjunct Pluto and Jupiter conjunct Neptune — both intense fire/water blends. Of course people expressing fire/water combinations positively are simply very warm, caring people with strong emotions.

Uranus is an important planet in her chart since it is the handle of the bucket, and much of her energy was directed toward being unusual, eclectic and bizarre.

Fred's girlfriend described her first meeting with his mother. Ruth was wearing a sweeping dressing gown, gobs of fake jewels, spoke with a southern accent and pretended to be from the deep South. Neither Gordon nor Fred corrected the false impression she gave. She seemed to have a need to act out roles, to perceive herself as someone whom she was not. Her Neptune/Jupiter conjunction in Leo perhaps was indicative of this.

Ruth Coe has a yod from Mercury in the 11th house to Uranus in the 6th and the Moon in the 4th. This, combined with the need for recognition shown by the stellium in the 10th house, indicates that when she was working (6th house), felt useful in the community (11th house) and was being noticed (10th house), she felt fulfilled and secure (4th house). When her modeling days were over, instead of making the necessary adjustments (the inconjuncts), she escaped into fantasy and feeling sorry for herself (Mercury conjunct Neptune).

In comparing her chart to her son's, we find some striking

similarities. He has Scorpio rising and the Sun opposed to Pluto; she has the Sun conjunct Pluto. They both have the nodes across the 2nd/8th house. He has a Mercury/Uranus trine; she has the inconjunct. He has Venus unaspected in the 2nd house; she has Mars in the 2nd without interplanetary aspects. Both have 10th house Plutos, illustrating the power struggle they engaged in. Both have the Ascendant ruler in Leo, implying that they both had the need to make grandiloquent gestures, to attract attention, to play the game of one-upmanship.

Fred's Moon conjuncts his mother's Sun/Venus/Pluto typifying a domination theme. The wide opposition to her Moon seems to connote a situation where she at times wanted to mother and at other times wanted him to mother her. The constant push-pull depicted by this aspect could have been the catalyst that catapulted them into their love-hate, screaming matches. Fred's Saturn is exactly conjunct her Mercury. She constantly berated him to make something of himself and would descend into her depressions when she felt he wasn't living up to what she expected of him. (Her Neptune conjuncts his MC.) (When not expressed positively, the potentials of Neptune include excessive expectations, wanting an unreachable ideal, a fantasy.) It seems both Fred and Ruth Coe were trapped, to some extent, in fantasies.

Her Jupiter/Neptune opposes his Sun/Mars, while his Neptune squares her 10th house conjunction. They hardly saw each other clearly and both fantasized the relationship. Her Saturn conjuncts his 11th house cusp. When he was a youngster, she went out of her way to be kind to his friends (Saturn trines the Moon). But when his friends could not in good conscience testify in his behalf, she threatened their lives (Saturn opposes Uranus).

Many innocent people have suffered from this man's actions — not just the victims, but the judge and prosecutor have lost status in the community (because of Ruth Coe's unfounded accusations) and Coe's family has disintegrated. His father has lost everything that it took him a lifetime to build up; his mother was institutionalized, and she and his father have moved away to try to make new lives for themselves. Could this all have been avoided? Perhaps if someone had read Frederick Coe's chart when he was a child and could have persuaded his parents to listen, he might have gotten some much-needed guidance and counseling.

We Have Choices

It is important to remember that the horoscope shows us the issues. How we handle those issues will make the difference — responsible action versus indulgence or self-pity. It is our choice. There are un-doubtedly people with patterns similar to Fred Coe's who are leading very positive lives. They may be in the business world, in competitive sports or other fields which channel the power drive (Saturn/Ascendant/Mars T-square; Saturn conjunct Pluto; Pluto opposed Sun). They utilize their imaginations creatively (Neptune in the 12th house trine Mars in the 3rd and the Sun) to create beauty in language, speaking, writing, advertising, promotion, etc. They meet the challenge of developing a personal ethical system (Jupiter in the 1st) which is moral and upright rather than self-indulgent. They express their uniqueness, rebelliousness and originality in helpful ways which can still be involved with joint resources or sexuality (e.g., fighting for ecology; writing letters, etc., against pollution; running for Congress on a platform of sexual equality or one to outlaw child pornography, etc.).

There are as many paths as there are souls in the Universe. We choose which roads we travel.

OUR HIGHEST PHILOSOPHICAL AND SPIRITUAL POTENTIAL

by Marion D. March

In most people's minds there is a very thin line between the words **spiritual/philosophical** versus *karmic*/**occult/metaphysical**. In fact, the title of this article could have been "An Esoteric Approach to Astrology," but the word esoteric immediately conjures past lives, reincarnation, astral travel, clairvoyance, etc. There is nothing wrong with reincarnation — in fact, I believe in it and would find life very difficult to bear if I thought this was the only chance I had! But I also feel that the time has come to explore those astrological paths that can be proven, or have proven themselves.

We can theorize that the sign of the Moon in a chart this time was the Sun sign in a previous life; but it will always be just that, a theory, and as such, at least for the time being, hard to substantiate.

Yet there are a multitude of symbols in astrology that have proven themselves over thousands of years, and a multitude of them can point us toward the highest evolvement possible in this lifetime. Astrology is a marvelous technique which can be used in so many different ways, and every one of them has a *raison d'être*, a value.

Many of us, when giving astrological consultations, use the holistic/humanistic approach. It is important to get insight into our psyche; to get to know and understand ourselves better; to find our strengths and weaknesses, our talents and aptitudes. But most of us stop right there. Rarely do we delve into the highest realms we could strive for. Of course there is a reason. Most people come to us with very definite problems, often in time of crisis when they need guidance to find the way out of specific dilemmas, and could care less about any kind of evolvement. Yet there are those chosen few (which is the true meaning of the word esoteric) who have come to the crossroads. They seem to have reached the material and concrete goals they set for themselves. Their stomachs are full, they have a roof over their heads, financial independence, standing in the community and all else they thought they longed for. Suddenly they realize: "Is that all there is? There must be more, but what is it? And especially, what is it for me?"

When we are faced with a person at such a point, a much deeper reading is necessary. There are several tools we can use. First of all we need to understand the basic language of astrology as symbolized by the **glyphs**. Each glyph has a very specific meaning which we tend to forget when swept up in our mundane counseling.

Glyphs

The glyphs consist of **straight lines, curves** and **circles**. Each has a definite import. The straight or **horizontal line** — is considered **physical** or **material** and manifests in a lower/earthy or higher/metaphysical and evolved way. The straight **vertical line** | is the line of **destiny** or **intellect**. The two lines crossing form the **cross of matter** +. The **full circle** ○ is considered **infinity** or **spirit**; the **semicircle** or **crescent** (in any direction)$\subset$ $\supset$ $\cup$ $\cap$ is the **soul force** or consciousness. The **curved upward stroke** $\subset$ is pouring out or **extroverted** when to the **right** and **introverted** $\diagdown$ when toward the **left**.

When interpreting a sign or planet in a higher or evolved way, we need to put these symbolic strokes to good use. Take the glyph for Libra as an example: ♎. The lower line is physical and material; the upper line is metaphysical; the small crescent in the upper line curves upward and shows pure and divine justice. The two lines never touch; they are detached, just as the higher nature of Libra is objective (air) and not attached to matter.

For additional understanding, let's look at Mercury's glyph ☿: the circle of spirit rising above the cross of matter, topped off by the crescent of consciousness. The line of destiny struggles upward to be manifested in higher or spiritual consciousness. If we understand the highest principle of Mercury and then interpret the sign it is placed in, we can easily see the possible evolvement of the mind. Mercury in Cancer would obviously have a different aim or goal than Mercury in Gemini.

Visualize the glyph for Cancer ♋. The two circles or spiritual forces are on the inside; the glyph begins and ends on a spiritual level. The symbol is all curves. There are no straight lines; Cancer is all emotion with none of the intellectual reasoning usually associated with Mercury.

The glyph also shows the taking and the giving, the protective and nurturing design.

Gemini ♊ on the other hand has the two vertical lines of destiny linked by the horizontal or physical lines — the dual lines of mentality linked by the physical on the lower and metaphysical on the higher level, able to bring the higher plane to the lower one. Mercury in Gemini can reach philosophical or spiritual evolvement through what the Hindus call *Jnana-Yoga*, namely, through reasoning and mental understanding, whereas Mercury in Cancer would find enlightenment through *Bhakti-Yoga*, the path of love and devotion.

These basic differences have to be kept in mind when we advise others. Let us look at the planet Mars: ♂. The circle is at the lowest point, the straight line is slanted upward, striving or driving to reach higher, yet ending in the barb of desire, penetration and testing. This upward line ending in a barb also symbolizes the concentrated, sexual energy of the penis. Thus Mars starts in spirit and tries to reach out and up, but is often held back by the animalistic instincts of desire and penetration.

Mars in Pisces could face a double dilemma. Pisces ♓ has the two crescents of consciousness back-to-back, tied by the line of matter. The line of matter is at midheight, able to reach above or below. The two crescents go in different directions, one looking backward into the past or subconscious, the other reaching toward the future — yet both are imbued with the compassionate quality of pouring out. We can interpret this as the crescent of finite consciousness of humanity versus the infinite consciousness of the universe, the line linking the two representing the Earth where the two forces meet — thus the struggle between body and soul.

To combine these feelings of dichotomy with Mars who tries to evolve yet often gets stopped by physical desires, we could be faced with double trouble. People who have this placement sometimes need much help in finding their priorities and much reassurance that to feel can be all right on any level. They may feel torn between the "'carnal" and the "spiritual," between self-assertion and self-sacrifice. Of course the entire chart must always be considered before a judgment can be made, but there is nothing wrong in finding fulfillment in earthy endeavors. A sexual encounter replete with feelings of love and giving can be as spiritual an experience to some people as meditation is to others. Not all of us are meant to retreat to the Himalayas or a convent in order to evolve. What we are and what we should reach for is imprinted in that moment in time when we are born, and, thank God, we and our needs are each totally unique.

Look at Everything

The symbolic meaning of the glyphs are obviously not the only points to look for in an esoteric interpretation. The houses play a very important role. Personally, I use the Koch table of houses, but I am a firm believer that astrologers should use the tools that work for them, so please don't feel that Koch is the only workable system; utilize whatever brings you results.

To better understand our role in life, we have to understand planets, signs and houses, as well as the qualities and elements, because in astrology every part taken apart is also part of the whole. The 1st house is not only the 1st house, it is also Aries and Mars and cardinal and fire and angular. We should never lose sight of the "whole" when giving any interpretation.

Qualities

In the qualities, **cardinal** stands for activity and **creation**, the doer of the zodiac. **fixed** stands for solidity and **preservation**, and **mutable** stands for interrelation and **transmutation**. The word transmutation needs to be understood in its proper context. Everything is born — creation; lives — preservation; and dies — but death only means a change in the form of the energy. The energy itself never dies. Form and matter are mortal; essence is immortal. Therefore we use the word transmutation instead of the commonly applied death or destruction.

Elements

The **elements** have the following significance:

Fire is the "reaching out" force, the spiritual rebirth, the growth potential in all its implications. Aries reaches out right now, Leo and Sagittarius reach out toward the future.

Earth is the land we live on — the physical, concrete reality as visualized by our five senses. Taurus's vision is realistic in a rather sensual, tactile and artistic way. Virgo's reality is practical and down to earth, but with enough mental orientation that it needs to analyze rather than just feel. Capricorn's concept is practical in a disciplined and responsible way but always colored by its background, upbringing and past experience. The material needs and urges are conditioned by what has gone before.

Air represents the atmosphere and gases that surround us, but it also represents the ether which fills all space and is part of the entire universe, is nonmaterial and yet has properties of its own. What other functions this universal medium may possess are yet to be discovered. Therefore air is yesterday, today and tomorrow, the element of the mind in all its ramifications. Gemini's mind can and wants to look at everything — past, present and future — and then in an unemotional, detached manner communicate its learning to all. Libra needs to experience today before deciding about tomorrow, to weigh other people's reactions before making a commitment one way or the other. Aquarius (like Gemini, made up of pure, straight, unemotional lines) not only understands the future but wants to discover it. Without a future to reach for, Aquarius resents the present, as the glyph well explains. Think of the angular lines representing electrical impulses or magnetism, the lower physical and the upper, metaphysical. Both end by pointing upward ♒. Like Libra, the lines never touch, showing detachment. The glyph has three full points and one unfinished one; these supposedly represent our four ways of communicating — first by foot, then by animal, the third by mechanical means and the fourth unfinished one would be the future way: by telepathy or brain waves.

Water constitutes 70% of the human body and therefore can easily outweigh the other elements. It is the primary element of the past, the absorption of that which was, be it ideas digested and absorbed as memories or our subconscious habit patterns. The three water signs are all curves, circles and crescents, seeking spiritual enlightenment but so imbued with instinct, intuition and sensitivity that, just like water, they embrace all, knowing no barrier and rarely using mind or reason.

They can be easily understood when we relate them to the three properties of water: in its liquid form, frozen as ice, or vaporous as gas or steam. Cancer relates to the liquid form of water. Since our body contains water as liquid, Cancer equates to our physical properties such as heredity, the absorption of the genes and genetic background. The collected thoughts or acquired habits are united with the genetic heredity through our parents. It is the home we chose for ourselves.

Scorpio equates with frozen water, fixed in its subconscious pattern, deeply rooted in its feelings. It shows our potential for really coming to grips with ourselves since it is the buried layer of the past. Pisces' emotions are closest to the surface; vapors and gases evaporate quickly and just as quickly can shed that which is bothersome. It is often considered the life lived just before and as such is supposedly easy to resolve.

Houses

Translating this into **houses**, we realize that the 4th, 8th and 12th are the houses of absorption or the past, the soaking up of feelings, emotions and memories; each in its own special way, relating it back to the qualities and elements. With the 4th house we should remember the protective design of the Cancer glyph, but let's also visualize the Moon ☽ : two crescents of consciousness linked on the lower (earth/home) level and above on the higher "true giving" level. The glyph is all curves (emotions), and since it is only a semi-circle, lives in the reflective light of the Sun. The symbol is turned backward, facing into that which was or is deep within.

The 8th house relates to Scorpio's frozen water, but we need to also keep the Pluto symbols in mind. Of the two glyphs used in the United States, ♇ represents the PL of Pluto and the initials of its discoverer, Percival Lowell. It shows the line of destiny intercepted by the physical line of matter, and on top the crescent of consciousness, turned back to face itself or look within. The other symbol ♆ sometimes referred to as Minerva, has the crescent of consciousness linked to the cross of matter, with the circle of infinity hovering above. At its highest level, matter would rise through the soul to regenerate as spirit. At its least evolved level, spirit would descend through the soul to manifest as matter.

The 3rd, 7th and 11th are the houses of detached and abstract mental processes. The 3rd house does it alone, the 7th house with someone and the 11th for someone.

The 2nd, 6th and 10th houses look for accomplishment in the here and now. The 2nd (succedent/earth) preserves that which exists and builds on that existing base. The 6th (cadent/earth) wants to transmute or change that which is into something more practical, more understandable, more usable. The 10th (angular/earth) works to create for itself a secure base on which to climb the ladder of earthly success.

Once the material success is reached, the 10th can become one of the most evolved houses. It is the highest point of the chart, representing the culmination of all that can be achieved and the consequences of the past. Also, because the cardinality of the 10th indicates individuals who are not afraid to work for what they want, the earth element, once it overcomes its material drive, can see "Reality" in its larger or total dimension. Many of our great philosophers, sages, psychics and saints have predominantly earth charts.

Saturn's glyph also needs to be studied: ♄. The cross of matter is the most elevated part of this symbol, Saturn representing matter in its purest sense. The crescent of consciousness curves first downward and inward, but ends with an upward and outward projection. Even on the most concrete level of earth, we have to first look within before we can reach out toward others and then finally reach toward evolvement. This last, upward stroke of Saturn is often neglected yet it is the most important factor, and whether we use it or not can determine our attitude toward Saturn as the great denier versus the positive teacher.

The 1st, 5th and 9th houses reach out to the future with great zest, enthusiasm and self-confidence. The 1st house, being angular, cares mostly about today, but give a 1st house planet a direction in which to head, and without a moment's hesitation it can be done, with vim and vigor. Since the Aries' spirit of pioneering is ever present, it may be done a bit differently than we intended. The 5th house is concerned with the immediate future, but being succedent and fixed, the approach has to be based on something that already exists, that is, tried and true. Then the Leo quality can take over by embellishing, embroidering and dramatically presenting everything in a different light. Point a 5th house planet in a higher direction, and it will give itself to that new goal with total heart and dedication.

The 9th house lives for tomorrow; the glyph for Sagittarius ♐ depicts the arrow shooting for the stars. But let's remember that even this lofty symbol has a straight line dividing the shaft, the lower half embodying the physical or animal nature of the centaur (half man, half beast). The barb at the end of the shaft can be the arrow denoting aspirations to reach infinity, or it can be the barb of human desires, holding the ideals to an earthy plane. The 9th house ideas and ideals can be restricted to the missionary who sees only one reality and expends much energy trying to force everyone else to see it the same way, or the truly spiritual person who knows that truth and enlightenment are within, to be found in our own superconscious mind.

By following the logic of an evolved delineation, we can understand what each astrological part, as well as the astrological "whole," stands for. Let's look at Jupiter in Virgo for one more example. ♃: the crescent of consciousness or soul force is higher than the cross of matter, but the crescent faces inward and can become self-oriented or self-indulgent. ♍ : Virgo's glyph shows three levels of consciousness: the conscious, the subconscious and the superconscious. The last stroke shows an outward motion, but — and here is Virgo's challenge — it is held back by the last line which goes not only inward but below the horizon. Thus, despite the three levels of consciousness, Virgo can become introversive and materialistic. The coils of energy may be kept from release by that last stroke, denoting a locked door. That locked door also relates to the 6th house of work and service, the practical application of the energies, and the constant effort to try to open that door, again and again. Once we find the key to the locked door, we can integrate the conscious, subconscious and superconscious to a harmonious, evolving whole (flowing like the glyph).

Aspects

The next areas to explore in an esoteric fashion are **aspects**. Probably all of us are familiar with the positive and negative keywords used for each aspect. Looking for the highest potential, we would naturally view an **opposition** as the key to **awareness**, and not the possible imbalance or pulling apart it also can indicate. The **square** would not be a **stumbling block** but a **stepping stone**, the tension or challenge illustrated by the square showing the impetus needed to achieve whatever the chart indicates that we can reach for. The **trines** depict flow and ease, especially if a square or opposition leads into them, suggesting energy to get the flow started. The **sextiles** denote the opportunity to communicate and to open doors rather than to scatter our talents.

A very difficult aspect to deal with, either in a regular or esoteric interpretation, is the **inconjunct** or **quincunx**. Here we deal with rather incompatible forces, leading from Aries/1st house/Active/fire/cardinal and "I" oriented to Virgo/6th house/passive/earth/mutable or Scorpio/8th house/passive/water/fixed. Fire is conjoined with earth or water — both earth and water can put out a fire. Aries hates to be put out or down!

How to solve this problem? In dealing with a 1st/6th house inconjunct we should see how the individual could take personal (1st house) action, by examining the mental and physical habit patterns (6th house) and through knowledge (6th house) make the appropriate adjustments or compromises. If it is a 1st/8th house quincunx, then the personal action (1st) should be directed into sexual or transformational areas (8th) through a deeper, psychological understanding (8th). If there are trines or sextiles leading to the planets involved in the inconjunct, they too should be brought into play. Esoterically this aspect is often called one of "testing" — if we pass the test, we may be ready for the next rung of the ladder, and the chart viewed in its entirety can give us the key.

The little used **quintile** aspect can also be helpful when looking for the highest potential. The orb should be very tight, no more than ½ ° in either direction. The quintile can indicate areas of spiritual talents and higher mind abilities and can show if we have the discipline

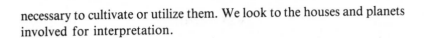

necessary to cultivate or utilize them. We look to the houses and planets involved for interpretation.

Arabic Parts

Some **Arabic Parts** can also help in delineating hidden or subconscious feelings — feelings which could illuminate blockage or indicate guidelines to spiritual evolvement. We need not aspect these parts, just interpret them by house position and sign. The three I use are: the **Part of Fortune**, the **Part of Spirit** and the **Web**.

First we need to consider what these parts really stand for. The **Part of Fortune** is calculated by adding the Ascendant to the Moon and subtracting the Sun. What are we really doing here? The Ascendant is our reality in this world, our physical body, the here and now. The Sun is our growth potential, the outreach of fire toward loftier goals. The Moon is our past, that which has gone before, as well as our inner feelings and emotions, many of them subconscious, based on memory. If we add the Moon to the Ascendant and take away the growth potential of the Sun, we are left with that which **is** and **was**: yesterday and today, tomorrow having been subtracted. So look at the Part of Fortune to interpret some of the deep, submerged and nearly always subconscious feelings of the past as we can apply them or work with them in the present.

The **Part of Spirit** on the other hand is calculated by adding the Sun to the Ascendant and subtracting the Moon. Here we have the reverse situation: today plus tomorrow, minus yesterday. The Part of Spirit can show us the spiritual and philosophical growth we are capable of, again not on a physical, but on a psychological, philosophical or spiritual level. Look to the sign involved to interpret if this growth potential is based on intellect, on feelings and emotions or on spiritual leanings.

The **Web** is calculated by adding Neptune to the Ascendant and subtracting the Sun. Neptune can be spiritual enlightenment or delusion, the rose-colored glasses or illusion. Since again we take away the future, namely the Sun, we are left with that which is. This can be the area where we are trapped into fooling ourselves, but it can become the way to our highest consciousness. Once we grasp the meaning of the parts, we can use any of them and interpret according to the planets involved, keeping in mind which one is added, which one subtracted. Since there are hundreds of parts, the potential is endless.

Progressions

For further esoteric interpretation, we should keep a careful watch on **progressions**. When an intercepted planet or house loses its interception, we can utilize the energies more directly, in a freer and more physical way. Whether house or planet, after having been intercepted for many years and then becoming "free," it seems to be terribly anxious to do its own thing, as if the energies have been pent up and can hardly wait to get going. The same applies to a planetary change of direction from retrograde to direct or vice versa. The seemingly outwardly oriented person now is able to look inward. And the inward-looking person can be more externally active. The tendency is for the individual to work toward balancing polarities. There is often a change in direction in the life area symbolized by the planet changing direction. Has a natal square become a trine by progression? This is an ideal time to use the energies of the square positively. Or does a trine now form a square or an opposition, urging it into action? Timing can be very important, in mundane as well as esoteric delineation. It is not only where and how we can evolve, but also when.

The important thing in this life is not so much where we are as in what direction we are going. The horoscope is your road map...let a more philosophical or spiritual approach to astrology show you the way.

INDEX

We calculate... You delineate!

CHART CALCULATIONS

Natal Chart wheel with planet/sign glyphs. Choice of house system: Placidus (standard), Equal, Koch, Campanus, Meridian, Porphyry, Regiomontanus, Topocentric, or Alcabitius. Choice of tropical (standard) or sidereal zodiac. Aspects, elements, planetary nodes, declinations, midpoints, etc. 2.00

Arabic Parts All traditional parts and more 1.00

Asteroids ⚳ ⚴ ⚵ ⚶ in wheel + aspects/midpoints ... .50

Asteroids ⚳ ⚴ ⚵ ⚶ + 15 new ones for 20th century only 1.00

Astrodynes Power, harmony and discord with summaries for easy comparison................ 2.00

Chiron, Transpluto (only one) in wheel............. N/C

Concentric Wheels Any 3 charts available in wheel format may be combined into a '3 wheeler' ...... 3.00 Deduct $1.00 for each chart ordered as a separate wheel.

Fixed Stars Robson's 110 fixed stars with aspects to natal chart 1.00

Fortune Finder more Arabic Parts — 97 ancient (Al Biruni) and 99 modern (Robert Hurzt Granite) 2.00

Graphic Midpoint Sort Proportional spacing highlights midpt. groupings. **Specify integer divisions of 360°** (1=360°, 4=90°, etc.) 1.00

Harmonic Chart John Addey type. Wheel format, harmonic asc. eq. houses. **Specify harmonic number** 2.00

Harmonic Positions 30 consecutive sets of positions **Specify starting harmonic number** 1.00

Heliocentric Charts Sun-centered positions 2.00

House Systems Comparison for 9 systems .... .50

Local Space Planet compass directions (azimuth & altitude) plus Campanus Mundoscope .... .50

Locality Map USA, World, Europe, S. Amer., Far East, Austl., Mid East and Africa map — choice of rise, set, and culmination lines or Asc., Desc., MC, IC lines for each map 6.00

Midpoint Structures Midpoint aspects + midpoints in 45° and 90° sequence....................... 1.00

Rectification Assist 10 same-day charts. **Specify starting time, time increment, e.g. 6 am, every 20 minutes** 10.00

Relocation Chart for current location. **Specify original birth data and new location**............. 2.00

Uranian Planets + halfsums..................... .50

Uranian Sensitive Points (includes Uranian Planets). 3.50

HUMAN RELATIONSHIPS

Chart Comparison (Synastry) All aspects between the two sets of planets plus house positions of one in the other 1.50

Composite Chart Rob Hand-type. Created from midpoints between 2 charts. **Specify location** 2.00

Relationship Chart Chart erected for space-time midpoint between two births 2.00

Interpretive Comparison Report Specify natal data for 2 births...................................... 8.00

COLOR CHARTS

4-Color Wheel any chart we offer in new, aesthetic format with color coded aspect lines 2.00

Local Space Map 4-color on 360° circle 2.00

Custom 6" Disk for any harmonic (laminated, you cut out) overlays on our color wheel charts 4.00

Plotted Natal Dial for use with custom 6" Disk ..... 2.00 **Specify harmonic #**

Custom Graphic Ephemeris in 4 colors. **Specify harmonic, zodiac, starting date.**

- 1 or 5 YR TRANSITS with or without natal positions 5.00
- 1 or 5 YR TRANSITS, NATAL & PROGRESSED 7.00
- 85 YR PROGRESSIONS with natal positions...... 10.00
- NATAL LINES ONLY (plus transparency).......... 4.00
- additional natal (same graph).................. 1.00
- additional person's progressions (same graph) 2.00

FUTURE TRENDS

Progressed Chart in wheel format. **Specify progressed day, month and year** 2.00

Secondary Progressions Day-by-day progressed aspects to natal and progressed planets, ingresses and parallels by month, day and year. **Specify starting year, MC by solar arc (standard) or RA of mean Sun** ....5 years 3.00
10 years 5.00
85 years 15.00

Minor or Tertiary Progressions Minor based on lunar-month-for-a-year, tertiary on day-for-a-lunar-month. **Specify year, MC by solar arc (standard) or RA of mean sun** ....1 year 2.00

Progressed Lifetime Lunar Phases a la Dane Rudhyar 5.00

Solar Arc Directions Day-by-day solar arc directed aspects to the natal planets, house and sign ingresses by month, day and year. **Specify starting year**. Asc. and Vertex arc directions available at same prices ....1st 5 years 1.00
Each add'l 5 years .50

Primary Arc Directions (Includes speculum) . .5 years 1.50
Specify starting year Each add'l 5 years .50

Transits by all planets except Moon. Date and time of transiting aspects/ingresses to natal chart. **Specify starting month.** Moon-only transits available at same prices................. 6 mos. 7.00
OR 12 mos. 12.00
summary only 6 mos. 3.50
summary only 12 mos. 6.00
calendar (9 planets OR Moon only) 6 mos. 7.00
calendar (9 planets OR Moon only) 12 mos. 12.00
calendar (Moon & planets) 6 mos. 12.00
calendar (Moon & planets) 12 mos. 20.00

Interpretive Transits. SPECIFY STARTING MONTH

- **Outer Planets** ♃♄♅♆♇ ....12 mos. 8.00
  Hard Aspects Only ☌☍□∠⚼
- **Outer Planets** ♃♄♅♆♇ ....12 mos. 10.00
  Soft & Hard Aspects △⚹⚺☌☍□∠⚼
- **9 Planets** ☉☿♀♂♃♄♅♆♇ ....6 mos. 15.00
  Hard Aspects Only ☌☍□∠⚼ 12 mos. 25.00
- **9 Planets** ☉☿♀♂♃♄♅♆♇ ....6 mos. 18.00
  Soft & Hard Aspects △⚹⚺☌☍□∠⚼ 12 mos. 30.00

Returns in wheel format. All returns can be precession corrected. **Specify place, Sun-return year, Moon-return month, planet-return month/year.** ....Solar, Lunar or Planet 2.00
13 Lunar 15.00

POTPOURRI

Winning!! Timing for gamblers, exact planet and transiting house cusps based on Joyce Wehrman's system. 1-7 days (per day) 3.00
8 or more days (per day) 2.00

Biorhythms Chart the 23-day, 28-day and 33-day cycles in ....Printed { per mo. .50 / 12 mos. 4.00 } black/white graph format.

4-Color Graph on our plotter .... Color 6 mos. 2.00

Custom House Cusps Table for each minute of sidereal time. **Specify latitude ° ′ ″** 10.00

Custom American Ephemeris Page Any month, 2500BC-AD2500. **Specify zodiac (Sidereal includes RA & dec.)**

- One mo. geocentric or two mos. heliocentric 5.00
- One year ephemeris (**specify beginning mo. yr.**) ... 50.00
- One year heliocentric ephemeris 25.00

Fertility Chart The Jonas method with Sun/Moon-squares/oppositions to the planets, for 1 year .... 3.00 **Specify starting month.**

Lamination of 1 or 2 sheets 1.00

Transparency (B/W) of any chart or map. Ordered at same time 1.00

Handling charge per order 2.00

SAME DAY SERVICE — Ask for Free Catalog

ASTRO COMPUTING SERVICES, Inc.
P.O. BOX 16430
SAN DIEGO, CA 92116-0430
NEIL F. MICHELSEN

(Prices Subject to Change)